Prospective Financial Statement Analysis

Prospective Financial Statement Analysis

Frank J. Kopczynski, PhD, CPA, CMA

John Wiley & Sons, Inc.

New York ● Chichester ● Brisbane ● Toronto ● Singapore

This publication is designed to provide accurate and authoritative information in regard to the subject matter covered. It is sold with the understanding that the publisher is not engaged in rendering legal, accounting, or other professional services. If legal advice or other expert assistance is required, the services of a competent professional person should be sought.

Library of Congress Cataloging in Publication Data:

Kopczynski, Frank J.
    Prospective financial statement analysis/Frank
  J. Kopczynski.
        p.   cm.
    Includes bibliographical references.
    ISBN 0-471-13455-4 (cloth : alk. paper)
    1. Financial statements.   I. Title.
  HF5681.B2K675   1996
  657´.32—dc20   95-44559 CIP

Printed in the United States of America

10 9 8 7 6 5 4 3 2 1

To my mother and father, Loretta and Frank, and to my
wife, Carol, for her assistance and support.

Summary Contents

Detailed Table of Contents

Preface

This book is about prospective financial statements—how to go about analyzing them, and, consequently, how to generate them. Surprisingly, there is little information available that addresses this important subject. The audience for this book includes CPAs, financial consultants, lawyers, bankers, financial analysts and cost accountants, venture capitalists, chief financial officers and vice presidents of finance, controllers, and strategic planners. The process model presented provides a methodology with which to approach this subject.

The traditional methods employed in the analysis of historical financial statements assume that the figures contained within the statements and presented for analysis are relatively verifiable and supportable. However, in the analysis of prospective financial statements, the results, contained within the statements and presented for analysis, will most likely not occur exactly as presented. The emphasis in this type of analysis needs to be on what might happen, and requires a totally different perspective and approach from those applied to the analysis of historical financial statements.

This book presents a generalized model which proposes a multiphase approach for the analysis process. The first four phases of the analysis process include: (1) qualitative, (2) quantitative, (3) strategic resources, and (4) sensitivity analysis. Evaluation, the final phase, rests upon the data obtained in the four previous phases.

Emphasis throughout is on the systems perspective. In addition to focusing on the interrelatedness of the phases in the analysis process, all the elements under examination in the prospective financial statements are brought together, kept together, and examined in such a fashion as to determine the influence of each upon the characteristics of the whole system—the business represented by the prospective financial statements.

The analysis of prospective financial statements hinges on this understanding of the firm as a system of interrelated subsystems and not as disjointed fragments. The systems prospective is the key to the process needed for proper analysis to take place.

This book approaches the subject of the analysis of prospective financial statements in a fashion that reflects major differences from previous works on the analysis of historical financial statements, including integrating the following:

- The use of the systems perspective
- An emphasis on what might happen
- The use of modeling, computers, and sensitivity analysis
- An emphasis on communications, qualitative issues, and assumptions
- An appreciation for art over technique
- An emphasis on risk and uncertainty
- A focus on context
- An understanding that change is the only real constant

In support of the process model for the analysis of prospective financial statements, also included in this book are discussions on communications, accounting information and standards, strategic planning, systems, modeling forecasting and sensitivity analysis, and traditional financial analysis.

A detailed case study using an actual start-up company is also included, as well as a computer diskette containing the LOTUS spreadsheet for the prospective financial statements presented for this start-up company together with the formulas for the quantitative financial analysis conducted.

Finally, I would like to acknowledge the assistance provided by Professor Richard Lindhe, recently retired from Northeastern University in Boston, Massachusetts, and Professor Herbert Otto of Plymouth State College in Plymouth, New Hampshire.

Frank J. Kopczynski
Canaan, New Hampshire
September 1995

About the Author

Frank J. Kopczynski, PhD, CPA, CMA, is President of Business Planning Associates in Canaan, New Hampshire, and has advised clients in management consulting matters for over 25 years. His engagements have included numerous banking proposals, feasibility studies, business and strategic plans, valuations, financial models, risk and decision analyses, systems and operation reviews, and business brokerings. His clients have spanned North and South America and the Pacific Rim and have included many of the Fortune 500, as well as banks, contractors, manufacturers, department stores, hospitals, retailers, restaurants, hotels, developers, mining firms, and other service and nonprofit organizations. He is currently also an Assistant Professor at Plymouth State College in Plymouth, New Hampshire, and has written many professional papers and articles. He has been a guest speaker before CPA Society and Bar meetings, the National Association of Accountants, the American Production and Inventory Control Society, and the Healthcare Financial Management Association. He is currently a member of the Institute of Management Accountants (and is on the New Hampshire chapter's Board of Directors), the AICPA, and the American Accounting Association.

CHAPTER ONE

Introduction

CHAPTER OUTLINE

1.1 THE NEED
1.2 THE CHALLENGE
1.3 THE GENERAL APPROACH
1.4 THE ANALYST
1.5 THE DIFFERENCES
1.6 CONCLUSION

1.1 THE NEED

How should an accountant or an analyst go about understanding and analyzing prospective financial statements? The analysis of prospective financial statements is quite different from the analysis of historical financial statements. Even though accountants regularly encounter prospective financial statements, they find themselves without the tools needed to address them properly. For example, what sort of analysis should one have undertaken in order to evaluate the figures for the projected budget deficits as developed by the Bush administration's Office of Manpower Budget (OMB) and the Congressional Budget Office (CBO) in 1989? (see Table 1-1)

How could we have known in 1989 which set of figures, as shown in Table 1-1, if either, was correct? Both sets of estimates consistently proved to be lower than the actual budget deficits experienced, and it appears that the tendency for inaccuracy within these estimates will continue. Although a full discussion of the myriad of possible reasons for these variances is

Table 1-1   Deficits Projected by the Office of Manpower Budget (OMB) and the Congressional Budget Office (CBO)

Year	OMB	CBO
1990	$123.8 billion deficit	$138 billion deficit
1991	$ 63.1 billion deficit	$138 billion deficit
1992	$ 25.1 billion deficit	$135 billion deficit
1993	$ 5.7 billion deficit	$141 billion deficit
1994	$ 10.7 billion deficit	$130 billion deficit
1995	$ 9.4 billion deficit	$118 billion deficit

(Adapted from J18, p. 98)

beyond the immediate scope of this chapter, an important point needs to be made. Although there is a lot written about dealing with very sophisticated forecasting tools and techniques in the professional literature, there is virtually nothing available providing guidance on approaching the actual analysis of prospective financial information such as these projected budget deficits. Nor are the types of prospective financial information frequently encountered by accounting or finance professionals in the daily course of their work addressed. For example, will the cash flow projected in a set of prospective financial statements of $1 million be available in a timely fashion for debt service next year, or will there be a negative cash flow, with a need for short-term borrowing (or, worse yet, bankruptcy)? This book seeks to help fill this need for a systematic approach for the analysis of prospective financial statements that can be used by CPAs and other analysts.

Financial analysts need to be equipped with techniques that will allow them to sort through the various forms of prospective financial information, and the assumptions that structure them. This book will go beyond the narrow confines of the CPA's role in the analysis of prospective financial statements as addressed by the AICPA. It will focus on the preparation and analysis of prospective financial statements from the perspective of a management consultant and business analyst.

Although this text will address prospective financial information in general, which is any financial information about the future (F10, p. 9), this information is often specifically presented in the particular form of financial statements, the two major categories of which are financial forecasts, and financial projections. These will be the focus of this work and are defined as follows:

A *financial forecast* should present:

. . . to the best of the responsible party's knowledge and belief, an entity's expected financial position, results of operations, and cash flows. (F10, p. 9)

A forecast is based on no significant change in circumstance.

A financial projection should present:

to the best of the responsible party's knowledge and belief, given one or more hypothetical assumptions, an entity's expected financial position, results of operations, and cash flow. (F10, p. 9)

A projection is based on the assumption of one or more significant changes.

1.2   THE CHALLENGE

The analysis of prospective financial statements presents some important challenges. This information, which is usually prepared by accountants, is presented on a regular basis to banks, potential investors, and business people, and is the basis upon which they make their decisions. But many of these analysts are attempting to apply the techniques and methodologies used in the analysis of historical financial information to prospective financial information. This just does not work.

Although there are a number of similarities between the analysis of historical financial information and prospective financial information, there are some distinct dissimilarities, which are important. The most important difference between the two is that historical financial information is analyzed based on the assumption that the numbers contained in them are relatively verifiable; whereas, prospective financial information must be analyzed using the assumption (given in the *Guide for Prospective Financial Information,* developed by the AICPA), that the actual results achieved will most likely vary from those presented in the prospective financial statements (F10, p. 112 and p. 140).

This very important difference leads to the need for an entirely different perspective and approach for the analysis of prospective financial information, a point that is seldom fully appreciated. CPAs tend to rely on the tools that have served them over the years, and these tools focus primarily on the historical, not the prospective.

1.3   THE GENERAL APPROACH

In order to help facilitate a proper analysis of prospective financial statements, this book begins with the nontraditional idea that the analysis process must be grounded in a new view of the firm. This new view is the systems view, in which the firm is seen as an assemblage of interrelated systems. All of these important subsystems of the organization are emphasized along with their interrelatedness. The purpose of using the systems view is to optimize the inflow of information for proper analysis and decision making. This is possible because the systems view describes the reality of how an organization actually works—a reality that has often been overlooked in the past. The main subjects of the various chapters of this book will address the most important subsystems of the firm, which are all elements in the systems view of the firm.

There needs to be an explicit recognition of the critical importance of assumptions relative to the ongoing dynamics of the business context, and of the variety of interacting (and sometimes conflicting) goals normally associated with the modern business firm. This book presents a process model in Chapter 2 that outlines the steps that should be taken for this type of analysis and helps to organize the various topics involved in a constructive way in order to enable the reader to draw reasonable and practical inferences concerning how to proceed. In subsequent chapters the text addresses a detailed discussion of these relevant topics in the following sequence:

Chapter 3	Communication	The Foundation
Chapter 4	Accounting	The Framework
Chapter 5	Prospective Financial Statements	The Standards
Chapter 6	Strategic Planning	The Context
Chapter 7	Systems	The Reality
Chapter 8	Modeling, Forecasting, and Sensitivity Analysis	Some Tools
Chapter 9	Financial Analysis	The Basics
Chapter 10	A Case Study	The Application

This book was written to help analysts understand and analyze prospective financial information and prepare meaningful prospective financial statements, including but not restricted to forecasts and projections—which are crucial for the planning and decision-making process. Figure 1-1 presents a conceptual overview of how the above-listed relevant facets fit into

Figure 1-1   Conceptual Overview of the Book

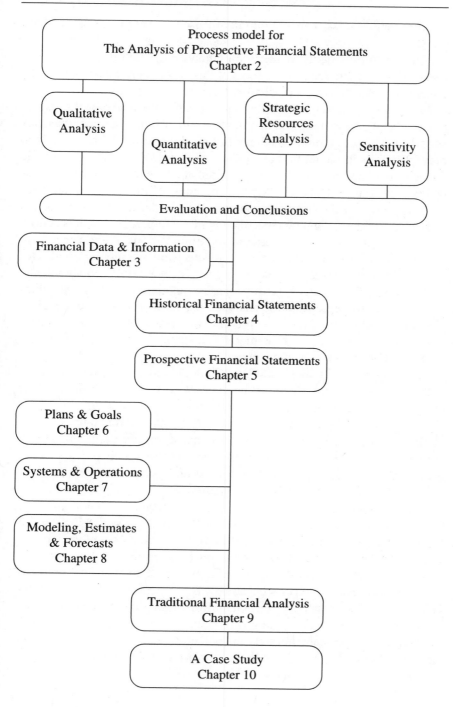

the complete process. The integration of these is the explicit task of Chapter 2.

In order to provide the reader with guidance through the many details that must be considered in the course of this work, a brief overview of the conceptual essentials of each chapter follows.

In order to address the special requirements of the analysis of prospective financial information, and in order to assure the integration of the many sorts of information and procedures involved, the task of Chapter 2 is to present a holistic model that assembles the input of the various analytic facets of the total process. It is holistic in that it integrates the basic methods of financial analysis with the systems view of the firm and the planner's attention to the business context. This model, however, is not an algorithm. It does not guarantee a reading of the future. Rather, it is heuristic in nature: it guides the process of examining various likely scenarios in a manner that assists rational planning and decision making. It provides for optimization, which is a reasonable goal where uncertainty is unavoidable.

The model that emerges has five phases: qualitative analysis, quantitative analysis, strategic resource analysis, sensitivity analysis, and evaluation and conclusions. Chapter 2 presents these in enough detail to allow for a basic understanding of the model. The components of the model are elaborated on in subsequent chapters.

Precisely because data have relevance if and only if they can influence decisions, the analyst's role must be understood within the framework of information processing and communication theory. The analyst's role is not limited to giving technical advice or arranging assorted data.

Hence, in Chapter 3, not only is a case made for this claim, but a basic communication-theoretic framework is laid for the heuristic process model presented in Chapter 2. This allows us to understand better the diverse facets of the firm, and how they fit together.

The day when an accountant could be qualified armed with nothing more than an adding machine is long since gone. It is necessary in today's world to be in touch with a great number of disciplines and much information in order to perform even their traditional functions properly.

This becomes even more important if, in fact, accountants are going to present themselves as experts capable of being part of the process to develop or analyze prospective financial information. Beyond the basic technical skills of traditional accounting, it is imperative for the contemporary accountant to understand not only the potential manipulations of accounting numbers but the theoretical basis from which these numbers were developed.

In Chapter 4, the basic concepts and principles embodied in what is called Generally Accepted Accounting Principles (GAAP) are examined with an eye to showing how these are integrated into the initial stages of the overall process of financial analysis. In effect, these principles serve as the foundation for the process; however, they do not mechanically determine the outcome.

It is also necessary to appreciate the standards that have been established by the AICPA for the preparation and examination of prospective financial statements. These standards are examined in Chapter 5. They are helpful guidelines and provide a general context in which to approach the process of generating sound prospective financial statements. But they only provide a starting point. If the process is to be viable, the analyst (or accountant) must extricate himself or herself from the mind-set of historical cost myopia, so very prevalent among the accounting community and its standards. By relating the rationale and dynamics of these standards to the communications foundation introduced earlier in Chapter 3 and the traditional accounting framework in Chapter 4, their employment as part of a larger analytic effort is justified. In succeeding chapters, then, the other "parts" necessary for this larger effort are developed—an effort that alone can ultimately lead to the formulation of prospective financial statements of direct value to the business planner, decision maker or analyst.

A process that began with an understanding of accounting information must now branch out to include other systems, which turns a complete financial analysis into an holistic endeavor. Expertise in strategic business planning is required to supply the next step in the total process, for it is that which provides an understanding of the context in which the prospective financial statements are developed. It is this context—the changing patterns of the business reality (often called the real world)—that gives life and meaning to numbers. Chapter 6 is a review and discussion of these principles of strategic business planning formulated from the perspective of the financial analyst, who must derive from his insights information pertinent to the development of prospective financial statements.

Just as the firm does not operate in a vacuum, it cannot usefully be viewed as a number of disjointed parts. Because it is an organic whole, it must be understood as a system of systems: that is, its various parts—production, personnel, management, and so on—need to be understood as subsystems having vital relationships to one another. Each part will have its operating parameters, goals, and objectives, which must be understood individually, but which must also be brought together, kept together, and viewed as a composite whole rather than fragmented, as the traditional analysis of financial information has done. This approach is called the systems perspective and is the focus of Chapter 7. It is essential in getting at those pieces of information needed to develop reliable prospective financial statements.

There are various tools that are important and even indispensable for a complete financial analysis. They include modeling, forecasting, and sensitivity analysis. Although not the only tools necessary for analyzing or generating prospective financial information, they are the important basic ones. They need to be understood in a way that is somewhat different from what much of the current literature presents in order to really be helpful with the analysis of prospective financial information. The systems view of the firm and its requirements for genuine prospective analysis are what guide their use here, and it is in this light that these tools are reviewed in Chapter 8.

The traditional approach to the analysis of historical financial information does, of course, provide an important and helpful starting point for the analysis of prospective financial information, but it has to be refined and adapted to the peculiarities and legal requirements of the analysis of prospective financial information.

In Chapter 9 the distinction between traditional and prospective financial analysis is sharpened, and the basic principles and procedures of the former are adapted and extended to satisfy the purposes and theoretical requirements of the latter.

1.4 THE ANALYST

Because of their experience with historical financial information, the AICPA and the accounting profession have assumed a major role in the generation and analysis of prospective financial information. But if one searches the professional literature, there is virtually nothing available on this important topic. This text seeks to help fill this void. Many of the individual topics presented here have been addressed before, but at the heart of this text is an appreciation that all these topics need to be brought together and holistically employed in viewing the firm as a system of systems if proper analysis is to take place.

Yet most analysts do not approach a business as a system of interrelated systems, let alone as a system involving qualitative as well as quantitative issues. There is much more to accounting and financial analysis than the simple manipulation of numbers. A symptom of the myopia of accounting today is that these topics are not viewed by most accounting professionals as integral to performing their professional tasks, although this view is slowly changing. Accountants often do not see a business in its interrelatedness to the environment, nor do they see the components of the business in their interrelatedness to each other. This missing view is called the systems perspective.

This book takes the systems perspective throughout. The firm is viewed as a system consisting of numerous subsystems. These subsystems are constantly kept in mind and are addressed as the subjects of the various chapters. The analysis process itself is a system and is presented as a model in Chapter 2. This analysis process is used to draw information from the various subsystems of the firm. The prospective financial information being analyzed should accurately reflect the various subsystems or elements of the firm. The analyst is in the middle of all three of these: the firm as a system; the analysis process as a system; and the prospective financial information being examined, which should accurately reflect the firm's systems (but often does not). These are all interrelated, and any comments made or information presented in the various chapters of this text will invariably apply to all these as well as to the analyst, regardless of the immediate focus of the point being presented.

The overall focus in this approach is on understanding the firm as a system of systems; the overall focus in more traditional approaches often ends up on the analysis process itself, and the generation of numbers upon which to base the conclusions reached. Because life is nonlinear and dynamic, there is no simple algorithm for the analysis of prospective financial information. One could attempt to present a very linear model, but it would have a major flaw—it would not apply to the real world, which is dynamic and complex. Rather, what is needed is a heuristic model, one which will provide rules of thumb to deal with the many open-ended sources of information which must be dealt with, and which are in a constant state of flux (I20, p. 209).

The subsystems of the firm as discussed in the various chapters of this text will still not perfectly describe the whole organization (system). But even though they present an incomplete and imperfect picture, it is considerably better than the old one, which focused only on the fragmented parts of the organization. Better to do the right thing less than perfectly than the wrong thing perfectly.

The analyst must have an intuitive understanding of and develop a solid foundation in many disciplines. For this reason a large number of seemingly diverse topics are introduced and discussed in this book. They provide important background information and help to develop the sense of the organization as a system of systems. Some topics could possibly be eliminated, and others possibly added. The text seeks to identify those issues and elements which this author believes are most important, presenting the information in such a way as to help develop a foundation for the analyst that will facilitate developing an intuitive understanding of the organization and its subsystems. There is a very real sense in which the analysis of prospective financial information is grounded in art as well as in science.

1.5   THE DIFFERENCES

The needs and challenges that have led to the writing of this book necessitate taking a very different perspective and approach for the analysis of prospective financial information, some important aspects of which include integrating the following:

- An emphasis on what might happen
- The use of the systems paradigm throughout
- A state-of-the-art approach, using modeling, computers, and sensitivity analysis
- An emphasis on communications, qualitative issues, and assumptions
- An appreciation for art over technique
- An emphasis on risk and uncertainty
- A focus on context
- An understanding that change is the only real constant

These important differences and their interrelatedness are reflected in the five-phase model presented for the analysis of prospective financial information.

An Emphasis on What Might Happen.   The emphasis in the analysis of prospective financial information needs to address what might happen rather than what has happened. The probable deviations from the figures in the projections and the interrelationships that drive these deviations should be of paramount importance in such an analysis.

The Systems Paradigm.   An important conclusion reached in this book is the need for incorporating the systems paradigm into all aspects of the process for the analysis of prospective financial information. The systems paradigm emphasizes the critical importance of the interrelationships among all the components of the projections being examined as well as among the techniques being used in the analysis process itself. Rather than fragmenting the system under examination into smaller and more easily managed components, prior to the analysis (as is currently common practice in the analysis of historical information), the individual elements are brought together, kept together, and viewed as a composite whole. This provides a methodology to determine the influence of each individual element on the characteristics of the system as a whole.

The prospective financial statements being examined must be seen in light of a systems perspective in order to maximize the meaningfulness of these statements. The proposed organization or firm presented in these financials is a system, and the various subsystems (elements) examined must each be understood in its role as part of this larger system if the analysis process is to be effective.

State-of-the-Art Approach.   My approach for the analysis of prospective financial information emphasizes financial modeling and the use of computers, which traditional financial analysis does not. This allows for the generating of a number of hypothetical scenarios for the analysis process. Moreover, the overall approach emphasizes the use of sensitivity analysis, thus bringing in the elements of risk and uncertainty. The importance of qualitative issues in the analysis process is also emphasized.

Communications.   An understanding of communications must be stressed in two senses: first, as the theoretic foundation of all the many lines of information flowing within the firm, between the firm and its environment, and between the analyst and decision maker; and, second, as the practical basis of the behavioral aspects of information. The second of these is the sense of communication that makes the ultimate process model in Chapter 2 a praxis-based model. The qualitative issues and the assumptions that underpin the prospective financial statements are as important to the analysis process as are the quantitative ones, if not more so. Analysts often tend to hide behind numbers, which in isolation have relatively little if any substantive meaning.

Art.   Another important aspect of the analysis of prospective financial information developed in this work is that there is an emphasis on art rather than on specific techniques. What this means is that analysis is really a very nonlinear exercise. There is continual need for feedback and recognition of the modifications that this nonlinear process demands. This is because of the mass of data encountered, all of which must be questioned.

Risk and Uncertainty.   Due to the fact that in the analysis of historical financial information the numbers used in general are assumed to be relatively accurate, the risk associated with the possibility of drawing incorrect conclusions is relatively predictable. The standard audit approach allows one to confirm the elements of the statements such that a person analyzing those statements can have a degree of comfort with the figures being used for the analysis process.

The analysis of *prospective* financial information is quite different and presents some very important technical challenges. As noted earlier, the projected results may very well not occur. There is no way of guaranteeing, with a confidence similar to that obtained with audited statements, the relative accuracy of the figures in prospective financial statements. Accordingly, the degree of uncertainty for each individual element in a prospective financial statement is greater than with historical financials. Overall uncertainty is cumulative and grows geometrically with the number of elements under examination, due to the compounding effect of the combinations and permutations of the potential errors. Therefore, the overall uncertainty with prospective financial statements must take on a radically greater importance in the analysis process, and the tools employed must be tailored to these special needs.

Context.   The approaches that serve the accountant/analyst well when analyzing historical financial information, although helpful in providing some basic techniques, are inadequate when addressing the analysis of prospective financial information. What is needed is a new broader perspective. In both types of analysis it is important to understand the context in which the business operates, but in prospective analysis it is unquestionably the heart of the matter.

For the analysis of historical financial information, the context is of secondary importance, because the numbers are assumed to be relatively verifiable, set and supportable. The opposite is true with the analysis of prospective financial information. Due to the above-mentioned uncertainties and their possible effects on the actual outcome(s), any individual figure contained within a prospective financial statement has a much lesser degree of relative importance because it is less reliable. Therefore, the prime focus within the analysis of prospective financial information needs to rest with the context in which that information is presented. Therefore, qualitative analysis of this information, once again, becomes equally if not more important than quantitative analysis.

Change.   Addressing the probability of change is another important element in the analysis of prospective financial information. Due to new technologies impacting communications, transportation, information, and virtually every aspect of our lives, the world is changing radically. Many business professionals and analysts have trouble with change. Although some minimal professional standards have been issued by the AICPA, little if any discussion has ensued on the topic of prospective financial information.

Should accountants be concerned with the future? Whether they want to or not, they will more and more be forced to deal with this issue. Therefore, they must confront the importance of the reality that all accountants and all businesses (in spite of the inevitable resistance to it) must be able to deal effectively with the future. This is why prospective financial statements are generated.

If the accountant is now not only to deal with historical financial statements but also to step into the role of an expert on prospective financial information, then a careful review of the accountant's preparedness for this role is in order. The AICPA's standards require that prospective financial statements "be prepared with appropriate care by qualified personnel" (F10, p. 19).

The primary qualification for dealing with prospective financial information is the ability to deal with and appreciate change. It might be difficult to define the exact rate of this change, but the reality is that change is inevitable, and the rate is increasing. John Naisbitt, in *Megatrends,* describes ten new trends transforming society. They are:

1. The shift in strategic resources from an industrial to an information society.
2. The coming sellers market and the new competition for the best employees.

3. The whittling away of middle management.
4. The continuing entrepreneurial revolution.
5. The emergence of the new variegated workforce.
6. The demographic revolution of working women.
7. The growing use of intuition and vision.
8. The mismatch between our educational system and the needs of the new information society.
9. The rising importance of corporate health issues.
10. The values of baby boomers, those born between 1946 and 1964, who are now populating the ranks of management. (E27, pp. 5–6)

These basic trends are pervasive and are still transforming the society in which we live. A financial analyst cannot function without at least acknowledging the existence of these ten hypotheses.

The realities of these trends have become even more apparent since the original book was first published. Further research has recently led Naisbett to postulate ten guidelines for reinventing the corporation. They are:

1. The best and brightest people will gravitate toward those corporations that foster personal growth.
2. The manager's new role is that of coach, teacher, and tutor.
3. The best people will want ownership—psychic and literal—in a company; the best companies are providing it.
4. Companies will increasingly turn to third-party contractors, shifting from hired labor to contract labor.
5. Authoritarian management is yielding to a networking, people style of management.
6. Entrepreneurship within the corporation—intrapreneurship—is creating new markets and revitalizing companies inside out.
7. Quality will be paramount.
8. Intuition and creativity are challenging the "It's all in the numbers" business-school philosophy.
9. Large corporations are emulating the positive and productive qualities of small businesses.
10. The dawn of the information economy has fostered a massive shift from infrastructure to quality of life. (E27, pp. 45–46)

These are the trends for the future of the corporation as seen by Naisbett. They will, if true, have a great impact on whether a business succeeds or not in the future, changing world. The analyst must understand the factors that will correlate with long-range business success in this changing world and marketplace. For example, Naisbett's point number 8 for reinventing the corporation is especially relevant to the artistic aspects of the financial-analysis process. If an accountant is to hold himself or herself forth as an expert in the analysis of prospective financial information and fails to appreciate fully the nonnumerical context in which this information must necessarily be viewed, then that accountant cannot properly perform the analysis. Understanding change is an integral part of understanding this context, and Naisbett is predicting where change is taking businesses.

1.6 CONCLUSION

The terms information, statements, and financial data are used often in this book. A fuller discussion of these terms will follow in subsequent chapters, but a brief introduction might prove helpful. Information is data which have the potential for influencing decisions (H21, p. 1). Statements, then, are selected financial information arranged and presented in a specific format, one in conformity with Generally Accepted Accounting Principles. In the specific case of prospective financial statements, they will be additionally separated by the results of careful systems analysis of the firm in the context of the changing business reality. Financial information is a subset of financial data; financial statements are a subset of financial information. Although the adjectives financial and accounting are used somewhat interchangeably in this text to qualify these terms, the adjective financial usually has a more global connotation. A strict distinction between the terms statements and information is often not followed in the literature, and so these terms are sometimes used interchangeably in the text when there is no danger of confusion. However, it is important to realize that they often signify different levels of analytic treatment.

The discussion in this text will not be restricted to prospective financial statements only, but will be more expansive in addressing prospective financial information in general, when appropriate, and thus go beyond the limited scope of many of the AICPA's standards.

Last, it is incumbent upon analysts to understand the multifaceted and interrelated nature of the many elements addressed in this book and the role that they play in the analysis of prospective financial information. Working with prospective financial statements requires an understanding of many elements and topics not considered when dealing with historical financials.

The text is not intended to provide all the answers to all the questions about this important topic. Rather, it is intended to be a practitioner's guide to the analysis of prospective financial statements.

The Analysis of Prospective Financial Statements— The Process Model

CHAPTER OUTLINE

- Step 1—Qualitative Sensitivity Analysis
- Step 2—Quantitative Sensitivity Analysis
- Step 3—Strategic (Total) Resources Sensitivity Analysis

2.7 PHASE 5—EVALUATION AND CONCLUSIONS

2.8 SUMMARY

2.1 INTRODUCTION

The base has now been prepared for the presentation of the model for the analysis of prospective financial statements. The factors to be covered have been discussed, and now they must be organized into a formal model that can be followed by the analyst.

The model will be divided into five basic phases:

Phase 1: Qualitative Analysis

Phase 2: Quantitative Analysis

Phase 3: Strategic (Total) Resources Analysis

Phase 4: Sensitivity Analysis

Phase 5: Evaluation and Conclusions

Each of these phases is comprised of pertinent steps that provide the precise mechanism for analysis.

Keep in mind the conditions that are likely to be faced. The basic information is usually prepared by accountants for presentation, often on a regular basis, to banks, potential investors, and business people. The work may apply traditional techniques, but an analysis based solely upon the techniques used with historical data will not work.

Remember that the organization is a system with many subsystems and that the analysis must reflect the interactive nature of those subsystems. Unless the organization weaves those elements together by its information/communication system and ties its decisions to its strategic path, the resources will not be utilized properly.

Later chapters will discuss in some detail the issues that relate to this model. They are vital to a thorough understanding of the process model and should be carefully pursued once you understand the basic template for the analysis.

Remember that there is no single approved process for analysis. Life is nonlinear and dynamic. The picture presented by the prospective statements is but a snapshot of a single point in a constantly changing vista. Any analysis must translate the clues presented by this single scenario into a reasonable feel for what is *likely* to happen. The analysis model as presented will not give a perfect picture, but it will give a better sense of what really matters than do traditional methods.

To understand the implications of this model as compared to traditional models, consider how this approach differs from that used with the analysis of historical financial information, integrating the following:

- An emphasis on what might happen
- The use of the systems paradigm throughout
- An approach using modeling, computers, and sensitivity analysis
- An emphasis on communications, qualitative issues, and assumptions
- An appreciation for art over technique
- An emphasis on risk and uncertainty
- A focus on context
- An understanding that change is the only real constant

Emphasis.   Prospective statements deal with what might happen rather than what has happened. The probable deviations from the presented data and the interrelationships that drive these deviations are of paramount importance.

Systems.   It is not enough to examine the parts separately; it is how those parts interrelate that makes the difference.

Approach.   This approach uses computer techniques, emphasizes sensitivity analysis, deals directly with risk and uncertainty, and recognizes explicitly the importance of qualitative issues.

Communications.   The model stresses the importance of communications not only in content but also in all those human elements that affect the process. Assumptions and qualitative issues must become the focus of the analysis process.

Art.   The art of analysis lies with the need to recognize and translate the clues inherent in the data.

Risk.   In the analysis of historical financial statements, the numbers can be confirmed; in prospective statements they cannot. The risk and uncertainty is greater, more important, and demands special attention.

Context.   In communications, context is all; in prospective financial statements, not only the context within the reports but the context of the organization's activities establishes the real message.

Change.   In historical statements what is done is done, but in prospective statements what may be is an ever changing thing. Therefore, the analysis must establish the likely trends as well as account for possible discontinuities. Qualitative analysis is a strong factor.

2.2   THE PROCESS MODEL

It is now time to build the model itself. The five phases referred to earlier provide the base, but before proceeding further, it might prove helpful to review the development and analysis processes for prospective financial statements graphically, as presented in Figure 2-1.

In this figure the developer takes all the relevant data and elements (the subjects of the various chapters in the text), starting with the most general and progressively "funneling" down to the more specific, and then generates the prospective financial statements. The statements, regardless of who might provide assistance in their preparation, are the responsibility of the parties who developed the underlying assumptions, usually management (F10, p. 10). A point that needs to be stressed is that the analysis process is separate and distinct from the development process. It follows the opposite flow, starting with the specific prospective financial statements to be analyzed and progressively taking a more global and open-ended perspective.

The process model for analysis developed and presented in the following sections of this chapter is heuristic. It will provide rules of thumb to deal with the many open-ended sources of potential information that must be dealt with, and which are in a constant state of flux (I20, p. 209). Figure 2-1 presents some of these sources as they relate to the development of the prospective financial information. But the analysis process is not limited to

Figure 2-1   The Development and Analysis of Prospective Financial Statements

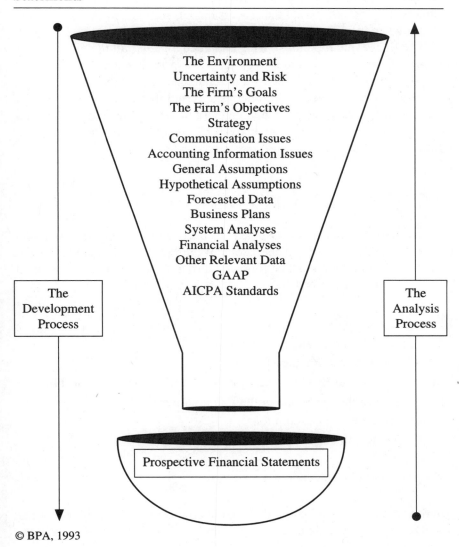

The Environment
Uncertainty and Risk
The Firm's Goals
The Firm's Objectives
Strategy
Communication Issues
Accounting Information Issues
General Assumptions
Hypothetical Assumptions
Forecasted Data
Business Plans
System Analyses
Financial Analyses
Other Relevant Data
GAAP
AICPA Standards

The
Development
Process

The
Analysis
Process

Prospective Financial Statements

© BPA, 1993

what was used in the development process. Any other sources of information that might provide insight into the prospective financial information can and should be used. Finally, just as no single element or organizational subsystem should be viewed in isolation or fragmented from the whole system, so, too, no phase or step in the analysis process for prospective financial information should be fragmented from any of the others. But, rather, all the phases and steps are part of the process model, and can only be truly meaningful when viewed as part of this composite whole.

The final evaluation must bring and keep together all the relevant elements of the process in order to examine them in such a fashion as to determine the influence of each upon the characteristics of the whole system, for it is the whole system that interests us and that is being used for the evaluation, not any one particular element or subsystem. This is the heart of the systems process for the analysis of prospective financial information.

2.3   PHASE 1: QUALITATIVE ANALYSIS

Before starting Phase 1, it is assumed that the practitioner already has a solid overview of the firm and its operations. Within Phase 1 there are seven distinct steps. Each step must be followed through and then blended with all the other steps. The steps are:

Step 1: Establish the General Context
Step 2: Review the Strategic Plan
Step 3: Examine the Business Plan
Step 4: Define and Examine the Systems and Their Interrelationships
Step 5: Determine the Scope of the Examination
Step 6: Examine the Assumptions
Step 7: Review the Preparation and Presentation

Step 1: Establish the General Context

In the process of establishing the general context, it is imperative that the analyst consider the elements of communication present in the operation. Following the concepts of Chapter 3, the analyst must examine the elements and components of the communication system required for the organization. This deals with the projected firm as reflected in the prospective financial statements.

Equally important is the presentation of the prospective financial statements themselves—they are part of the communication process.

The material in Chapter 4 provides the basic analytical framework for establishing the general context for accounting information. To do so it is necessary to examine:

- Conformity of the statements with GAAP
- The objectives of the financial statements
- The qualitative characteristics of the accounting information
- The basic assumptions made
- The basic principles applied
- The basic modifiers used

These basic issues help to confirm that the requirements of GAAP are met and set the context for the presentation and understanding of financial information. This allows the analyst to establish a correct perspective on the value of the information contained in the statements.

Step 2: Review the Strategic Plan

The strategic plan, with its various components, creates the context of the firm's operations, and so the analyst must review and understand it. Sections 6.2, 6.3, and 6.4 present an overview of this process and its important related elements.

Step 3: Examine the Business Plan

Since the business plan encompasses the way in which management expects to implement the firm's strategy, the firm must have a grasp of it. Reviewing the business plan is a vital part of the analysis process. Section 6.5 addresses the differences between the global plans developed in the strategic planning process and the detailed business plans that must be developed. It is imperative that the analyst consider the strategic plan and the business plan as a unit. Unless they are coordinated, the firm will lose direction.

Within this step of the analysis process is the need to examine the various business functions and their roles. In the start-up organization, there should be evidence that these functions have been included in the plans. An area often overlooked is the necessity of a viable information system.

Another area of concern is the forecasting process. It is necessary for the organization to have an ongoing forecasting process. Continuous change requires continuous scanning and a mechanism to relate information gathered to appropriate action.

Step 4: Define and Examine the Systems and Their Interrelationships

The overall perspective in the analysis must be in the systems context. This requires a sensitivity to the components and subsystems of the organization and their interrelatedness. Thorough analysis requires that the elements be brought together, kept together, and viewed as a composite whole.

Each subsystem must be considered as the whole for its parts, and as part of its larger system. Analysts need to develop a feel for organizations as systems, and Chapter 7 provides an introduction to this important component of the analysis process.

Step 5: Determine the Scope of the Examination

How much study is necessary for the analysis to be complete? This, too, requires judgment. Consider Section 5.4 and its list of procedures to help in providing guidance for determining the scope of the examination.

Step 6: Examine the Assumptions

Assumptions underlie all financial statements, but are especially critical to prospective statements. To understand the statements it is necessary to understand and evaluate these assumptions. Section 5.4 presents some specific procedures that can be used to evaluate the assumptions reflected in prospective financial statements.

Step 7: Review the Preparation and Presentation

Section 5.4 provides specific procedures for reviewing the presentation of prospective financial statements. Use them as a checklist in the analytic process. Some of the items in the checklist apply equally in Phase 2 of the analysis process—quantitative analysis.

2.4   PHASE 2: QUANTITATIVE ANALYSIS

The four main steps of quantitative analysis are:

Step 1: Familiarization with and Review of Model
Step 2: Traditional Financial Analysis
Step 3: Discriminant (Bankruptcy) Analysis
Step 4: Valuation

Step 1: Familiarization with and Review of Model

The first step in the quantitative process is to develop an understanding of the model. Where spreadsheets are used, this clearly requires having the actual computer model available for analysis. Although the AICPA suggests that analysis should be conducted primarily from the hard-copy printouts of the prospective statements, assumptions underlying prospective statements differ from those basic to historical information. The standard compilation report for both a forecast and a projection that does not contain a range states:

> There will usually be differences between forecasted and actual results, because events and circumstances frequently do not occur as expected and those differences may be material. (F10, p. 111)

The emphasis in the analysis of prospective financial information must focus on what *might* happen, unlike the analysis of historical financial information, which deals with what *has* happened. Deviations should be expected and become the heart of the analysis. This includes the cause of the deviations as well as their identity.

With the spreadsheet computer model in hand, the first step is a quick walk-through. It is important to get a feel for the layout and a sense of the process of information development. Is there a natural flow from top to bottom and from left to right in the spreadsheet? Without a proper natural flow, cell input is likely to be random and encourage errors.

Next are the initial arithmetic tests using the hard-copy printout of the model. Using a simple calculator, a quick and acceptable test of the arithmetics involved can be made. Remember that accuracy in this regard does not imply value for the numbers involved.

The review should then examine the drivers of the various cells. This requires an understanding and facility with the functions of spreadsheets. Typically this involves a version of Lotus or some similar spreadsheet program, such as Excel. The process requires reconstructing the logic behind the development of the various elements of the model. Most cells are dependent on another cell for their computations.

Having confirmed the initial mathematical accuracy and a sense of the functions that drive the model, it is time to test the model itself. This requires changing various inputs of the original model to see if it maintains its arithmetical accuracy. For example, does the balance sheet equation remain in balance? Many models use an arithmetic approach rather than an algebraic one and do not allow a generalized approach. Even the smallest change in an element may require hours of editing to reflect that change properly.

Since projected financial statements depict conditions highly related to change, the computer programs should be capable of reflecting such change and the analyst should weigh the results with this in mind. Indeed, the analyst should require access to the model programs and, if they are not available, should insist on multiple runs of the prospective financial statements showing the effects of possible variations in the important assumptions.

Step 2: Traditional Financial Analysis

The first step in traditional financial analysis consists of choosing benchmarks and targets. Typically they have three sources:

1. Historical figures
2. Industry norms
3. Various budgets and targets

The approach for this type of analysis is covered in Sections 9.3 and 9.4. The general categories available are:

• Horizontal analysis
• Vertical analysis
• Ratio analysis

After identifying the desired approach(es) and ratios, the analyst should use the spreadsheet for calculation on a period-by-period basis. The test is for ballpark figures and time consistency. When a significant deviation occurs, assumptions should be reviewed and business plans examined.

Step 3: Discriminant (Bankruptcy) Analysis

The use of discriminant analysis is up to the analyst. It does provide a good basis for reference. The formula presented in this text is for manufacturing firms and is skewed toward older, more established firms and may be unsatisfactory for start-up situations. It is presented in Section 9.3.

Step 4: Valuation

A common practice today is to value organizations and their elements on the basis of the present value of future after-tax cash flows. Future values can also be used and are more consistent with the perspective of prospective financial statements. Difficulties arise in the choice of interest rates and the exclusion of other significant resources. Section 9.3 presents a brief discussion of this topic, which is addressed in depth in most management accounting texts.

2.5   PHASE 3: STRATEGIC (TOTAL) RESOURCES ANALYSIS

The Statement of Financial Accounting Concepts as discussed in Chapter 4 recognizes the importance of all resources of the organization. In Chapter 6 the importance of qualitative goals and objectives and the resources associated with them is discussed. Here, too, is noted the potential discrepancies between promulgated strategic objectives and detailed business plans.

All the resources needed to sustain goals and objectives must be reflected in the business plan. An absence of needed resources suggest either that the goals are not important or that a serious flaw exists in the process.

For goals to have meaning, several guidelines apply:

1.   They must be clear, direct, and understood.
2.   They must be attainable.
3.   They must be translated into concrete factors. (F54, p. 5)

The third guideline is especially significant and often ignored.

Goals are often screened out based upon difficulty of measurement, resulting in the omission of important qualitative goals. One approach to the quantification of qualitative factors follows (F54, pp. 5–6):

> Well managed firms establish goals in terms of sales levels, personnel levels, and both physical and nonphysical resources. It is not uncommon to see at least some of them spelled out in financial reports.
>
> Thus a firm may have such goals as a 20% increase in sales dollars, a 15% increase in building space, a 10% increase in public recognition. We can depict this array as a set:
>
> $$A, B, C, \ldots\ldots\ldots\ldots n$$
>
> where each item in the set represents a goal as stated.
>
> We can further depict the desired change in resources (these goals become resources for the firm's future) by setting the present value of each resource at 100. Then the desired 20% increase in, say, A would be shown as
>
> $$A_n = 1.2A_o$$

This provides a way of addressing the various goals of a business as a set. Setting targets in such a fashion allows the incorporation of both physical and nonphysical elements into the business plans in a concrete form, thus perfectly complementing the strategic-planning process.

As identified above, the goals themselves become a set of resources for the firm's future. These resources and their budgeted levels can be viewed in the form of a matrix, in which the letters represent subsets of resources (F54, p. 6):

year	0	1	2	3	4	5
	A_0	A_1	A_2	A_3	A_4	A_5
	B_0	B_1	B_2	B_3	B_4	B_5
	C_0	C_1	C_2	C_3	C_4	C_5
	-	-	-	-	-	-
	-	-	-	-	-	-
	n_0	n_1	n_2	n_3	n_4	n_5

If A were the resource, cash, we would budget for it in the usual way but $A_1 \ldots A_5$ would be presented as percentages of A_0. Indeed, by setting all initial resource levels at 100, the desired or expected values of the resources in subsequent years would be set at some percentage of 100. In assessing the results of decisions, projected-end sets caused by the decision are compared to desired-end sets. In this way it is possible to include all elements directly in the decision model and relate each one to the desired results.

Since each individual element (resource) does not have the same relative value (utility) in the firm's strategy, a weighted average approach can be used (with changing weights over time). This approach would allow for the computation of a single measure for the total utility of all the firm's resources at any point in time. This approach is consistent with the systems perspective because all the resources are viewed as a composite whole, with the single measure indicating their current status.

2.6   PHASE 4: SENSITIVITY ANALYSIS

The three main steps in sensitivity analysis are:

Step 1: Qualitative Sensitivity Analysis
Step 2: Quantitative Sensitivity Analysis
Step 3: Strategic (Total) Resources Sensitivity Analysis

Sensitivity analysis is discussed in Section 8.3. Although the static component of analysis is important, it is even more important to examine just how the prospective financial statements respond to change, which is what this phase of the analysis addresses.

Step 1: Qualitative Sensitivity Analysis

The discussion of various issues in the qualitative analysis section are predicated upon a static review of the information presented. However, the figures exactly as presented in the prospective financial statements are not likely to occur. The qualitative components of the analysis emphasize the context of both the construction of the statements and how they are expected to function.

Therefore, a sensitivity analysis needs to be applied to these components examining the effect of changes in the context in which the prospective financial statements are assumed to function. This is the proverbial "what if" type of analysis usually applied to quantitative information. This is important because it is the qualitative information that underpins the quantitative information.

Step 2: Quantitative Sensitivity Analysis

Quantitative sensitivity analysis requires addressing the issues discussed in Chapter 8. Three kinds of sensitivity are relevant:

1. Numerical sensitivity
2. Behavioral sensitivity
3. Strategic sensitivity

Numerical sensitivity is concerned with the specific arithmetical changes within the model when subjected to change. All financial models exhibit arithmetical sensitivity.

Behavioral sensitivity relates to changes in the model when subjected to variations in parameter values or relationships within the model. The implications can be more far-reaching than with numerical sensitivity. The analyst must be aware if patterns of behavior fluctuate substantially over probable ranges of activity.

Strategic sensitivity examines the possibility of changes in model-based policy conclusions with reasonable changes in the model.

The three types of model changes used to facilitate sensitivity analysis are discussed in Chapter 8:

1. Parameter changes
2. Structural changes
3. A combination of these two (H37, p. 191)

These constitute the mechanical changes that can be made to the actual model in an effort to test the various types of sensitivity within the model.

Step 3: Strategic (Total) Resources Sensitivity Analysis

Strategic or total resource sensitivity examines changes in the total resources matrix presented in Section 2.5 (Phase 3 of the analysis process).

In the section on quantitative sensitivity analysis above, there was a discussion of the possible effects on policy or the strategic plan due to possible changes within various elements of the plan itself. This is called strategic sensitivity—a similar-sounding topic to strategic resources sensitivity. Strategic resources sensitivity is concerned with the effects on the outcome of the specific prospective financial statements under analysis due to changes or modifications in major assumptions. The set of these outcomes (and future resources), which can include both qualitative and quantitative elements, is the focus in this area of analysis.

Policy affects outcomes, but outcomes can affect policy and this condition is encountered in a nonlinear dynamic environment in which feedback plays an important role. These two similar but distinct types of sensitivities are a reflection of the interrelatedness seen when using the systems approach. In fact, in this process model, a number of the analyses are interrelated.

2.7 PHASE 5: EVALUATION AND CONCLUSIONS

The final phase in the process requires the analyst to examine and assess the significance of the results and information obtained in the previous phases. Can the firm "exploit the opportunities and meet the threats that the environment is presenting" (C12, p. 154) in the way that the prospective financial statements indicate? Do the prospective financial statements appear workable and do the assumptions provide a reasonable basis for the projections or forecasts?

If there are deviations, will they be material? Given the systems perspective, are the net results—given the probable deviations in assumptions—acceptable in light of the initial projected or forecasted results?

There is no single appropriate, simple method for arriving at any conclusions. The analyst must understand the "scientific use of the imagination" coupled with a "material basis" upon which to develop any speculations (C7, p. 162).

Finally, the CPA performing any of the services as outlined in Chapter 5 will also have to conform to AICPA standards as presented in that chapter.

2.8 SUMMARY

This chapter has addressed the importance and interrelatedness of the many components within the process for analysis of prospective financial statements. It should be noted that the process must use as much art as techniques, methodologies, and specific activities.

Methods applied to the analysis of historical statements are inappropriate for the analysis of prospective statements. Historical statements reflect what has happened; prospective statements tell only what might happen. This fact means that new and different tools must be applied to this developing area.

The model for the analysis of prospective financial statements has been developed and briefly discussed. Now is the time to proceed with a more detailed discussion of the topics presented in the process model.

CHAPTER THREE

Communication— the Foundation

CHAPTER OUTLINE

3.1   INTRODUCTION

This chapter identifies, defines, and emphasizes the role of communication in the operation of an organization and relates that role to the process of analyzing prospective information. The communication subsystem is one of the most important and pervasive in the firm and must be understood for proper analysis to take place, for it provides the foundation on which the many other subsystems of the firm rest.

Unless the various elements of the organizational system obtain necessary information, they cannot perform their functions properly. If the information they receive is not effectively communicated, the information will be distorted and the resulting behavior will be inappropriate. Clearly, then, the design and prospective use of the internal information/communication system is of vital interest to the analyst. So, too, is both the information to be provided to external interests *and* its process of communication.

The study of communication is a most complex one and this text is not the vehicle for a truly in-depth look at it. Here will be an introduction to the field as it relates to the analysis of prospective financial statements. What is provided should alert the analyst to the type of communication issues that are relevant as well as the need to deal with them.

As suggested above, this chapter will focus on the role of communication in the operation of the organization. But there are other equally important communication processes at work and of concern. They include the critical communication processes between the firm and the business environment, as well as between the analyst and the whole process for the generation and analysis of the prospective financial information. The comments made within this chapter will apply equally to these other processes. Each is a special case or instantiation of the general communication model that will be presented and discussed.

If, indeed, there can be no information without communication, then the process of communication should be understood. Figure 3-1 (C24, p. 4) depicts this process.

The sender is, in the case of the forecasted report, the organization responsible for generating the report. The coder is the accountant who translates the message into symbols for transmission (*all* messages are encoded).

The channel is the report, which may be formal or informal, oral or written. This channel has a capacity, as do all channels, and the purpose is not to send as much data as possible, but rather to optimize the information received. All messages are decoded, and this may be done by the receiver or by an agent whose message the receiver must still decode.

Figure 3-1   The Communication Process

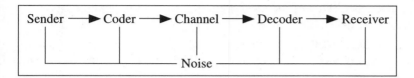

Noise is anything that distracts the message being received as sent, and can take many forms. Too much data can become noise.

The point is that prospective financial information is subject to the rules of communication and, if it is to be effective, due consideration must be given to the communication process.

Communication Theory

To understand the relevant communication needs it is advisable to look at communication theory. To maintain an appropriate focus, let us consider the three levels of communication.

Three Levels of the Communication Problem
The real question in information is that of its appropriateness for decisions. These decisions are the ones that will be made "by the decision maker and not, indirectly, by the designers" (H21, p. 23).

There can be many problems in understanding a transmitted message. These problems can all affect the communication and therefore are relevant to any consideration of financial information, whether historical or prospective.

> When we read a text, or listen to a speech, we are aware not only of the individual words and phrases but also of a broad, overall effect. We appreciate the word or symbolic patterning and rhythm, the prevailing length or shortness of words, the simplicity or complexity or the grammar; we may glean some understanding of our writer's or speaker's social background. All such properties may be brought to our attention though we may not perform detailed analysis while reading or listening. (K2, pp. 110–111)

A basic traditional discussion and analysis of the communication problem was conducted by Shannon and Weaver. Weaver made note of three levels of the communication problem. They were as follows:

- Level A: The technical problem deals with how accurately the symbols of communication can be transmitted. The primary concern is with the accurate transmission of the message rather than with meaning, relative value, purpose, or importance.
- Level B: The semantic problem deals with how precisely the transmitted symbols convey the desired meaning. Here the main concern is with how the message has been interpreted rather than the intended meaning of the message or the accuracy of its transmission.
- Level C: The effectivity problem deals with how effectively the received meaning affects the conduct of the recipient. Psychological and emotional reactions are relevant in this level of analysis. (H21, p. 23)

The three levels of the problem are levels of increasing complexity. Although much of the early work in communications theory focused on Level A, which was a technical problem, most of the study today focuses on levels B and C, the issues of semantics and effectivity. All three levels are of interest to the analyst. There are various perspectives that the analyst must take. On the one hand is the examination of the systems within the projected organization. Its operations are reflected (or should be) in the prospective financial statements. On the other hand, another part of the analysis requires an appreciation for the realities of the present, and the communications that are being made by the designer of those prospective financial statements. What are their immediate objectives? The promulgated projected objectives are articulated and reflected within the prospective financial statements. But what, in fact, are the real objectives and goals that are motivating the creation of the prospective financial statements?

The recent challenges within the savings and loan and banking industries demonstrate this problem. Much of the financial information that the bankers relied upon, although purportedly reflecting proposed activities, had very little to do with reality. In fact, the real purpose of many of those communications was only to secure the loans in question. The failure of the analysts was really due to entirely missing the purposes of those documents. This resulted not only in the failures of the projected enterprises, but also in the failures of many financial institutions as well.

The Communications Model
There has been a lot written about communications theory. The five parts of the communications model are:

- An information source, which produces a message or a sequence of messages for the destination. The message may be sent via telegraph, radio, telephone, television, face-to-face communication, or other means.
- A transmitter, which operates on the message in some way to produce a signal suitable for transmission over the channel (this process is called encoding). For example, if the message is sent by telephone, the operation consists of changing sound pressure into a proportional electrical current.
- The channel is the medium to transmit the signal from transmitter to receiver. For example, it may consist of a pair of wires, a band of radio frequencies, or a beam of light.
- The receiver, which reconstructs the message from the signal (this process is called decoding).
- The destination (or recipient), which is the person or object for whom the message is intended. (H21, p. 24)

A detailed schematic of the communication model is shown in Figure 3-2.

Following through the model, an information source selects and produces a message. The message is sent through a transmitter. The transmitter changes the messages into a signal, which conveys the message. The channel is the medium from the transmitter to the receiver. The receiver re-

Figure 3-2   The Communication Model

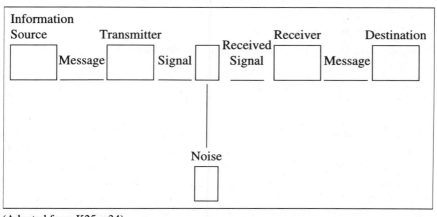

(Adapted from K25, p34)

constructs the message and it is then conveyed to the destination intended. Noise exists throughout the model and is any form of distraction that could interfere with the signal.

The Value of Information

Another important issue is the value of information. "When we talk about the value of information, it is obvious that value is determined by the context of the situation" (H21, p. 18). It is said that there is little value in the information when not much is gained by the extra information. Information is the reduction in the degree of uncertainty about a situation (H21, p. 17). A large part of the concept of value deals with perception. This presents some real problems for many accountants. Most practitioners come from a strongly positivist background in which absolutes are often assumed. Information is generated as if it has some absolute meaning in and of itself.

This is particularly true for less sophisticated users of those figures. The real value of information is only in the usefulness of that information. The systems within the environment have to accommodate communication needs. But, more important, the analyst, in addition to having to ascertain whether the systems are adequate to accommodate the communication needs, must also be sensitive to the context in which the communication document that is being analyzed is presented. The reality is that numbers are only symbols and reflect the ideas of the persons who generated the prospective financial statements. They are not necessarily representative of any physical reality. This concept presents problems for many accountants. Many of the numbers encountered in the analysis of prospective financial statements are based on pure expediency. They are not necessarily based on any physical reality. It is the challenge of analysis to sort through these potentially important limitations to understand the information presented.

The Analyst's Role

Much of accounting and finance revolves around the assumption that analysts are primarily technical specialists. Although this is a very important component of the accountant's responsibilities, there are other equally if not more important functions that the analyst must perform.

There are three facets to the accountant's role: technical specialist, information specialist, and communication specialist. Traditionally, the accountant/analyst's role has focused on technical proficiency. However, to continue without a full understanding of the implications of the other facets of the role would be foolhardy. One of the objectives of this chapter is to understand these roles better.

A better understanding of the role that the accountant/analyst plays will hinge upon an appreciation of the fact that within the analysis process there are two communication systems that are important. The first deals with the actual systems that are proposed to support the initiatives described in the prospective financial statements under examination. This is a primary concern of the analyst, and is one the analyst has to appreciate. There is no approved solution for an ideal communication system. Rather, what is important is that the managers and developers of the prospective financial statements have a sensitivity themselves for the importance of the communication function within the organization. Given the dynamic environment that we find ourselves in, this is becoming a more important aspect of any business plan. Failure to accommodate the realities of dealing with information would show a great naïveté on the part of the preparers of the prospective financial information.

The second communication system deals with the prospective financial statements themselves. They are developed and presented as a communication of information on the part of the firm, and must be understood and treated as such.

Accounting as the Language of Business

Communication is concerned with the transmission of information (H21, p. 22). Accounting is the language of business (H21, p. 5). There are a number of challenges with the use of accounting as a language. They include:

- Meaning
- The effectiveness of a message
- The specific organization that the information relates to
- The control systems of the organization
- The internal and external environments
- Key information points
- Advancing technology
- The measurement of those financial figures
- Specific systems employed (H21, pp. 5–10)

Meaning.   Accounting has often been described as being the language of business. The ability to understand the meaning of accounting information is not always simple. The general opinion of the accounting community and the FASB has been that accounting reports are primarily intended for sophisticated users. The results of recent court cases challenge this myopic and dangerous opinion and imply a much broader range of users than the accounting community is currently willing to acknowledge.

A challenge also arises due to the myriad of standards that now exist (and that are regularly being generated). It is becoming more and more difficult for even a CPA to understand fully all the implications of certain accounting information. The language of accounting is daily becoming more complex due to these numerous new rules. This presents some real challenges especially in the area of analysis of information, and even more so if that financial information happens to be prospective financial information (H21, p. 6).

Effectiveness.   The second point, concerning the effectiveness of a message, is quite important. It is the measure of the ability of the message to influence behavior. We often find that there is inconsistency between the message, even when understood, and the resultant behavior. This challenge presents even more difficulty when we are dealing with prospective financial information.

What are the intentions of the sender of the message? How do we go about interpreting what those intentions are? When dealing with historical financial information, the latitude and potential confusion are almost overwhelming. When dealing with prospective financial information, the number of alternative interpretations available is many times that of historical information. The proper approach for analyzing this information presents a real challenge.

The Organization.   Another important component of information has to do with the specific organization to which the information relates. Again, with historical information we have a set of relative constants/givens. With prospective financial information, the organization is an even greater concern because this information often deals with a start-up operation that does not yet exist. Even when it is not a start-up organization, one should anticipate that the nature of the existing organization could change radically from its present configuration. The organizational context for information becomes crucial to understanding that information. With many of the components of the prospective financial statements themselves defined only as assumptions, the analyst is confronted with a very serious challenge. To understand the ramifications of the many potential variations in these assumptions requires real skill.

Control. All organizations have some form of control system. In the analysis of prospective financial information we are once again challenged with anticipating appropriate control systems to accommodate various systems and subsystems within an organization. The organization itself, at the point in time of the generation of the prospective financial statements, might not yet even exist. The complexity of the potential systems within the plan, the changes that might be required, and the organizational structure and culture that might evolve all present real challenges to analyzing the system of control.

The accounting process is primarily concerned with informational controls (H21, p. 8). But prospective financial information does not concern itself with only informational matters. Rather, a large concern of the prospective financial statements is with financial and operational uncertainties. The ability to analyze and anticipate the control needs within an environment that in itself is conditionally defined presents some major challenges and requires careful analysis.

The Environments. An understanding of the internal and external environments is crucial to understanding the communication function. The responsiveness to these environments within the context of a historical financial information system is in itself quite important, but it is even more so in a situation in which the real focus of the information has to do with the future. The need to focus on the environments and monitor them on a continuous basis is very important. The specific environmental factors that should be considered will be covered more thoroughly in Chapter 6. Even though the analyst might be dealing with a specific prospective financial statement for a specific point in time, the reality is that the viability of that plan in the future will be dependent upon the ability of the organization to be responsive to the signals coming from the above-mentioned environments.

Information Points. There are certain key bits of information that are essential for the success of any organization. They have been called critical success factors. These bits of information are essential for the running and analysis of an existing organization. With prospective information the challenge becomes even greater.

The analyst must anticipate which of the drivers will be most important for the success of the organization. To identify the specific elements presents a challenge, not only for the person or persons responsible for the development of the prospective financial statements, but even more so for the analyst who must have a real appreciation for business in general and for the specific industry under examination in particular. Businesses appear to run one way on paper, but another way in reality. The "critical mass" necessary to execute a business plan successfully is a combination of many different variables. The ability to balance and counterbalance the various strengths and weaknesses is essential for the manager and the analyst alike.

Technology. Another element within the external and internal environment that always presents a challenge for communication is advancing technology. Just a few years ago it was possible to exist in a relatively static environment as far as technology was concerned. We are now confronted with such dynamic, powerful, and often conflicting forces that it is almost impossible to adapt easily. Within an organization the ability to convey information associated with new technologies in a timely fashion is almost impossible. This can require the complete and effective reeducation of major segments of a particular organization's workforce. Often there is no one available to provide this function within the organization itself, but it must be done. One way to deal with rapid obsolence is to create and maintain strong information/communication links with both suppliers and customers.

Prospective financial statements seek to present a view of the future activity of an organization. How well that activity will be accomplished will be determined to a large extent by the ability of the organization to handle information, and handle it effectively.

Measurement. The question of measurement always presents some difficulty. What do the figures in the prospective financial statements really mean? What do the different inventory alternatives imply? What are the implications of the various alternatives available for depreciation? Along with the concept of measurement comes the question of the meaning of that information and whether that meaning has been intentionally distorted to present a biased picture. The analyst is presented with the challenge of sorting through the various techniques that have been embraced by the preparer of the financial statements in order to appreciate the real meaning behind the information.

Systems. Finally, the specific systems employed within an organization will have a large impact on the information and communication. How well an organization has adapted to the importance of information and how well it has anticipated its information needs will determine how viable the prospective financial statements are. The analyst has to look to these factors in performing the analysis.

Although it is beyond the scope of this chapter to go into a detailed discussion of these topics, they are nonetheless very important and essential to understanding the subject of information and communication.

Without a full appreciation of the context in which the prospective financial statements are presented, the analyst will be at a disadvantage in performing his or her function. In order to address this important topic, my discussion of communication will address three major areas. They are:

- The technical aspect of information theory
- The semantic aspect of information theory
- The effectivity aspect of information theory

3.2 THE TECHNICAL ASPECT OF INFORMATION THEORY

One consistent problem in the analysis of prospective financial information is the failure to differentiate between data and information. Too often this results in the failure to analyze effectively.

One definition of information is as follows:

. . . data which have the potential for influencing decisions. This means that information is not random. It has purpose and that purpose is defined in the context of a particular decision or a particular kind of decision. (H21, p. 1)

Some communications specialists are concerned only with the replication of symbols. The analyst must be concerned with the replication of meaning. The technical aspect of information theory is concerned with the efficient and effective transmission of information.

Information theory must therefore deal with:

- The accuracy of the transmitted symbols
- The effects of noise on reception
- The capacity of the channel
- The matching of information content and channel capacity (H21, p. 17)

The four issues alluded to above are concerned with sending and receiving through communication channels.

The coding process can be used to increase the efficiency of the communications sent. Coding must keep in mind the designated receiver. It can affect the meaning and attitude of the receiver as well as increase the accuracy of the transmitted symbols.

Anything that interferes with the transmission of the message is noise. Because the communication model applies to all three levels of communication, noise is not limited to interference with the physical transmission. It can also have a psychological basis (H21, p. 19). It is impossible to eliminate noise from a system totally. An acceptable level is determined using the conceptual approach of cost/benefit analysis. As with many of the problems discussed, a large part depends on the human element, and that human element is not always readily quantifiable (H21, p. 19).

One tool that is used to address the problem of noise is redundancy. We are all familiar with redundancy in terms of repeating an important point of a lecture. The same process is used in communications in order to focus and overcome some of the problems associated with noise (H21, p. 22).

Another important point is that of the capacity of a channel. The channel is important to communication. When one attempts to "crowd too much over a channel" (K25, pp. 26–27), a problem will ensue. All channels have a capacity and it cannot be exceeded. As Weaver states:

> Here again a general theory at all levels will have to take into account not only the capacity of the channel but also the capacity of the audience. If one tries to overcrowd the capacity of the audience, it is probably true, by direct analogy, that you do not, so to speak, fill the audience up and then waste only the remainder by spilling. More likely, and again by direct analogy, if you overcrowd the capacity of the audience you force a general and inescapable error and confusion. (K25, p. 27)

3.3 THE SEMANTIC ASPECT OF INFORMATION THEORY

An appreciation for the nature of communication theory obviously leads one to focus on the issue of meaning. Within the context of prospective financial statements meaning becomes quite important. The people preparing and using prospective financial information have their own biases. These can particularly bear upon the ultimate meaning being conveyed.

The semantic issue of communication is concerned with the replication of meaning, not the replication of symbols. Encoding and decoding can easily impact meaning. Also, different symbols can be used to convey the same meaning.

Section 3.2 focused on the technical issues of the transfer of information between senders and receivers. This section is concerned with the issue of meaning. Some of the areas discussed include:

- Meaning
- Language
- Indexing
- Word Shortening
- Latent Meaning
- Nonverbal Behavior
- Abstractive Relevance
- Information Distortion (H21)

Meaning

"Semantics is the study of meaning—not the meaning of the dictionary, but the meaning transmitted to the recipient of the message" (H21, p. 39). The focus must not be on the translation that should be made but rather on the translation that will most likely be made.

Language uses symbols to convey meaning. Meaning is most effectively conveyed when language clearly depicts what it represents with its symbols. The more concrete the message is, the more easily it is understood.

However, language tends to get more abstract over time. A relevant example of this is the desire for increased precision, often accompanied by the increased use of mathematics, which itself is an increase in the use of abstraction. This works against clearer communication.

Communication involving numbers is often presented in an effort to increase precision, assuming increased accuracy. In fact, such communication finds itself in a dynamic tension between the goal of increased precision and the process of increased abstraction.

Language

It is always possible that messages will be misunderstood, and one of the most commonly accepted reasons for misunderstanding is that of language. But the problems of language can be even more challenging when analyzing financial information, and especially when analyzing prospective financial information. It is important to understand the particular message presented in the form of prospective financial information as well as the system within which the projected organization will be functioning, and its ability to deal with the important question of meaning.

Much has been written concerning organizations and their ability to perform a variety of business functions. However, little has been written about the ability of organizations to function in the context of the information flows that all modern organizations are dependent upon. It is a myopic response (given the many problems of our current economy that can be traced to problems of information), because many businesses still are not emphasizing the importance of this crucial component of an organization.

Much has also been written on the technical issues of planning, organizing, directing, and controlling, as well as about the need for good communication within an organization, but little focuses on the specific impact on all phases and roles in the business of the changing communication paradigm. This is especially true with the accounting function, one of the primary information systems within an organization. It is actually frightening to realize that most accountants still do not view their function primarily as communication specialists. They still focus on the performance of technical accounting tasks.

Is there any wonder that there are problems with the transmission of meaning throughout the information systems in most organizations? The organizational structure must accommodate this important function if it is to survive in the perilous waters of today's global economy.

The analyst must be particularly sensitive to this issue in the analysis of prospective financial information, the preparation of which is often conducted without the modelers being privy to the strategic issues that generated the concepts behind the numbers. This discontinuity between the strategic planning process and the actual technical generation of these figures often makes them quite suspect. A question arises as to how the financial models that support the prospective financial statements are generated. Who was the person actually responsible for the generation of those models? How can a person not privy to the subtleties of the particular business be assigned the task of reducing the most subtle of interrelated concepts to a tangible form in a financial model? A model reflects all the aspects of a plan and yet is often inconsistent with the strategic plan. For these reasons the issue of meaning in the communication of the prospective financial statements themselves is important.

Language is the background that influences all that we do (H21, p. 41). People are not as free to act as they often believe. To a degree, much of what is said and done is influenced by the prevailing language. Thinking is constrained by the dictates of the language in which it is done. This is true even with technical languages such as accounting.

A lot of this has to do with the cultural context in which the language has evolved and is used. Culture can be defined as "the total personality that emerges from its members interpersonal transactions" (J1, p. 3). These interpersonal transactions to a large extent dictate the meaning of language. Culture is a code of behavior; language is the vehicle through which the code operates. But organizations can have more than one culture. The multicultural environment of business is greatly impacted by the diversity of its "spoken" languages. An understanding of the dynamic nature of language is essential for an understanding of communication and meaning.

The issue of language and its role for the accountant and analyst is important.

A language has not been invented or set up at some time, by authority, like a card-index coding system, but has steadily moved with the history of the community, changing as social conditions change. It has been described as "the mirror of society." It represents a continuous growth, for all human experience is a continuous process. (K2, p. 73)

In fact, all the various activities within the organization—including accounting, finance, production and marketing, among others—can be viewed as subcultures. Any effort at communication within these subcultures needs to be sensitive to the language that has evolved and is evolving. Even more important, problems of communication and understanding will arise as these subcultures interact with other segments of society.

Part of the benefit of the Statements on Financial Accounting Concepts is the development of a common ground for the basic concepts upon which all financial theory and practice ultimately rests. We do not formally consider the communications problem when we discuss GAAP in Chapter 4, so now we must in order to provide a better understanding of the context in which GAAP should function. A poor understanding of this issue can create some very important problems.

The meaning of the words within our language in general is arbitrated by the dictionary. The meaning in accounting and finance is not so easily established. The community of financial and accounting professionals accept the GAAP outlined in Chapter 4, but a vast segment of the users and generators of financial and accounting information are not very conversant with the conceptual foundation for these principles. This becomes especially important when applying these principles to prospective financial statements. The accounting profession is required to conform to these principles in the performance of most of their services. Others are not so professionally constrained. Therefore, the possibility if not probability exists for people, especially nonaccountants, to present information that is inconsistent with the General Principles. This inconsistency can arise either as a consequence of mistakes or intentional misrepresentations.

The challenge for the analyst is to sort through the myriad of possibilities that exist concerning the information being analyzed. An understanding of the motivations and cultural context in which the prospective financial information have been framed is essential for the financial analyst. Without this understanding, the conveyance of meaning can and probably will be lost.

Indexing

Indexing is concerned with the context of the communication, which is established in a wide variety of ways. The preceding word or sentence helps to establish context.

Meaning can be changed based upon the surrounding information. "Context . . . is a form or phase of indexing" (H21, p. 47).

Basically, the use of indexing sets up the communication. As a stimulus that predisposes the message for a particular meaning, indexing can be achieved through emphasis of certain descriptive adjectives. Without indexing, many of the words or messages that follow would have a totally different meaning. The subsequent message, when divorced from the preceding picture/index, would not convey the same meaning.

The use of the term *bottom line* is a good example of this. This term usually implies, according to Lindhe (F55, p. 8), a final result—a clarity of purpose and result. A greater accuracy is implied than is usually warranted. This index can greatly influence the message that follows.

The importance of indexing is apparent in the format for the presentation of financial information. The analyst has to be sensitive to this setup. The information conveyed may be presented with indexing that attempts to lead the reader/analyst in a desired direction. This leading needs to be appreciated. The analyst must be able to ascertain through the analysis process whether the indexing is in fact leading to valid conclusions concerning the message.

This process presents a challenge for the analyst. Much of what is presented as financial information is in fact part of a sales pitch. Most accountants are insensitive to the strong influence of marketing in the presentation of financial information. A sensitivity to the selling of ideas needs to be comprehended if the analyst is going to be successful in his/her endeavors.

Word Shortening

Word and sentence shortening present another means of impacting meaning. Over time, subcultures go through a process of deriving terms in usage that are common to that particular group, but are probably not understood by other groups. The use of such terms can provide increased efficiency among professionals when there is a common acceptance of the meaning of the truncated term or word. Terms such as GAAP, ROI, and SG and A are good examples. But these shortenings also provide the opportunity for problems with the conveyance of meaning. This is particularly true in the use of prospective financial information.

Latent Meaning

Latent meaning relates the information to either the sender or receiver of information. This is due to an experience on the part of one party in the process and not the other. Without a shared experience the meaning becomes confused. Most have encountered this situation. When a certain experience is shared by a particular group of people, the implications of that prior experience are immediately understood by the members of that group with only a very quick or slight allusion. An outsider, not privy to these particular experiences, does not necessarily share in the full measure of the message in that communication.

This presents some challenges for the analyst. The information presented in prospective financial statements often represents months if not years of prior work. The preparer of that information tries to embody in a few lines of a financial model the ideas and concepts that have evolved over possibly thousands of hours of effort. It is not an easy task to encapsulate the full experience and meaning of those concepts within a limited number of mathematical symbols in a model. The potential for problems in understanding the implications of latent meaning is great. The analyst needs to be sensitive to the full implications of the context in which the information has been developed and is presented.

Nonverbal Behavior

Another issue that can impact on the meaning of a message is nonverbal behavior. The analysis of prospective financial information is usually thought of in the context of written information. Analysis usually revolves around prospective financial statements. Therefore, this issue may be considered by many as not relevant to the analysis process. But, in fact, it can provide an important source of information especially in the development of the scope of the examination.

It is very common for the analyst to get together before, during, and after the completion of major segments of the analysis with various concerned parties. In these get-togethers certain important cues can be gathered, such as:

- Tone of voice
- Facial expression
- Rate of speech
- Propinquity with others
- Relaxation or tension (H21, p. 50)

These cues can assist the analyst in developing a comfort with the information presented. There is an assumption among analysts that if information is not on paper and not in the form of numbers, then it has little or no value. This assumption is totally wrong. A sophisticated analyst, like a good detective, will seek to elicit information from any and all sources available. Face-to-face contact with the people responsible for financial statements can prove very helpful.

It is particularly important to elicit the degree of confidence in the numbers. Often the person who created the financial model is not the same person who developed the strategic or business plans. One can elicit a lot of information if that preparer is another professional with similar credentials to your own—for example, a CPA. Empathy with another professional can help to establish an important bond. This bond can help to facilitate nonverbal communication: the subtle lack of comfort with some suspect components of the prospective financial statements or the willingness to provide supporting documentation (or not). These responses to questioning about the prospective financial statements can lend comfort or discomfort to the analyst. It is common to find most CPAs uncomfortable with the exaggerations that are sometimes incorporated into prospective financial statements. This can be an important source of information and should not be overlooked in the analysis process.

Abstractive Relevance

Abstractive relevance can also impact meaning. This concept implies that messages can be sent if the recipient is conditioned to see them. An example of this is that of a blinking red light, which indicates caution or danger. The light is what is important. It might appear in a number of different locations. For example, it could be located above the road, or on a sawhorse next to the road. Many of the particular features related to that light are not relevant. The shape, the size, the intensity, the container, are all irrelevant features. The important feature is the color red. The important message is one of caution or danger.

In the same way, meaning can be influenced by certain elements of a prospective financial statement. There is a problem in reading too much or too little into some of these signs. The analyst has to be sensitive to this information and careful about how it affects the message.

An example of this for the analyst might be an expected professional level of presentation. The prospective financial statements might be framed by a person much less sophisticated than the analyst. The telltale signs of this lack of sophistication could influence the analysis of the information. It is very easy to be distracted by what appears to be deficiencies in form, techniques, or methods of presentation. These might indicate some substantive problems with the prospective financial information. On the other hand, they could have nothing to do with the validity of the financial information. This tendency toward abstractive relevance needs to be appreciated in the analysis of prospective financial information (H21, p. 51).

Information Distortion

The last element to be considered in terms of possible impacts on meaning is that of information distortion. There are three types of information distortion. They are:

- Stretch distortion
- Fog distortion
- Mirror distortion

Stretch distortion is "demonstrated by the trick mirror that makes us taller or shorter than reality" (H21, p. 52). In fact, it is not uncommon to find information made to look "taller or shorter" than it actually is. The analyst has to be sensitive to these distortions, whether intended or not.

In fog distortion,

> . . . information is lost or fogged over because of the inability of the processor which transfers the information from one conducting medium to another to respond to the largest or smallest element in the input. (H21, p. 52)

Fog distortion can exist knowingly or unknowingly. A photograph of a field can show a beautiful barn on the horizon but fail to show the presence of germs which are also present. "A message can contain a warning which the recipient cannot recognize" (H21, p. 52). On the other hand, a moderate amount of distortion can be helpful. This is because it could help to focus on those elements of the message that are most important.

A problem arises when the analyst and, ultimately, the reader of the prospective financial statements is caught in intentional fogging in which the preparers of the financial statement attempt to emphasize certain elements and minimize others. It is common to find that these efforts at overemphasizing or underemphasizing usually directly benefit the preparer of the financial statements, and are intentionally framed into the prospective financial information.

The third type of distortion is mirage distortion, which

> . . . provides "information" that is not present, but is likely to be construed as pertinent information. (H21, p. 53)

Often, analysts and users of financial information "tend to see what we expect to see" (H21, p. 53). What we think we are seeing and what we actually are seeing are not always the same thing. It is important to be careful not to be led into assuming more than is actually present.

3.4 THE EFFECTIVITY ASPECT OF INFORMATION THEORY

Thus far, the discussion of communication has focused on the technical and semantic issues of communication. Now we will address the effect that the messages transmitted have on the recipients.

Effectivity may be thought of as the effect the message has upon the receiver of that message. That effect will be determined by all that has preceded the message in terms of the receiver. In a sense, that effect will be established by the attitude which the receiver has toward the message—the mental condition or "mental set" of the receiver. The mental set is established by:

1. Instruction—formal and informal
2. Environment
3. The form of the message
4. The transmittal system
5. Knowledge available about the source. (H21, pp. 61–62)

Instruction

Part of the attitude that the receiver has toward the message has to do with instruction received. Some instruction is informal, some formal. Both constitute a predisposition toward how the message is received (H21, p. 62).

This predisposition due to instruction is especially important for the analyst. Sometimes he or she is encouraged to a certain conclusion concerning the prospective financial statement. The analyst has to be sensitive to this and not let his or her objectivity be swayed by this instruction.

Environment

Another part of the mental set of the receiver is the environment. The sense and feel of the environment become part of the mind-set of the receiver. These predispose the receiver to receiving the data in a certain fashion (H21, pp. 64–65).

As with instruction, it is necessary for the analyst to be aware of this mental set and not allow it to interfere with his or her analysis.

The Form of the Message

Form can affect meaning. Many aspects of the message can affect how it is received, such as the leaders, trailers, color, letter size, and case. All of these have the ability to affect the message (H21, pp. 66–67).

The impact of form is often missed by analysts. They are not conscious of how the presentation of financial information can influence their (and all users') acceptance or rejection of that information. A sensitivity to these predispositions needs to be appreciated in the analysis function.

The Transmittal System

The transmittal system can affect the mind-set of the receiver. Whether we use written or oral communication, telephone, computer networks, or facsimile machines, all of these have significant and different impacts on the receiver. Another related issue has to do with the timing of the receipt of the message. For instance, whether one is using a real time system or not for responses to inquiries about the prospective financial statements can also have an impact on the communication (H21, pp. 68–70).

The effects of these potential variants within the transmittal system and their impact on the analysis process need to be appreciated by the analyst if he/she is to perform the analyst's function properly.

Knowledge About the Sources

Prior knowledge about a source predisposes us to certain expectations. Those expectations have a definite impact upon our receiving of a message (H21, pp. 71–72).

Prior knowledge can greatly impact all of us and our interpretation of the messages received. This is of particular importance for the analyst. Prior knowledge can be favorable or unfavorable, but both subvert the objective performance of the analysis function.

3.5 SUMMARY

This chapter has emphasized the importance of communications in both the operation of the organization and the analysis of the prospective statements of that organization.

No analyst is likely to be a true expert of the field of communications, but all can be sensitive to the implications of communication and reasonably aware of the kind of clues to seek. Good sense and sufficient study of the organization can provide the insights needed to deal effectively with the issue. The analyst should be aware of both the complexities involved and the benefits to be derived by a sensitive examination of the communications factor.

Accounting—The Framework

4.1   INTRODUCTION

In order to provide consistency in accounting information, the accounting profession has established a canon of principles and assumptions that serve to define and provide the framework for acceptable practices. The body of these principles and assumptions is called Generally Accepted Accounting Principles (GAAP). Some of these principles are general; some are specific. This chapter presents the basic conceptual framework of accounting and the general structure of GAAP. It is upon these concepts and principles that all the practices and techniques of accounting rest.

The accounting information system, a vital component of the firm's communication system, is another important subsystem of the firm that must be understood for proper analysis of prospective financial statements to take place. It relies heavily on GAAP. Although this book addresses how to examine prospective financial information, the guidelines of GAAP are still important. Without an understanding of the rules that govern the presentation of financial information in general, the examination and analysis of prospective financial information is impossible because its presentation must also conform to the same principles that apply to historical financial information.

Additionally, an understanding of these rules provides a better understanding of the prospective component of the financial information under examination. Due to the fundamental nature of these principles and assumptions, they are especially important to the analysis of prospective financial information. Prospective financial information is much more open-ended in terms of content and meaning than is historical financial information. An understanding of the general foundations of GAAP helps in understanding the underpinnings of the specific prospective financial information as presented, as well as in establishing a grounding in the general context in which the numbers presented need to be understood and analyzed.

The implications of the assumptions of GAAP also need to be understood. Assumptions permeate all accounting information. Too often even accounting professionals tend to view financial information as if it were in some sense absolute. In reality there are tiers of assumptions that underpin all financial information. Any meaning that accounting information has can be appreciated only in light of a thorough understanding of the assumptions upon which it is based.

4.2   TO "PRESENT FAIRLY IN CONFORMITY WITH GAAP"

One of the most widely acknowledged functions of a CPA (and also a basic form of financial analysis) is the audit function. The independent auditor's unqualified opinion includes the following: "In our opinion, the financial statements referred to above present fairly in all material respects, the financial position of X company as of (at) December 31, 19XX, and the results of its operations and cash flows for the year then ended, in conformity with Generally Accepted Accounting Principles" (F20, par. 1).

What the auditor is really doing is attesting as to whether the financial statements in question follow the basic canon of accounting. This canon, as stated earlier, is called GAAP, but who created this canon? What does it encompass? What "tests" are included? What are the principles and assumptions that allow us to understand the meaning behind the figures in accounting statements? An understanding of the answers to these questions will help the analyst to understand better all financial information, including prospective financial statements.

There has been a lot of discussion about this topic in the past two decades, and even more disagreement and confusion. In order to clarify what GAAP means, the Auditing Standards Board issued the *Statement on Auditing Standards No. 52* in 1987. This was called the "Omnibus Statement on Auditing Standards—1987," subtitled "The Meaning of Present Fairly in Conformity with Generally Accepted Accounting Principles in the Independent Auditor's Report" (F18). Subsequent to *SAS 52, SAS 69* was issued in the spring of 1992, entitled "The Meaning of Present Fairly in Conformity with Generally Accepted Accounting Principles in the Independent Auditor's Report" (F20). *SAS 69* incorporates *SAS 52* and extends, elaborates, and clarifies many of the points raised in *SAS 52*. According to *SAS 69,* the sources of established accounting principles that are generally accepted in the United States are derived as follows:

> Independent auditors agree on the existence of a body of generally accepted accounting principles, and they are knowledgeable about these principles and in the determination of their general acceptance. Nevertheless, the determi-

nation that a particular accounting principle is generally accepted may be difficult because no single reference source exists for all such principles. The sources of established accounting principles that are generally accepted in the United States are:

a. Accounting principles promulgated by a body designated by the AICPA Council to establish such principles, pursuant to rule 203 (AICPA, Professional Standards, vol. 2, ET sec. 203.01) of the AICPA Code of Professional Conduct. Rule 203 provides that an auditor should not express an unqualified opinion if the financial statements contain a material departure from such pronouncements unless, due to unusual circumstances, adherence to the pronouncements would make the statements misleading. Rule 203 implies that application of officially established accounting principles almost always results in the fair presentation of financial position, results of operations, and cash flows, in conformity with generally accepted accounting principles. Nevertheless, rule 203 provides for the possibility that literal application of such a pronouncement might, in unusual circumstances, result in misleading financial statements. (See paragraphs 14 and 15 of SAS No. 58, Reports on Audited Financial Statements [AICPA, Professional Standards, vol. 1, AU sec. 508].)

b. Pronouncements of bodies, composed of expert accountants, that deliberate accounting issues in public forums for the purpose of establishing accounting principles or describing existing accounting practices that are generally accepted, provided those pronouncements have been exposed for public comment and have been cleared by a body referred to in category (a). For purposes of this statement, the work cleared means that a body referred to in subparagraph (a) has indicated that it does not object to the issuance of the proposed pronouncement.

c. Pronouncements of bodies, organized by a body referred to in category (a) and composed of expert accountants, that deliberate accounting issues in public forums for the purpose of interpreting or establishing accounting principles or describing existing accounting practices that are generally accepted, or pronouncements referred to in category (b) that have been cleared by a body referred to in category (a) but have not been exposed for public comment.

d. Practices or pronouncements that are widely recognized as being generally accepted because they represent prevalent practice in a particular industry, or the knowledgeable application to specific circumstances of pronouncements that are generally accepted. (F20, par. 5)

The above general definition of what constitutes GAAP applies to both governmental and nongovernmental entities. The following discussion relates specifically to nongovernmental entities. *SAS 69* goes on to discuss the specific sources of established accounting principles for nongovernmental entities:

For financial statements of entities other than governmental entities—

a. Category (a), officially established accounting principles, consists of Financial Accounting Board (FASB) Statements of Financial Accounting Standards and Interpretations, Accounting Principles Board (APB) Opinions, and AICPA Accounting Research Bulletins.
     Rules and interpretive releases of the Securities and Exchange Commission (SEC) have an authority similar to category (a) pronouncements for SEC registrants. In addition, the SEC staff issues Staff Accounting Bulletins that represent practices followed by the staff in administering SEC disclosure requirements. Also, the Introduction to the FASB's *EITF Abstracts* states that the Securities and Exchange Commission's Chief Accountant has said that the SEC staff would challenge any accounting that differs from a consensus of the FASB Emerging Issues Task Force, because the consensus position represents the best thinking on areas for which there are no specific standards.

b. Category (b) consists of FASB Technical Bulletins and, if cleared by the FASB, AICPA Industry Audit and Accounting Guides and AICPA Statements of Position.

c. Category (c) consists of AICPA Accounting Standards Executive Committee (AcSEC) Practice Bulletins that have been cleared by the FASB and consensus positions of the FASB Emerging Issues Task Force.

d. Category (d) includes AICPA accounting interpretations and implementation guides ("Q's and A's") published by the FASB staff, and practices that are widely recognized and prevalent either generally or in the industry.
     In the absence of a pronouncement covered by rule 203 or another source of established accounting principles, the auditor of financial statements of entities other than governmental entities may consider other accounting literature, depending on its relevance in the circumstances. Other accounting literature includes, for example, FASB Statements of Financial Accounting Concepts; APB Statements; AICPA Issues Papers; International Accounting Standards of the International Accounting Standards Committee; Governmental Accounting Standards Board (GASB) Statements, Interpretations, and Technical Bulletins; pronouncements of other professional associations or regulatory

agencies; Technical Information Service Inquiries and Replies included in AICPA Technical Practice Aids; and accounting textbooks, handbooks, and articles. The appropriateness of other accounting literature depends on its relevance to particular circumstances, the specificity of the guidance, and the general recognition of the issuer or author as an authority. For example, FASB Statements of Financial Accounting Concepts would normally be more influential than other sources in this category. (F20, par. 10–11).

SAS 69 establishes a hierarchy for GAAP. In so doing it specifies the sources of these accounting principles that are "generally accepted" in the United States for the purpose of issuing an auditor's report. This is the CPA's canon.

GAAP does little to address the details of real cost patterns. Whether costs are ever purely fixed or variable, how changes in technology over time conflict with the concept of consistency in presentation, how accounting depreciation differs from the expected useful lives of the assets, are all topics that GAAP fails to address.

However, these topics are often the heart of the process of the analysis of prospective financial information. GAAP can deal in abstractions; the analysis of prospective financial information must deal in reality. This search for reality often requires research far beyond what GAAP might demand.

Prospective financial statements must deal with reality over the perception of reality, which is where GAAP often stops. Real income is often quite different from accounting income. How changes in total resources affect the firm over time is very important to the analysis of prospective statements.

A danger exists in letting the rules of GAAP take precedence over reality; for example, take the automobile industry in the late 1970s. Many "accounting expenses," according to GAAP, such as those for research and development, are really investments in the firm's long-term future. Income can be manipulated to the detriment of the firm's health.

Accounting assets are not resources in themselves, but only become resources when coupled with human help (other resources) and the intent to use those assets in a planned strategy to achieve the firm's goals. These limitations on GAAP need to be kept in mind as we start our detailed discussion concerning its various characteristics.

4.3   FINANCIAL STATEMENTS

The above discussion addressing what constitutes GAAP focused specifically on financial information presented in the firm's financial statements. A complete set of financial statements for a period should include:

- Financial position at the end of the period
- Earnings (net income) for the period
- Comprehensive income (total nonowner changes in equity) for the period
- Cash flows during the period
- Investment by and distributions to owners during the period (F46, par. 13)

These are the basic vehicles for presenting the relevant financial information for a company. Entities can choose to present some of this information in combined statements (F46, par. 14). This is acceptable as long as the appropriate information is presented.

A complete discussion of financial statements is beyond the scope of this work. The *Statement of Financial Accounting Concepts No. 5* provides a more thorough discussion for the interested party (F46).

4.4   CONCEPTUAL FRAMEWORK

Thus far we have briefly discussed the concept of Generally Accepted Accounting Principles and who creates them. This section presents (1) the objectives of financial statements, and (2) the qualitative characteristics of accounting information.

Objectives of Financial Statements

The objectives of financial reporting as presented in the *Statement of Financial Accounting Concepts No. 1* are:

- Information useful in investment and credit decisions
- Information useful in assessing cash flow prospects
- Information about enterprise resources, claims to those resources, and changes in them (F42, par. 32–54)

Information Useful in Investment and Credit Decisions

The first objective of financial reporting should be to provide "information that is useful to present and potential investors and creditors and other users in making rational investment, credit, and similar decisions" (F42, par. 34). The emphasis of this first objective is on information that is useful for decision making. This basic objective is sometimes overlooked by CPAs. It should be noted that the Statements for Financial Accounting Concepts (in which these three objectives are listed) appear in the lowest tier in the hierarchy for GAAP according to *SAS 69*. An understanding of accounting information, whether historical of prospective, needs to focus on this objective. Financial information is important because it assists interested parties in making better decisions.

This importance and its relationship to decision making is of particular concern for prospective financial information. With historical information it is possible to emphasize somewhat the recording and stewardship functions of accounting and downplay the role of decision making. It appears that this is all too often overemphasized. However, *Concept Statement No. 1* makes it clear that the first objective of financial statements relates to decision making. The Financial Accounting Concepts were primarily structured to assist with the understanding of historical financial statements. If this function is important for historical information, it is even more important when dealing with prospective financial information.

Information Useful in Assessing Cash Flow Prospects

In addition to providing information useful for investment and credit decisions, another objective of financial statements is to provide information useful in assessing cash-flow prospects. The ultimate test of the success of a business is its ability to generate cash. The value of a business is determined by either applying present value or future value adjustments to after tax cash flows (G32, p. 14). Therefore, the ability to assess cash-flow prospects is of great importance.

It is interesting to note that the word *prospects* was used in this objective. Although addressing historical financial information, ultimately the objective emphasized the prospective. Once again the guidance in the *Concept Statement* focuses on another element that is apparently all too often overlooked in assessing historical financial information. Providing information to assess the future is an important objective of historical information as well as prospective financial information. The context and structure of all financial information needs to address the future. The analysis of all financial information must be sensitive to this objective.

Financial reporting should provide information to help present and potential investors, creditors, and other users in assessing the amounts, timing and uncertainty of prospective cash receipts from dividends or interest and the proceeds from the sale, redemption or maturity of securities and loans. (F42, par. 37)

Although accrual accounting is important, this second objective of financial reporting focuses on cash flows.

Information About Enterprise Resources, Claims to Those Resources, and Changes in Them

The next objective of financial reporting focuses on the resources of an enterprise. It is interesting to note that the FASB chose to address those resources necessary for the conduct of the business. The focus on resources and changes in them is the focus of business. For too long we have taken a very narrow view of business and not concerned ourselves with a total resources perspective. This perspective needs to be embraced if we are truly to understand the analysis of either historical or prospective financial information.

Financial reporting should provide information about the economic resources of an enterprise, the claims to those resources, and the effects of transactions, events and circumstances that change the resources and claims to those resources. (F42, par. 40)

This objective focuses on the resources of a firm and the evaluation of information "about the enterprise's performance during a period" (F42, par. 41).

Financial reporting should provide information about how management of an enterprise has discharged stewardship responsibility to owners (stockholders) for the use of enterprise resources entrusted to it. Management of an enterprise is periodically accountable to owners not only for the custody and safekeeping of enterprise and resources but also for their efficient and profitable use and for protecting them to the extent possible from unfavorable economic impacts of factors in the economy such as inflation or deflation and technological and social changes. (F42, par. 50)

"Society may also impose broad or specific responsibilities on enterprises and their managements" (F42, par. 50). The systems perspective which we will be addressing later in this text emphasizes the fact that businesses do not exist or operate in a vacuum. A common business philosophy assumes that even if businesses do not exist in a vacuum, they should do everything they can to attempt to insulate themselves from social responsibility. *Concept Statement No. 1* emphasizes that, in fact, the "ostrich mode" that seems to have sufficed as a paradigm for business for so long is an unacceptable model. Although beyond the scope of the specific discussion of the *Concept Statement,* it is important to note that companies are becoming, and will continue to become, more involved in the global economy. It is becoming more apparent that corporations are in fact perceived as having responsibilities to a multitude of publics. This responsibility enlarges the definition of just what those resources are that are of relevance to the corporation.

For generations the water table in the communities in which many corporations were located was not considered a relevant resource of those specific companies. For this reason those saw fit to contaminate and destroy the environments in which they were located through pollution. It is now becoming apparent that society is no longer submitting to this wanton indifference to the responsibilities of the corporation. The concept of a total resources approach to planning was addressed in Chapter 2 of this text.

Qualitative Characteristics

Statements on Financial Accounting Concepts No. 2 focuses on the qualitative characteristics of accounting information. It presents, discusses, defines, and interprets a number of important qualitative characteristics for accounting information.

These qualitative characteristics are important for our study because they not only provide an understanding of the general context in which financial information and statements are constructed but also provide some important considerations for the analysis of prospective financial information. This importance will be seen in the following discussion on these qualitative characteristics. They are presented in a figure that *Statement No. 2* calls the hierarchy of accounting qualities (see Figure 4-1, which is an adaptation of this figure). These characteristics are:

- Understandability
- Decision usefulness
- Relevance
    Predictive value

    Feedback value
    Timeliness
- Reliability
    Verifiability
    Neutrality
    Representational faithfulness
- Comparability
- Consistency (F43, par. 32 and Figure 1)

Thus, the most important characteristics in the hierarchy are "understandability" and "usefulness for decision making" (F43, par. 32). As with the objectives for the financial statements discussed in the previous sections, once again usefulness for decision makers is identified as one of the most important elements within the hierarchy. These characteristics are constrained by two important concepts:

- Benefits need to exceed costs (F43, par. 133–144)
- Materiality (F43, par. 123–132)

These elements form the general context of qualitative characteristics of accounting information. The information can be either historical or prospective. It should be noted that *Statement No. 2* technically addressed historical financial information. Figure 4-1 shows the interrelationship among the accounting qualities. Additionally, it establishes a functional sequence for organizing and viewing the qualitative aspects of accounting information, including the need for constraints.

Although Figure 4-1 is adapted from *Statement No. 2* itself, there is quite a bit of debate as to whether this figure appropriately presents the proper interrelationships among the qualitative elements. A fuller discussion of this topic is beyond the scope of this work, but could prove to be valuable to the accounting profession.

The following will briefly discuss the various qualitative accounting characteristics presented in Figure 4-1, and, in particular, emphasize those concepts most important to the analysis of prospective financial information.

Usefulness and understandability are defined as user-specific qualities. "Financial reporting should provide information that can be used by all—nonprofessionals as well as professionals—who are willing to learn to use it properly" (F43, par. 40). Understandability is defined as "The quality of

Figure 4-1   A Hierarchy of Accounting Qualities

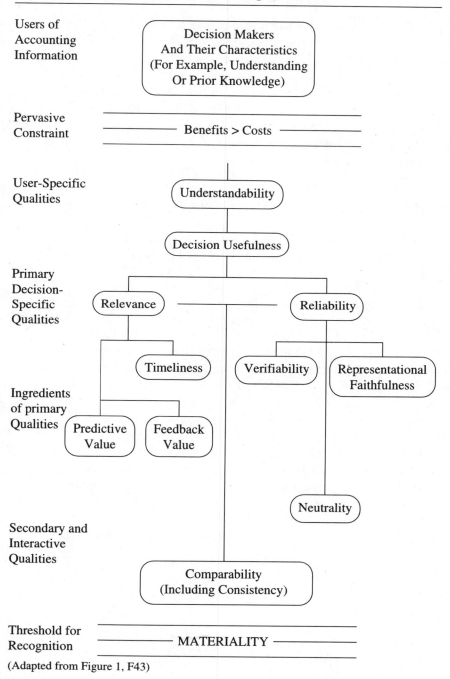

(Adapted from Figure 1, F43)

information that enables users to perceive its significance" (F43, glossary). Usefulness and understandability link the users of financial information to decision-specific qualities.

The primary decision-specific qualities are defined as relevance and reliability, with comparability (including consistency) identified as a secondary and interactive quality (F43, Figure 1). Relevance is defined as:

> The capacity of information to make a difference in a decision by helping users to form predictions about the outcomes of past, present, and future events, or to confirm or correct prior expectations. (F43, glossary)

Reliability, on the other hand, is defined as:

> The quality of information that assures information is reasonably free from error and bias and faithfully represents what it purports to represent. (F43, glossary)

Reliability and relevance, primary decision-specific qualities, are both equally important for accounting information. When looking at any financial information, especially as an analyst, these two characteristics become focal in assessing the value or importance of that information. The analysis of prospective financial information in particular requires an assessment of the relevance and reliability of all the information presented. These characteristics, in fact, become a conceptual threshold with which to gauge the importance of that information, and should help to define the scope of the examination as well as provide a focus to the analysis process.

Comparability is "The quality of information that enables users to identify similarities in and differences between two sets of economic phenomenon" (F43, glossary). Consistency, a component of comparability, is "Conformity from period to period with unchanging policies and procedures" (F43, glossary).

Three aspects of relevance are identified in *Statement No. 2*. They are:

1. Predictive value
2. Feedback value
3. Timeliness

Predictive value deals with the future. "Without an interest in the future, knowledge of the past is sterile" (F43, par. 51). Information is relevant if it can "reduce uncertainty about the situation" (F43, par. 52). Feedback value has to do with information on past performance provided as a basis for prediction (F43, par. 52). *Timeliness* is defined as "Bringing information to a decision maker before it loses its capacity to influence decisions" (F43, glossary). If we do not have information available when needed, then the information becomes irrelevant.

Reliability, as defined earlier, is "The quality of information that assures that information is reasonably free from error and bias and faithfully represents what it purports to represent" (F43, glossary). Three aspects of reliability are important. They are:

1. Representational faithfulness
2. Verifiability
3. Neutrality

Representational faithfulness is defined as "Correspondence or agreement between a measure or description in the phenomenon that it purports to represent (sometimes called validity)" (F43, glossary). There are degrees of representational faithfulness. Given the question of uncertainty and sophistication in today's business world, it becomes quite difficult to assess the faithfulness of accounting representations of an economic phenomenon. An important component of representational faithfulness is *completeness* (F43, par. 79). Completeness is "The inclusion in reported information of everything material that is necessary for faithful representation of the relevant phenomenon" (F43, glossary).

The second aspect of reliability is *verifiability.* Verifiability is "The ability through consensus among measurers to ensure that information represents what it purports to represent or that the chosen method of measurement has been used without error or bias" (F43, glossary). Verifiability is concerned with guaranteeing that the numbers presented actually represent what they purport to represent (F43, par. 81). Some call this characteristic objectivity.

APB Statement No. 4 established a criterion for determining if information is verifiable. It is if it "would be duplicated by independent measures using the same measurement methods" (F43, par. 82).

The third aspect of reliability is neutrality. *Neutrality* is defined as "Absence in reported information of bias intended to obtain a predetermined result or to induce a particular mode of behavior" (F43, glossary).

Neutrality does not mean "without purpose," nor does it mean that neutrality should be without influence on human behavior. Accounting informa-

tion cannot avoid affecting behavior nor should it. But rather it is supposed
to ensure that the information is balanced. (F43, par. 100)

Reliability is essential in order to perform sensitivity analysis. How
much things can change before a different decision is reached is dependent
on just how reliable the measurements under examination are.

Comparability and consistency, which Figure 4-1 describes as secondary
and interactive qualities, are important aspects of usefulness. *Comparability*
is "The quality of information that enables users to identify similarities in
and differences between two sets of economic phenomenon" (F43, glossary). *Consistency* is "Conformity from period to period with unchanging
policies and procedures" (F43, glossary).

The heart of the discussion thus far has revolved around the importance
of certain qualitative characteristics of accounting information. All these
qualitative characteristics help to define what makes information useful for
decisions. This is extremely important for the analysis of prospective financial information. As we start to create a context in which to view financial information in general, and, more particularly, with which to
analyze prospective financial statements, it is necessary first to develop an
appreciation for those characteristics that the information we are examining should be providing or should embody.

Although the *Statements on Financial Accounting Concepts* focus primarily on historical financial information, the translation to prospective financial information is easily achieved.

A fuller understanding of the qualitative characteristics of accounting
information provides the basis for interpreting the meaning of the information that will be examined. Additionally, and probably more important,
it provides a context in which to view the numbers included in the perspective of prospective financial statements.

4.5 STRUCTURE OF GAAP

For the purpose of the discussion in this section, the various topics concerning the structure of GAAP have been organized into three categories.
They are:

1. Assumptions
2. Principles
3. Modifiers

Basic Assumptions

Business Entity Concept

APB Statement No. 4 discusses the business entity concept. This concept is the basic assumption that the financial figures presented are for a specific business. These figures must clearly separate and distinguish between the activities and resources of a business entity and those of the owners of that entity. For example, a person may be a sole proprietor and owner of a retail clothing store. The person as an individual, and that person's individual financial activities, must be treated separately from the activities of the clothing store (F4, AC sec. 1022.17).

The practitioner must be especially wary of violations of this concept when dealing with a small, closely held business.

Going Concern or Continuity Concept

The going concern concept is the assumption that the business will continue for an indefinite period of time (F4, AC sec. 1022.17). Without this assumption, all the financial information would become relatively meaningless except in very special situations. The business that the financial information relates to might in fact no longer even be in existence. This would make the whole process of creating financial statements somewhat absurd, and potentially very misleading.

This is important in the analysis of prospective financial information because those entities described in prospective financial statements must necessarily be assumed to have an ongoing and continuous existence, unless otherwise explicitly stated. With prospective financial information, if the going concern concept does not apply, those statements could be materially misleading.

Time Period Concept

The time period concept assumes that financial information is presented for a specific and limited period of time, usually a twelve-month period (F4, AC sec. 1022.17). The time period concept is important because financial statements must be presented in artificially segmented periods of time. These periods of time can be months, quarters, years, or some other appropriate unit.

There are a number of important implications that ensue as a consequence of this assumption. Most important is the need for various estimates to present fairly the results of operations and the financial position of the entity for the period leading up to and including the cutoff date ending the period. The method of constructing these estimates is really the topic of accrual accounting.

Stable Dollar Concept

Statements on Accounting Concepts No. 5 states that it is assumed that the monetary unit is in "nominal units of money, that is, unadjusted for changes and purchasing power of money over time. . . . An ideal measurement scale would be one that would be stable over time" (F46, par. 71). The reality is that with "inflation or deflation" the monetary unit is not usually stable, and this can present misleading figures. It is a simplyfing assumption that the analyst must be especially aware of with prospective financial statements.

However, given the assumption of a stable dollar, the financial statements that are presented (both historical and prospective) necessarily assume that the dollar is in fact stable. This provides the context in which to view the statements under examination properly.

Basic Principles

The basic principles of accounting information include the historical cost principle, the revenue recognition principle, the expense recognition principle, the matching principle, the consistency principle, and the full disclosure principle.

Historical Cost Principle

Exchanges are made and recorded at an actual point in time in accounting records. The values for the exchange at that point in time are called the historical cost. There are some modifications, for instance with inventories and investments being adjusted, short- and long-term receivables being reported at other than historical cost figures (current cost, current market value, net realizable value, and present value of future cash flows), the general assumption in accounting figures is that the figures in financial statements are recorded at historical costs or proceeds. This is discussed in detail in *Statements on Financial Accounting Concepts No. 5* (F46, par. 67).

Revenue Recognition Principle

Statement of Financial Accounting Concepts No. 5 discusses the heart of accrual accounting: that revenues are recognized when earned, not when cash is received (F46, par. 83). Revenues are "realized when products (goods or services), merchandise, or other assets are exchanged for cash or claims to cash" (F46, par. 83). Revenues are considered to be earned when "the entity has substantially accomplished what it must do to be entitled to the benefits represented by the revenues" (F46, par. 83).

For example, if one buys a can of corn, the grocery store will, at the point of sale when cash is exchanged for the can of corn, have both realized and earned the revenue for the transaction. Additionally, if you have a credit account at the same grocery store and buy the same can of corn and it is put on account, the owner of that store will again have both realized and earned the revenue at that time, but no cash will have been exchanged.

The analyst needs to ensure that this concept is followed with prospective financial information, in which liberties are often taken with the timing of the earning of revenues.

Expense Recognition Principle
Statements of Accounting Concepts No. 5 states, "Expenses and losses are generally recognized when an entity's economic benefits are used up in delivering or producing goods, rendering services, or other activities that constitute its ongoing major and central operations, or when previously recognized assets are expected to provide reduced or no further benefit" (F46, par. 85).

The logic pursued in the previous section concerning revenue recognition applies equally here. The issue does not focus on cash, but rather on those activities that must substantially be complete in order to recognize the expenses. This is a difficult concept for those not conversant with accrual accounting.

With prospective financial information it is important to establish the timing of these events. There is a tendency to be overly optimistic on the part of many people who generate prospective financial information as to when both the revenue and the expense events are complete. This needs to be carefully considered by the analyst, and accurate assumptions concerning this timing must be clearly reflected in the prospective financial statements.

GAAP does little to establish if the expenses as reported actually reflect the use of the firm's resources consumed in the process of generating revenues. Depreciation is a good example of this. GAAP is only concerned with a consistent schema for reflecting depreciation in the financial statements, and not whether the depreciation really reflects the actual timing of the consumption of the assets.

Matching Principle
According to *Statements of Accounting Concepts No. 6,*

Matching of costs and revenues is simultaneous or combined recognition of the revenues and expenses that result directly and jointly from the same transactions or other events. In most entities, some transactions or events result simultaneously in both a revenue and one or more expense(s). The revenue and expense(s) are directly related to each other and require recognition at the same time. (F47, par. 146)

The real purpose of the matching principle is to reflect an accurate estimate of income for a period of time. If, in fact, the revenues and expenses related to the generation of those revenues are not represented in the results of operations for the same period, the information presented will necessarily be misleading. The financial analyst needs to be careful to assess whether this important principle has been consistently followed in the prospective financial statements. One example of a violation of this concept that is easily overlooked is the accruing of income taxes associated with a specific year. Although income taxes, especially for a start-up organization, might not be due until some future point in time, they need to be recorded when actually incurred.

This important distinction between when the cash is actually paid for an expense and when the expense is in fact incurred must be considered in order to represent this information accurately in the prospective financial statements.

Consistency Principle
Consistency is an important characteristic of accounting information. The consistency principle requires that a business entity conform "period to period with unchanging policies" (F43, glossary).

It is important that the entity use the same policies from period to period. This is even more important for prospective financial statements. The policies that underpin the development of the prospective financial statements must also be consistent with the historical policies if both types are being presented and if the information is to be meaningful.

Often the modeler of prospective financial information is not fully conversant with all the subtleties and applications of the various accounting and operating policies within the firm and might view the accounting policies reflected in the prospective financial statements as separate and distinct from those which are currently in use within the company. This could cause the prospective financial information to be substantially misleading. Therefore, careful attention to these details is important. Comparability, as we discussed earlier, is closely related to consistency. It is important, when we make comparisons from historical to prospective, or from period to period within the prospective financial statements, that the figures are consistently presented. Without this characteristic, the statements can indeed become quite misleading.

Additionally, given the quickly changing environments firms find themselves in today, there is a current debate as to whether financial information in general can truly conform to the consistency principle. Nonetheless, the analyst assumes it to apply even with these limitations.

Full Disclosure Principle

APB 4 and *SAS 32* require that full disclosure of all relevant information be presented in the financial statements (F4, AC sec. 1024.34).

Statement of Financial Accounting Concepts No. 2 discusses the importance of representational faithfulness (F43, par. 63–80). An important component of the reliability of financial accounting information, one of the elements of representational faithfulness is completeness (F43, par. 79–80). Without full disclosure, the reliability of the information is definitely impacted, due to the incompleteness. Conformity to the necessity for completeness of information is really a corollary to the various financial accounting concepts discussed earlier in this chapter.

Basic Modifiers

The basic modifiers of accounting information include benefits greater than costs, materiality, conservatism, and industry practices.

Benefits Greater Than Costs

Gathering and transmitting of information must be viewed in the dynamic tension of the real world between the costs associated with gathering that information and the benefits that accrue as a result of these efforts. In *Statements of Financial Accounting Concepts No. 1* and *No. 2* there is a lengthy discussion about the realities of the practical world and the need to weigh the various trade-offs in the pursuit of any information (F42, par. 23) and (F43, par. 133–144).

Too often, in practice, regulatory agencies and organs ignore the implications of the costs that are incurred as a consequence of many of their requirements. This is in part due to the fact that none of those costs accrue to either the legislators, regulators, or agencies involved. However, businesses often hide behind the cost/benefit shield in order to avoid or forestall certain actions.

This problem is encountered in a very realistic way by the analyst. Often the information that should be carefully constructed in a prospective financial statement is in fact constructed rather haphazardly. When questioned, the designers of the prospective financial statements often fall back on what effectively is a cost/benefit argument, suggesting that the information is in fact not that relevant, or that the estimates are adequate for the purposes of the specific projection or forecast.

Additionally, when cost/benefit analysis is pursued, all qualitative and quantitative costs and benefits must be included in the analysis. This "total resources" approach is seldom pursued and the resultant conclusions reached are greatly limited by this omission.

The analyst must be careful not to be led by the generators of financial information and their assumptions concerning this important modifier. The assessment as to costs and benefits needs to be made by the analyst without permitting inappropriate influence by the biases of the generators of that financial information.

This argument is often used as a ruse to avoid either examination of substantial material weaknesses in a projection or sloppy work in the preparation of the financial information.

Materiality
Statements of Accounting Concepts No. 2 defines *materiality* as

> The magnitude of an omission or misstatement of accounting information that, in the light of surrounding circumstances, makes it improbable that the judgment of a reasonable person relying on the information would have been changed or influenced by the omission or misstatement. (F43, glossary)

In making any type of decision, one is consistently confronted with the need to make judgments about materiality (F43, par. 123). This is even more common in the area of financial information. It has been of particular interest to auditors for many years. How one goes about defining what is in fact material has presented a great challenge over the years. Although some of the official pronouncements do provide some minimal guidelines, in general it is a decision that must be made based on the experience and expertise of the accountant in the case of historical financial information, or the analyst in the case of prospective financial information.

This issue becomes of particular import in the analysis of prospective financial information. The concept of the cumulative impact of uncertainties on materiality comes into play. There is usually a good degree of confidence with most of the figures in historical financial statements under examination. Therefore, the cumulative effect of the uncertainty with the entire statement is small, or at least able to be estimated. The materiality of any of the individual elements in isolation is able to be judged with reasonable comfort concerning the reliability of the figures.

This is not necessarily the case with prospective financial information. The effect of a series of potential variations in certain figures under consideration presents a real problem. Any single variation in and of itself might not be considered important, but when viewed in the cumulative context, given the overall greater degree of uncertainty, it might present a substantial concern, in combination with the potential variations in the other elements under examination.

Due to the tentativeness of almost all the figures under consideration within prospective financial information, the analyst must adjust his or her concept of materiality to address this totally different situation that one encounters than when dealing with historical financial information. Care must be taken to reflect uncertainty in the analyst's assessment of materiality properly.

Conservatism
Statement on Accounting Concepts No. 2 defines *conservatism* as:

> A prudent reaction to uncertainty to try to ensure that uncertainty and risks inherent in business situations are adequately considered. (F43, glossary)

Conservatism is referred to in *Concepts No. 2* as prudence (F43, par. 92). Business activity is surrounded by uncertainty and one must necessarily be prudent in order to minimize misstatement. Given the reality of uncertainty, conservatism anticipates and modifies for what might be possible errors. The intention is that if an error is made, it should be such as to minimize its negative impact (F43, par. 95).

A problem arises due to the nature of double-entry accounting. When an effort is made to accommodate one account, it always affects another account. This means that if one makes adjustments showing less profit, the balance sheet is affected and potentially misrepresented in the opposite direction. The benefit of conservatism accrues when all the parties involved are using the same adjustments—somewhat similar to the process for rounding off of numbers. Otherwise, it can actually confuse matters.

This problem, though, can present some challenges in the analysis of prospective financial information because it is open to misuse and abuse in the construction of this information. The practitioner must be careful to be attuned to any material modifications to prospective financial information when in fact this modifying convention is referred to as a justification.

Industry Practices

There are some industry practices that do not conform to more common and prevalent accounting practices. These exceptions to common practice are few and far between, but when they do occur the industry practice is often used in order to "present fairly in all material respects" the financial statements (F20, par. 5d).

The real concern here needs to be with the ultimate use for financial statements. If they are going to be used basically for internal use or with third parties with whom direct negotiations will ensue, the problem is minimized. But when the use is not limited and in fact will be for "general use," then these practices can pose some real problems. It is best to identify these practices clearly in the summary of the significant accounting policies and procedures.

4.6 SUMMARY

Accounting information forms the foundation for all financial analysis. A full appreciation of the assumptions that underpin financial figures is essential in order to be able to proceed even with the most basic form of analysis. The overview presented in this chapter of the basic concepts and principles that govern accounting information in the United States is important. These principles and concepts are the meat and potatoes of the analysis process.

The very general nature of the principles discussed in this chapter can lead to a wide variation in the specific application of alternative and equally acceptable Generally Accepted Accounting Principles. Some examples of these alternatives include:

- Income Recognition on Long-term Contracts—percentage-of-completion, completed-contract.
- Inventory Valuation—acquisition cost, lower-of-cost-or-market, standard cost.
- Inventory Cost Flow Assumption—first-in, first-out (FIFO); weighted average; last-in, first-out (LIFO).

- Investments in Securities—acquisition cost, lower-of-cost-or-market, equity.
- Depreciation—straight line, declining balance, sum-of-the-years'-digits.
- Mineral Resource Exploration and Development Costs—successful efforts costing, full costing.
- Leases—operating lease, capital lease.
- Foreign Currency Translation—all-current, monetary/nonmonetary.
- Corporate Acquisitions—purchase, pooling of interests. (E33, p. 145)

The wide variety of specific applications of the various principles can present a real challenge for the analyst.

The topics discussed in this chapter raise the question of information and communication. There is a tendency sometimes to assume that financial information stands like a fortress—strong and alone, cast in cold, hard granite. In fact, the heart of the value of all information relates back to the earlier-stated first objective given in the section on the Statements on Financial Accounting Concepts: financial information is provided for the purpose of assisting in making better business decisions (F42, par. 34–36). Due to the importance of this objective and the fact that good decisions must draw upon a wide range of potentially variable inputs, analysts must be fully aware of the important role that the assumptions, principles, and modifiers play in the analysis process.

CHAPTER FIVE

Prospective Financial Statements—The Standards

CHAPTER OUTLINE

5.4 ILLUSTRATIVE EXAMINATION PROCEDURES
- Procedures to Determine the Scope
- Procedures to Evaluate Assumptions
- Procedures to Evaluate Preparation and Presentation

5.5 SUMMARY

5.1 INTRODUCTION

This chapter will primarily address the AICPA's standards for:

- The issuance of prospective financial statements
- Various accounting services available for prospective financial statements
- Some procedures for use in examining prospective financial statements

The process for the generation of prospective financial information is another subsystem of the firm. The model presented in this chapter basically follows the standards of the AICPA, which are restricted to complete statements. The scope of the overall book is more expansive and addresses prospective financial information in general. Although this chapter focuses on the standards as presented by the AICPA, the prospective financial information that you might be asked to analyze might not necessarily conform to these standards. These standards provide a helpful context in which to start the analysis of prospective financial information, but they provide only an initial reference point. Still, it is useful to start the study of this process with the guidelines that have already been developed and as they have evolved within the accounting profession.

The topic of prospective financial information and its analysis has been addressed on a number of occasions by the AICPA. There are five documents that addressed financial forecasts and projections that were issued prior to the now-current standards. These were:

1. *Guidelines for Systems for the Preparation of Financial Forecasts,* Management Advisory Services Guideline No. 3 (March 1975).

2. *Presentation and Disclosure of Financial Forecasts,* Statement of Position 75-4 (August 1975).

3. *Guide for a Review of a Financial Forecast* (October 1980).

4.   *Report on a Financial Feasibility Study* (October 1982).
5.   *Guide for Prospective Financial Statements* (1986) (F11)

These five documents have been superceded by the current three authoritative statements, which are:

1.   *The Statements on Standards for Accountants' Services on Prospective Financial Information,* "Financial Forecasts and Projections" (1985) (F22)
2.   *Guide for Prospective Financial Information* (1993) (F10)
3.   *Statement on Standards for Attestation Engagements,* "Reporting on Pro Forma Information" (1988) (F25)

These three documents provide the current authoritative guidance concerning prospective financial information. The *Guide for Prospective Financial Information* (1993) (F10) will be referred to as the *Guide* for the remainder of this text. *The Statements on Standards for Accountants' Services on Prospective Financial Information* was prepared by The Financial Forecast and Projections Taskforce and defines *prospective financial statements* as

> Either financial forecasts or financial projections including the summaries of significant assumptions and accounting policies. Although prospective financial statements may cover a period that has partially expired, statements for periods that have completely expired are not considered to be prospective financial statements. Pro forma financial statements and partial presentations are not considered to be prospective financial statements. (F22, p. 4)

Financial forecasts are defined as

> Prospective financial statements that present, to the best of the responsible party's knowledge and belief, an entity's expected financial position, results of operations, and changes in financial position. A financial forecast is based on the responsible party's assumptions reflecting conditions it expects to exist and the course of action it expects to take. A financial forecast may be expressed in specific monetary amounts as a single point estimate of forecasted results or as a range, where the responsible party selects key assumptions to form a range within which it reasonably expects, to the best of its knowledge and belief, the item or items subject to the assumptions to actually fall. When a forecast contains a range, the range is not selected in a

biased or misleading manner, for example, a range in which one end is significantly less expected than the other. (F22, p. 5)

Financial projections are defined as

Prospective financial statements that present, to the best of the responsible party's knowledge and belief, given one or more hypothetical assumptions, an entity's expected financial position, results of operations, and changes in financial position. A financial projection is sometimes prepared to present one or more hypothetical courses of action for evaluation, as in response to a question such as "What would happen if . . . ?" A financial projection is based on the responsible party's assumptions reflecting conditions it expects would exist and the source of action it expects would be taken, given one or more hypothetical assumptions. A projection, like a forecast, may contain a range. Minimum presentation guidelines for prospective financial statements are set forth in Appendix A of this Statement. (F22, p. 5)

In discussing prospective financial information it is important to understand the anticipated use that will be made of the information. Prospective financial statements may be either for "general use" or "limited use."

"General use" of prospective financial statements refers to the use of the statement by persons with whom the responsible party is not negotiating directly, for example, in an offering statement of an entity's debt or equity interests. Because recipients of financial statements distributed for general use are not able to ask the responsible party directly about the presentation, the presentation most useful to them is one that portrays, to the best of the responsible party's knowledge and belief, the expected results. Thus, only a financial forecast is appropriate for general use. (F22, p. 6)

However, prospective financial statements might be for "limited use."

"Limited use" of prospective financial statements refers to use of prospective financial statements by the responsible party alone, or by the responsible party and third parties with whom the responsible party is negotiating directly. Examples include use of negotiations for a bank loan, submission to a regulatory agency, and use solely within the entity. Third-party recipients of prospective financial statements intended to limited use can ask questions of the responsible party and negotiate terms directly with it. Any type of prospective financial statement that would be useful in the circumstances would normally be appropriate for limited use. Thus, the presentation may be a financial forecast or a financial projection. (F22, pp. 6–7)

Specific knowledge of the proposed use of the prospective financial statements goes beyond just sorting into the two above-mentioned categories. It is also helpful in determining how to interpret and view much of the information gained in the analysis process.

The majority of the material presented in this chapter will closely follow the above-mentioned authoritative statements and will provide an important reference for the analysis process.

5.2 ISSUING PROSPECTIVE FINANCIAL STATEMENTS

There are two issues of concern in the issuing of prospective financial statements. They are:

1. Preparation
2. Presentation

Guidelines are presented within the *Guide For Prospective Financial Information* that address both of these topics.

Preparation Guidelines

There are a number of guidelines that are applicable to the preparation of financial forecasts. A list of these eleven general guidelines and the references within the *Guide* are presented below (F10, p. 18).

1. Financial forecasts should be prepared in good faith.
2. Financial forecasts should be prepared with appropriate care by qualified personnel.
3. Financial forecasts should be prepared using appropriate accounting principles.
4. The process used to develop financial forecasts should provide for seeking out the best information that is reasonably available at the time.
5. The information used in preparing financial forecasts should be consistent with the plans of the entity.
6. Key factors should be identified as a basis for assumptions.
7. Assumptions used in preparing financial forecasts should be appropriate.

8. The process used to develop financial forecasts should provide the means to determine the relative effect of variations in the major underlying assumptions.

9. The process used to develop financial forecasts should provide adequate documentation of both the financial forecasts and the process used to develop them.

10. The process used to develop financial forecasts should include, where appropriate, the regular comparison of the financial forecasts with attained results.

11. The process used to prepare financial forecasts should include adequate review and approval by the responsible party at the appropriate levels of authority.

Presentation Guidelines

In any presentation of prospective financial information, it is important to ascertain the intended use for the financial statements. This will be the primary determinant as to whether a financial forecast or a projection would be the appropriate prospective financial statement.

For the remainder of this text the discussions will use the term forecast in a generic sense when referring to either type of prospective financial statement. If there are material differences between the guidelines for forecasts or projections these differences will be indicated. Otherwise the discussions will focus on prospective financial statements in general.

It is important to appreciate who is responsible for the financial forecast. This is similar to the requirements for historical financial statements. The responsible party is usually but is not necessarily management another party—for instance it could be someone who is considering acquiring a business (F10, p. 10). As with historical information, it is important for the responsible party to determine whether there is a reasonable basis for the prospective financial information. For a projection the basis does not necessarily have to be reasonable but the hypothetical assumptions must necessarily be "consistent with the purpose of the projection" (F10, p. 25).

The issue of responsibility as seen by the courts differs greatly from the standards as presented by the AICPA. Accountants, both those internal to the firm and any third parties performing an attest function, have potential legal exposure due to their involvement with any prospective financial information.

There are minimal presentation guidelines that are required by the *Guide*.

These parallel the information needed in historical financial statements. The elements required in a minimum presentation include:

1. Sales or gross revenues
2. Gross profit or cost of sales
3. Unusual or infrequently occurring items
4. Provision for income tax
5. Discontinued operations or extraordinary items
6. Income from continuing operations
7. Net income
8. Primary and fully diluted earnings per share
9. Significant changes in financial position
10. A description of what the responsible party intends the financial forecast to present, a statement that the assumptions are based on the responsible party's judgment at the time the prospective information was prepared, and a caveat that the forecasted results may not be achieved.
11. Summary of significant assumptions
12. Summary of significant accounting policies (F10, p. 36)

If any of the above-listed items are not included then you could have a partial presentation that would not be appropriate for general use. But "if the omitted applicable item is derivable from the information presented, the presentation would not be deemed to be a partial presentation" (F10, p. 36).

Many published reports include valuable prospective financial information that does not conform to the standards for a minimum presentation and therefore technically should not be appropriate for general use. In fact this demonstrates one of the many problems with these standards.

Additionally it is important that the forecast or projection include the date of completion (F11, p. 36). The assumptions need to be appropriate as of that date. A summary of the significant accounting policies used in preparing (F10, p. 37) the prospective financial information should be disclosed. The concept of materiality applies to prospective financial information as well as to historical statements, and accordingly there is an "expected range of reasonableness of the information" (F10, p. 38).

It is important that all significant assumptions and the basis for those assumptions should be disclosed to assist the user (F10, p. 39) in better understanding the statements.

Assumptions disclosed should include:

a.   Assumptions about which there is a reasonable possibility of the occurrence of a variation that may significantly affect the prospective results; that is, sensitive assumptions.

b.   Assumptions about anticipated conditions that are expected to be significantly different from current conditions, which are not otherwise reasonably apparent.

c.   Other matters deemed important to the prospective information or its interpretation.

d.   . . . the responsible party should identify which assumptions in the projection are hypothetical. In addition, if the hypothetical assumptions are improbable, the disclosure should indicate that. (F10, p. 39)

It is important that particularly sensitive assumptions be disclosed, although it is not always easy to know which will be sensitive to all the various conditions possible. These would include:

a.   An assumption with a relatively high probability of a sizable variation, or

b.   An assumption for which the probability of a sizable variation is not as high but for which a small variation would have a large impact. (F10, p. 39)

A frequently applied but not always clearly articulated assumption is that "current conditions [will] prevail" (F10, p. 40). Examples of the current conditions prevailing include an absence of war, earthquakes, and so forth. But there are situations in which this assumption might not be appropriate—for instance, if the locale in which the business is located is, in fact, undergoing a civil war or the high probability of one. There are many other systemic changes that can occur and have an impact on the prospective financial statements that need to be considered in the analysis process, given the dynamic nature of the world in which we live.

The introduction to the assumptions in the prospective financial statements should make it clear that the list is not all-inclusive. It should clearly identify who the responsible party (or parties) is, and should present the fact that the assumptions are judgments made at the time when the prospective financial statements were prepared. It should clearly identify the fact that the prospective results may not be attained (F10, p. 40).

The period to be covered is usually "at least one full year of normal operations . . ." but it might include multiple years. "However, no minimum or maximum period of time is specified . . ." (F10, p. 41).

It is important to clearly differentiate between the prospective financial statements and any historical information included with them, so that there can be no possibility of confusing the two. (F10, p. 46) It usually is not expected that the prospective financial statements will be updated. It should be understood that when a responsible party does uncover errors that were made in preparing the prospective financial statements the statement should be withdrawn if it is likely that any of the current users will rely on the erroneous information (F10, p. 47).

It is interesting to note that not requiring the updating of prospective financial statements except if the "users would expect prospective statements to be updated" (F10, p. 47) is another professional caveat provided by the AICPA that the courts have concluded has little place in the real world. The AICPA seems insistent on forcing the examination of prospective financial statements into the model for the examination of historical financial information, which in itself is currently under rigorous scrutiny by various agencies, regulatory bodies, and the courts.

5.3 ACCOUNTANTS' SERVICES ON PROSPECTIVE FINANCIAL STATEMENTS

There are three types of services on prospective financial statements that should be considered.

1. Compilations
2. Examinations
3. Agreed-upon procedures

Compilations

Definition
Compilations are one of the three types of professional services that are discussed in the *Guide*. A compilation is a type of professional service that involves:

a. Assembling, to the extent necessary, the financial forecast based on the responsible party's assumptions.

b. Performing the required compilation procedures, including reading the financial forecast with its summaries of significant assumptions and accounting policies and considering whether they appear to be (1) presented in conformity with AICPA presentation guidelines and (2) not obviously inappropriate.

c. issuing a compilation report. (F10, p. 99)

Standards

As with all services performed by a CPA there are various standards that apply. The standards for compilations include:

a. The compilation should be performed by a person or persons having adequate technical training and proficiency to compile a financial forecast.

b. Due professional care should be exercised in the performance of the compilation and the preparation of the report.

c. The work should be adequately planned, and assistants, if any, should be properly supervised.

d. Applicable compilation procedures should be performed as a basis for reporting on the compiled financial forecast.

e. The report based on the accountant's compilation of a financial forecast should conform to the applicable guidance in chapter 14. (F10, p. 99)

Procedures

There are some general procedures that must be followed in the performance of a compilation. Where applicable the accountant should:

a. Establish an understanding with the client, preferably in writing, regarding the services to be performed. (F10, p. 100)

b. Inquire about the accounting principles used in the preparation of the financial forecast.

   i. For existing entities, compare the accounting principles used to those used in the preparation of previous historical financial statements and inquire whether such principles are the same as those expected to be used in the historical financial statements covering the forecast period. (F10, p. 101)

    ii. For entities to be formed or entities formed that have not commenced operations, compare specialized industry accounting principles used, if any, to those typically used in the industry. Inquire about whether the accounting principles used for the financial forecast are those that are expected to be used when, or if, the entity commences operations. (F10, p. 101)

c. Ask how the responsible party identifies the key factors and develops its assumptions. (F10, p. 101)

d. List, or obtain a list, of the responsible party's significant assumptions providing the basis for the financial forecast and consider whether there are any obvious omissions in light of the key factors upon which the prospective results of the entity appear to depend. (F10, p. 101)

e. Consider whether there appear to be any obvious internal inconsistencies in the assumptions. (F10, p. 101)

f. Perform, or test the mathematical accuracy of the computations that translate the assumptions into the financial forecast. (F10, p. 101)

g. Read the financial forecast, including the summary of significant assumptions, and consider whether

    i. The forecast, including the disclosures of assumptions and accounting policies, appears to be presented in conformity with the AICPA presentation guidelines for a financial forecast, which appear in section 400. (F10, p. 101)

    ii. The forecast, including the summary of significant assumptions, appears to be not obviously inappropriate in relation to

        a. The accountant's knowledge of the entity and its industry.

        b. The expected conditions and course of action in the forecast period. (F10, p. 101)

h. If a significant part of the prospective period has expired, inquire about the results of operations or significant portions of the operations (such as sales volume) and significant changes in financial position, and consider their effect in relation to the financial forecast. If historical financial statements have been prepared for the expired portion of the period, the accountant should read such statements and consider those results in relation to the financial forecast. (F10, p. 101)

i. Confirm his or her understanding of the forecast (including assumptions) by obtaining written representations from the responsible party.

Because the amounts reflected in the forecast are not supported by historical books and records but rather by assumptions, the accountant should obtain representations in which the responsible party indicates its responsibility for the assumptions. The representations should be signed by the responsible party at the highest level of authority who the accountant believes is responsible for and knowledgeable, directly or through others, about matters covered by the representations. The representations should include a statement that the financial forecast presents, to the best of the responsible party's knowledge and belief, the expected financial position, results of operations, and changes in financial position for the forecast period, and that the forecast reflects the responsible party's judgment, based on present circumstances, of the expected conditions and its expected course of action. If the forecast contains a range, the representations should also include a statement that, to the best of the responsible party's knowledge and belief, the item or items subject to the assumptions are expected to actually fall within the range and that the range was not selected in a biased or misleading manner. (F10, pp. 101–102)

j.   Consider, after applying the above procedures, whether he or she has received representations or other information that appears to be obviously inappropriate, incomplete, or otherwise misleading and, if so, attempt to obtain additional or revised information. If he or she does not receive such information, the accountant should ordinarily withdraw from the compilation engagement. (Note that the omission of disclosures, other than those relating to significant assumptions, would not require the accountant to withdraw; see paragraph 14.09.) (F10, pp. 102–103)

The above standards do not relieve the CPA from following the standards established for working with historical financial information.

If the accountant is addressing a projection and not a forecast, the paragraph (i) above is amended by the *Guide* to state that:

The accountant should confirm his or her understanding of the projection (including assumptions) by obtaining written representations from the responsible party. Because the amounts reflected in the statements are not supported by historical books and records but rather by assumptions, the accountant should obtain representations in which the responsible party indicates its responsibility for the assumptions. The representations should be signed by the responsible party at the highest level of authority who the accountant believes is responsible for and knowledgeable, directly or through others, about matters covered by the representations. The representations should include a statement that the financial projection presents, to the best of the responsible party's knowledge and belief, the expected financial position, results of operations, and changes in financial position for the projection period given the hypothetical assumptions, and that the projection reflects its judgment, based on present circumstances, of expected conditions and its expected course of action given the occurrence of the hypothetical events. The representations should also (1) identify the hypothetical assumptions and describe the limitations on the usefulness of the presentation, (2) state that the assumptions are appropriate, (3) indicate if the hypothetical assumptions are improbable, and (4) if the projection contains a range, the representations should also include a statement that, to the best of the responsible party's knowledge and belief, given the hypothetical assumptions, the item or items subject to the assumption are expected to actually fall within the range and that the range was not selected in a biased or misleading manner. (F10, p. 102)

Working Papers
Although there is no specific form or content for the working papers, there are certain general guidelines that are appropriate. The working papers should indicate that:

a.   The work was adequately planned and supervised.
b.   The required compilation procedures were performed as a basis for the compilation report. (F10, p. 103)

Report
The compilation report should include:

a.   An identification of the financial forecast presented by the responsible party.
b.   A statement that the accountant has compiled the financial forecast in accordance with standards established by the American Institute of Certified Public Accountants.
c.   A statement that a compilation is limited in scope and does not enable the accountant to express an opinion or any other form of assurance on the financial forecast or the assumptions.

d.   A caveat that the forecasted results may not be achieved.

e.   A statement that the accountant assumes no responsibility to update the report for events and circumstances occurring after the date of the report. (F10, p. 111)

The date of the report should be the date that the compilation is completed. (F10, p. 112). If the CPA compiles a prospective financial statement for an entity of which he or she is not independent this should be disclosed after the last paragraph of the report.

Sometimes there are modifications to the standard report that are appropriate. This might occur when management chooses to omit the summary of significant accounting policies, and would be presented as an additional paragraph in the report.

Examinations

Definition
An examination of prospective financial information is a professional service that involves:

1.   Evaluating the preparation of the financial forecast.
2.   Evaluating the support underlying the assumptions.
3.   Evaluating the presentation of the financial forecast for conformity with AICPA presentation guidelines.
4.   Issuing an examination report. (F10, p. 119)

Basis for Reporting
The purpose of the examination is to provide the CPA with a reasonable basis for reporting on whether in his or her opinion:

a.   The financial forecast is presented in conformity with AICPA guidelines.

b.   The assumptions provide a reasonable basis for the responsible party's forecast. (F10, p. 119)

The standards do not preclude more exhaustive efforts on the part of the analyst, but only set up the minimum guidelines that must be followed.

Planning

The planning of an engagement requires developing an overall strategy for the conduct of an engagement. It is necessary to have an appropriate foundational knowledge for developing the plan. Some factors that must be considered in the planning process include:

a. The accounting principles and the type of presentation to be used,

b. The anticipated level of attestation risk related to the financial forecast,

c. Preliminary judgments about materiality levels,

d. Items within the financial forecast that are likely to require revision or adjustment,

e. Conditions that may require extension or modification of the accountant's examination procedures,

f. Knowledge of the entity's business and its industry,

g. The responsible party's experience in preparing financial forecasts,

h. The length of the period covered by the financial forecast, and

i. The process by which the responsible party develops its financial forecast (F10, p. 120)

This list, which is provided by the AICPA, omits and ignores the issues of business organization and strategy that are deemed by this author to be of vital importance to the analysis process. This important topic will be discussed in Chapter 6.

Areas of Focus

Although an overall knowledge of the industry is important, there are usually a number of areas that are key to the achievement of the results depicted in the prospective financial information. Some of these key areas include:

a. The availability and cost of resources needed to operate. Principal items usually include raw materials, labor, short-term and long-term financing, and plant and equipment. (F10, p. 120)

b. The nature and condition of markets in which the entity sells its goods or services, including final consumer markets if the entity sells to intermediate markets. (F10, p. 120)

c.   Factors specific to the industry, including competitive conditions, sensitivity to economic conditions, accounting policies, specific regulatory requirements, and technology. (F10, p. 121)

d.   Patterns of past performance for the entity or comparable entities, including trends in revenue and costs, turnover of assets, uses and capacities of physical facilities, and management policies. (F10, p. 121)

The resources referred to in the first item above must include many other important and often overlooked items, such as the skills of the workforce and the reputation of the firm under examination.

Extent of Procedures

There are a variety of specific procedures that can be applied. These will be discussed later in this chapter. But in determining the extent to which various procedures should be performed the CPA has to make an evaluation of a number of important considerations, including:

a.   The nature and materiality of the information to the financial forecast taken as a whole,

b.   The likeliness of misstatements,

c.   Knowledge obtained during current and previous engagements,

d.   The responsible party's competence with respect to financial forecasts,

e.   The extent to which the financial forecast is affected by the responsible party's judgment—for example, its judgment in selecting the assumptions used to prepare the financial forecast, and

f.   The adequacy of the responsible party's underlying data. (F10, p. 121)

Procedures

The actual procedures selected depend to a large extent on the experience of the CPA performing the examination The length of time covered by the projection must be determined. How the projection is developed is also important. There are a number of general procedures necessary to evaluate the assumptions. The CPA has to be able to conclude that all of the key factors that might materially affect the operations have been explicitly identified. In the case of a projection this would be qualified by the effects of the hypothetical assumptions (F10, pp. 121–123).

In dealing with prospective financial information, the CPA must be careful not to allow in any way (either in the work performed or in the statements presented) the conclusion that any particular outcome is expected.

This is because:

a.   Realization of the financial forecast may depend upon the responsible party's intentions, which cannot be examined,

b.   There is substantial inherent uncertainty in the assumptions,

c.   Some of the information accumulated about an assumption may appear contradictory, and

d.   Different but similarly reasonable assumptions concerning a particular matter might be derived from common information. (F10, p. 124)

As in any accounting process, in choosing the assumptions to be examined it is necessary to apply a cost/benefit analysis, which should include an examination of both quantitative and qualitative factors. A CPA should concentrate on those areas that are:

1.   Material to the prospective amounts

2.   Especially sensitive to variations

3.   Deviations from historical trends

4.   Especially uncertain (F10, p. 124)

Once the specific assumptions that need to be examined have been chosen, it is necessary to evaluate these assumptions. These assumptions need to be examined and the support for them properly understood and appropriately questioned. Some important lines of questioning include:

a.   Whether enough pertinent sources of information about the assumptions have been considered. Examples of external sources the accountant might consider are government publications, industry publications, economic forecasts, existing or proposed legislation, and reports of changing technology. Examples of internal sources are budgets, labor agreements, patents, royalty agreements and records, sales backlog records, debt agreements, and actions of the board of directors involving entity plans (F10, p. 124)

b.   Whether the assumptions are consistent with the sources from which they are derived (F10, p. 124)

c.   Whether the assumptions are consistent with each other (F10, p. 124)

d.   Whether the historical financial information and other data used in developing the assumptions are sufficiently reliable for that purpose.

Reliability can be assessed by inquiry and analytical or other procedures, some of which may have been completed in past examinations or reviews of the historical financial statements. If historical financial statements have been prepared for an expired part of the prospective period, the accountant should consider the historical data in relation to the prospective results for the same period, where applicable. If the financial forecast incorporates such historical financial results and that period is significant to the presentation, the accountant should make a review of the historical information in conformity with the applicable standards for a review (F10, pp. 124–125)

e.   Whether the historical financial information and other data used in developing the assumptions are comparable over the period specified or whether the effects of any lack of comparability were considered in developing the assumptions (F10, p. 125)

f.   Whether the logical arguments or theory, considered with the data supporting the assumptions, are reasonable (F10, p. 125)

There are many sources of support for various assumptions. They may include market surveys, engineering studies, general economic indicators, industry statistics, trends and patterns developed from an entity's operating history, and internal data and analyses accompanied by their supporting logical argument or theory. (F10, p. 125)

Additionally, it may be necessary to consider the income tax treatment of certain prospective transactions, as the firm is likely to pursue them. Where this is the case it is important for the CPA to be satisfied as to the appropriateness of the assumptions. This could even include obtaining a tax opinion, which could come from the entity's tax counsel, another accountant, or the IRS.

It is also necessary to evaluate the preparation and presentation of the prospective financial statements. In order to do this the CPA must perform procedures that will provide reasonable assurance that the:

a.   Presentation reflects the identified assumptions. (F10, p. 126)

b.   Computations made to translate the assumptions into prospective amounts are mathematically accurate. (F10, p. 126)

c.   Assumptions are internally consistent. (F10, p. 126)

d.   Accounting principles used in the financial forecast are consistent with the accounting principles expected to be used in the historical financial statements covering the prospective period and those used in the most recent historical financial statements, if any. (F10, pp. 126–127)

e.   Presentation of the financial forecast follows the AICPA guidelines applicable for such statements. (F10, p. 127)

f.   Assumptions have been adequately disclosed based upon AICPA presentation guidelines in chapter 400. (F10, p. 127)

There are times when the CPA will feel that the work of a specialist would be helpful. Examples of these specialists include engineers, economists, investment bankers, and architects (F10, p. 128). Guidance for using specialists is presented in *SAS No. 11, Using the Work of a Specialist*. As with any type of procedure this determination is made at the discretion of the examining accountant.

It is important to be aware of the fact that the results of a prospective financial statement are often highly dependent on the actions of the statement's user—for instance, a bank providing a loan. The achievement of the prospective financial information would be dependent on whether or not that user (the banker) authorizes the granting of that loan. In this situation it is very difficult for the CPA to obtain support for these assumptions (F10, p. 128).

This can present some real difficulties in issuing an examination report. If he or she is dealing with a single important assumption (for instance, the granting of a bank loan, which would result in obtaining needed funds) the CPA can develop an adequate assurance to issue an examination report. However, when there is a variety of potential outcomes, it might be inappropriate to issue the report.

Bankers may follow a set of rules that the analyst/accountant also accepts—for instance, a current ratio of 2 to 1. These rules in themselves may determine whether or not a loan is granted, and they may have little to do with the viability of the plans. Every time it is encountered, the rule forces failure upon the firm seeking funds. But the rule itself rather than the firm might be the problem—a type of self-fulfilling prophecy.

Working Papers

As with the compilation procedures it is important that there be appropriate working papers in connection with an examination. Although the specific contents and form might vary, minimally they should indicate that:

1. The work was adequately planned and supervised.
2. The process by which the entity develops its financial forecast was considered in determining the scope of the examination.
3. Sufficient evidence was obtained to provide a reasonable basis for the accountant's report. (F10, p. 128)

Report

The CPA has a standard report that must be issued when the examination of a prospective financial statement is completed. The important components for this report include:

a. An identification of the financial forecast presented.
b. A statement that the examination of the financial forecast was made in accordance with AICPA standards and a brief description of the nature of such an examination.
c. The accountant's opinion that the financial forecast is presented in conformity with AICPA presentation guidelines and that the underlying assumptions provide a reasonable basis for the forecast.
d. A caveat that the forecasted results may not be achieved.
e. A statement that the accountant assumes no responsibility to update the report for events and circumstances occurring after the date of the report. (F10, p. 139)

Agreed-Upon Procedures

A CPA may be asked to perform agreed-upon procedures on a prospective financial statement. In such cases, it is important, given the specialized nature of the engagement, that the users of the prospective financial information be involved in the development of both the scope and the procedures of the engagement. The report must be restricted to specified users, and the prospective financial information must include a summary of all significant assumptions (F10, p. 155).

The technical training and proficiency must be similar to that necessary for conducting compilations or examinations.

Procedures

The procedures are generally limited to those agreed upon by the CPA and the user. This is because the user will take responsibility for their appropriateness and adequacy. However, mere reading of the financial forecast does not constitute a procedure sufficient to permit an accountant to report on the results of applying agreed-upon procedures to it (F10, p. 155).

The development of the procedures requires interaction between the CPA and the user. This requirement can be satisfied by applying one of the following or similar procedures:

1. Discussing the procedures to be applied with legal counsel or other appropriate designated representatives of the users involved, such as a trustee, a receiver, or a creditor's committee.
2. Reviewing relevant correspondence from specified users.
3. Comparing the procedures to be applied to written requirements of a supervisory agency.
4. Distributing a draft of the report or a copy of the client's engagement letter to the specified users involved with a request for their comments before the report is issued. (F10, p. 155)

Working Papers
As with compilation and examination procedures, the content and form of the working papers may vary considerably. They ordinarily should indicate that:

1. The work was adequately planned and supervised.
2. The agreed-upon procedures were performed as the basis for the report. (F10, p. 155)

5.4   ILLUSTRATIVE EXAMINATION PROCEDURES

The procedures discussed in the previous sections of this chapter were somewhat general in nature. In order to expand on these some illustrative examination procedures will be covered in this section. They include:

1. Procedures to determine the scope of an examination
2. Procedures to evaluate assumptions
3. Procedures to evaluate preparation and presentation

Procedures to Determine the Scope of an Examination

The following list spells out some illustrative examination procedures that can be used to assist in determining the scope of an examination.

a.   Obtain knowledge of the entity's business by
   i.   Interviewing entity personnel and other individuals knowledgable about the industry.
   ii.   Consulting AICPA guides, industry publications, textbooks, and periodicals.
   iii.   Analyzing financial statements of the entity and of other entities in the industry. (F10, p. 129)

   The accountant may have previously obtained some or all of this knowledge through experience with the entity or its industry. (F10, p. 129)

b.   In obtaining knowledge of the entity's business, consider
   i.   Resources needed by the company (availability and cost)
      Material
      Labor
      Capital
      Fixed assets (for example, capacity of plant and equipment) (F10, p. 129)
   ii.   Markets served by the company (nature and condition)
      Intermediate markets
      Final consumer markets
      Entity's market share
      Advertising and marketing plans (F10, p. 129)
   iii.   Factors specific to the industry
      Competitive conditions
      Sensitivity to economic conditions
      Accounting policies
      Specific regulatory requirements
      Technology (F10, p. 129)
   iv.   Patterns of past performance for the entity or comparable entities
      Trends in revenue and costs
      Turnover of assets
      Uses and capabilities of physical facilities
      Management policies (F10, p. 129)

   When resources needed by a company are considered, real resources beyond those that traditionally are accepted and that the AICPA enumerates here must be included. These additional real resources can include such things as employee skills, the reputation of the firm, or the firm's location.

Additionally, when an accountant considers the resources needed by a company, that consideration must include an examination of the firm's strategy and organization. These are often the most important elements to be investigated and should be added to the AICPA's list.

c.   Obtain or assemble the financial forecast, together with a list of the significant assumptions and their descriptions. (F10, p. 130)

d.   Review the process used in preparing the financial forecast to obtain an understanding of the rationale by which key factors are identified and assumptions are developed and of the process by which assumptions are translated into prospective data. The accountant would look for answers to such questions as these:

  i.   Is preparation of the financial forecast adequately documented to permit tracing through the process? The accountant may decide to prepare a brief outline of the process used to develop the financial forecast. (F10, p. 130)

  ii.   Has the process been used in the past to generate financial forecasts, and if so, was it effective? (F10, p. 130)

  iii.   What procedures provide reasonable assurance that all significant factors are included in the assumptions? (F10, p. 130)

  iv.   What procedures provide reasonable assurance that the financial forecast is based on assumptions approved by the responsible party? (F10, p. 130)

  v.   What are the methods for collecting, calculating, and aggregating prospective data? (F10, p. 130)

  vi.   What methods identify and quantify the impact of variations in assumptions? (F10, p. 130)

  vii.   What are the procedures to effect changes in accounting principles and reflect them in the financial forecast? (F10, p. 130)

  viii.   If the process used to develop financial forecasts has been in operation or used in the past, are there procedures to compare prior prospective amounts with the historical results for the same period and analyze the differences where applicable? (For example, differences in forecasted amounts and actual results should be analyzed to ascertain that identified causes are considered.) Are the procedures used to adjust the process, where applicable, as a result of such analysis? (F10, p. 130)

ix. What are the responsible party's review and approval procedures? (F10, p. 130)

x. How are errors prevented or detected? (F10, p. 130)

e. Identify any models and techniques that are used. If possible, obtain a description of them. (F10, p. 130)

f. Having reviewed the process by which the responsible party develops its financial forecasts, analyze its strengths and weaknesses by comparing it with the guidelines outlined in Chapter 6 (F10, p. 130)

g. Consider the competence of the entity's personnel involved in the process, including their degree of authority, prior experience with the entity and industry, and understanding of both the entity's plans and the process, in relation to their functions in the process and in entity operations. (F10, p. 130)

h. Review documentation of both the financial forecasts and process to develop them or otherwise investigate whether there is

   i. Review and approval by the responsible party

   ii. Determination of the relative effect on variations in major underlying assumptions

   iii. Use of appropriate accounting principles and practices (F10, p. 131)

i. Test significant elements of the process designed to prevent or detect errors, including clerical errors (F10, p. 131)

j. Where applicable, review the entity's documentation of the comparison of actual results with amounts contained in previous financial forecasts (if any) for that period and consider

   i. Whether the comparison was performed using correct, comparable data and whether analyzed differences were documented and appropriately supported,

   ii. Whether the process was adjusted where appropriate,

   iii. Whether the procedures to develop financial forecasts in the past have reflected the entity's plans properly, and

   iv. Whether any consistent biases have been observed (F10, p. 131)

k. Based on the knowledge obtained in the foregoing procedures, design the examination procedures for evaluating the assumptions and the preparation and the presentation of the financial forecast (F10, p. 131)

Procedure to Evaluate Assumptions

Specific examination procedures that can be used to evaluate assumptions include:

a. Identify key factors upon which the financial results of the entity appear to depend. (F11, p. 138)

   i. Evaluate both the assumptions listed in the financial forecast and the more detailed data included in the underlying documentation to determine the completeness of the list. Factors to consider include:

      Risks inherent in the business.

      Sensitivity to variations.

      Pervasiveness of the impact of particular factors on the various assumptions (F11, p. 138)

   ii. Obtain financial forecasts of similar entities, if available, and consider whether the key factors covered by the assumptions therein are covered in the client's statements.

   iii. Analyze prior-period financial results to help identify the principal factors that influenced the results. If any interim historical results are available, consider any significant deviations from historical patterns and investigate the causes.

   iv. Review any public statements, formal plans, and the minutes of board of directors' meetings, noting any significant decisions regarding plans, contracts, or legal agreements.

   v. Question the responsible party regarding possible additional factors or changes in assumptions about factors.

   vi. Using the knowledge of the entity and its industry, investigate any particularly risky or sensitive aspect of the business—market trends, competitive conditions, pending laws and regulations, social, economic, political and technological influences, and dependence upon major customers and suppliers. (F10, p. 131)

b. Evaluate whether the assumptions are suitably supported.

   i. Evaluate the support for the assumptions, giving special attention to specific assumptions that are

      Material to the prospective amounts

      Especially sensitive to variations

Deviations from historical patterns

Especially uncertain

ii. For key assumptions, obtain a list of internal and external sources of information that the entity used in formulating the assumptions. On a test basis, evaluate whether the information was considered in formulating the assumptions.

iii. Trace assumptions about selected key factors to the support for the assumptions to determine whether the indicated sources of information were actually used and evaluate the suitability of existing support. If the information is taken from internal analysis, consider the need for testing the supporting information.

iv. Review any available documentation of the responsible party's plans, such as budgets, spending estimates, policy statements, contractual agreements, among others, and inquire about those plans, goals, and objectives, and consider their relationship to the assumptions.

v. Investigate alternative sources of support for the assumptions and evaluate whether the preponderance of available information supports each significant assumption.

vi. Inquire about and analyze the historical data used in developing prospective amounts to assess

    (i). Whether it is comparable and consistent with the forecast period.

    (ii). Whether it is sufficiently reliable for the purpose.

vii. If historical financial statements have been prepared for an expired part of the prospective period, read the historical data and consider them in relation to the prospective results for the same period.

viii. If the financial forecast is based on the historical financial results for part of the forecast period and that part is significant to the presentation, make a review of the historical information in conformity with applicable standards for a review.

ix. Consider alternative approaches to the development of the assumptions. For example, if the sales assumption was developed by aggregating individual salespeople's estimates, consider comparing the assumptions to historical patterns. Also consider trying other models and techniques.

x. Evaluate whether the presentation extends to time periods for which suitable support for assumptions is not available, considering

The nature of the entity's industry

Patterns of past performance for the entity or comparable entities

xi. Where appropriate, consider confirming with external sources information supporting the assumptions. (For example, if the backlog of sales orders is significant to the financial forecast and is not adequately supported, consider sending written confirmation request to customers.)

xii. If the support for key assumptions comes from experts, such as lawyers, engineers, economists, investment bankers, and architects

Consider their professional standing

Consider using the work of another expert in the field.

Review the data and plans the entity submitted to the expert for consistency with the financial forecast and supporting data.

xiii. If the assumptions about the tax treatment of prospective transactions are sensitive, obtain support for their appropriateness by

Analyzing prospective transactions in the context of applicable tax laws or

Obtaining an opinion as to such matters from the entity's tax counsel or another accountant and applying the procedures in SAS No. 11, paragraphs 5-8.

xiv. Obtain a representation letter from the responsible party.

xv. Consider obtaining a letter from the client's legal counsel, as of the report date, covering

Litigation, claims and assessments

Legality of any major changes planned (such as marketing considerations, environmental impact or patents) and other matters (such as the impact of new laws affecting the industry) (F10, pp. 131–133)

Procedures to Evaluate Preparation and Presentation

Some examples of specific examination procedures to assist in evaluating the preparation and presentation of a financial forecast include:

a. Test the mathematical accuracy of the computations made in translating the assumptions into prospective amounts. (F10, p. 133)

b. Evaluate whether data have been appropriately aggregated by—

    i. Evaluating the appropriateness of mathematical equations, statistical techniques, or modeling procedures. *Comment:* This investigation should include looking at patterns of behavior and investigating whether the data described are appropriate. Sometimes additional research is required in order to pursue this.

    ii. Recomputing on a test basis.

    iii. Tracing aggregate amounts to the financial forecast. (F10, p. 133)

c. Determine whether the listed assumptions are those used in preparing the financial forecast. (F10, p. 133)

d. Determine whether the effects of each assumption on all of the related prospective amounts have been reflected in the presentation. (F10, p. 133)

e. Determine whether any assumption contradicts or is inconsistent with another. (F10, p. 133)

f. Review the relationship between financial and other relevant data using appropriate mathematical or judgmental methods. (F10, p. 133)

g. Review adjustments made in the data, considering whether they are justified and reasonable in relation to other information and whether their impact has been properly reflected in the financial forecast. (F10, p. 134)

h. If historical data for part of the forecast period are included in the financial forecast, trace the amounts from the books, records, and other indicated sources to the financial forecast. (F10, p. 134)

i. Determine whether the presentation is in conformity with the presentation guidelines in section 400, considering the following:

    i. Is the financial forecast presented in the format of the historical financial statements expected to be issued? If not, are the required items presented?

    ii. Are the accounting principles used:

Consistent with those used in the historical financial statements, if any?

Consistent with those expected to be used in future financial statements (including expected changes in accounting principles)?

Generally accepted accounting principles or based on another comprehensive basis of accounting?

iii. Is the basis of accounting used:

Consistent with that used in historical financial statements, if any?

Reconciled with the historical methods where different, or are the differences described?

iv. Are the assumptions adequately disclosed?

v. Are particularly sensitive assumptions identified?

vi. If the impact of a variation is disclosed, is it appropriately stated?

vii. Is the financial forecast appropriately distinguished from historical financial statements? (F10, p. 134)

5.5 SUMMARY

The above discussion on the issuance of prospective financial information has focused on the following:

1. The various levels of accountant's services for the financial statements
2. Various examples of procedures that can be applied

These discussions provide some helpful checklists with which to view prospective financial information. However, the application of the techniques must be tailored to the specific project at hand.

Basically the procedures in this discussion have been developed by the AICPA. The intention of this chapter is to present the general guidelines that the organization suggests using in the analysis process.

However, in many cases, the financial information that an accountant deals with will not necessarily conform to the guidelines presented in this chapter, and therefore he or she must be flexible enough to recognize and accommodate these differences. In fact, most of the prospective financial information dealt with has not been prepared or presented in strict conformity with these guidelines. These guidelines therefore present a helpful context in which to view the process, but they only provide a general theoretical framework and an approach limited to complete prospective financial statements as defined by the AICPA.

Not only must the analyst be flexible in accepting the format of prospective financial information, but the entire model and process presented in this chapter must be approached with consummate flexibility.

Unlike what often happens with the application of the standards for the examination of historical financial information, the process described in these statements must be radically particularized for each firm examined. There is no one single set of important facts that apply to all firms. The important drivers of success for each firm must be identified and their implications understood, and then the focus of the analysis process itself must be adjusted to address them. This requires a great degree of flexibility, which will not be found in the rote application of some standard set of procedures.

CHAPTER SIX

Strategic Planning—
The Context

CHAPTER OUTLINE

The Life Cycle for Entrepreneurs
Capital
6.6 SUMMARY

6.1 INTRODUCTION

One of the most important and least used tools in the analysis of prospective financial statements is an understanding of the strategy that underpins the prospective financial information. Strategic plans are really the heart of the prospective financials. In fact, prospective financial statements are meaningless without them.

This chapter presents an overview of the strategic and business planning processes that will help with a better understanding of the context in which prospective financial information must be viewed. Planning itself constitutes another important subsystem of the firm.

It is interesting to note that most analysis performed on prospective financial information in fact does not focus on the strategic plans. These plans should provide the context in which the prospective financials were developed and greatly help in understanding them. However, most analysis focuses instead on the arithmetical and algebraic integrity of the information, and on the use of specific techniques, methodologies, and processes. Letting these tools become the focal point of the analysis process should be scrupulously avoided.

Although there are innumerable approaches attempting to describe the strategic planning process (some quite structured, others almost purely intuitive), this text will use a relatively basic and linear model in our discussion. What is important for our purposes is the prospective financial statements under examination and how they relate to the firm's stated strategy. A diagram of the strategic planning process model used in this text is presented in Figure 6-1.

There is general agreement on the basic components of strategic planning among most planners. These components are all contained in Figure 6-1. Disagreement does arise as to the way that the components should be arranged and just how they work together in real-world situations. But our focus is not on exactly *how* the strategic planning process works, but more importantly on just *what* the strategic plans for a firm are and what their relationship is to the specific prospective financial statements under examination. The exact planning process used will vary by firm, but a documentation and understanding of the specific steps taken and their

Figure 6-1 Strategic Planning Model

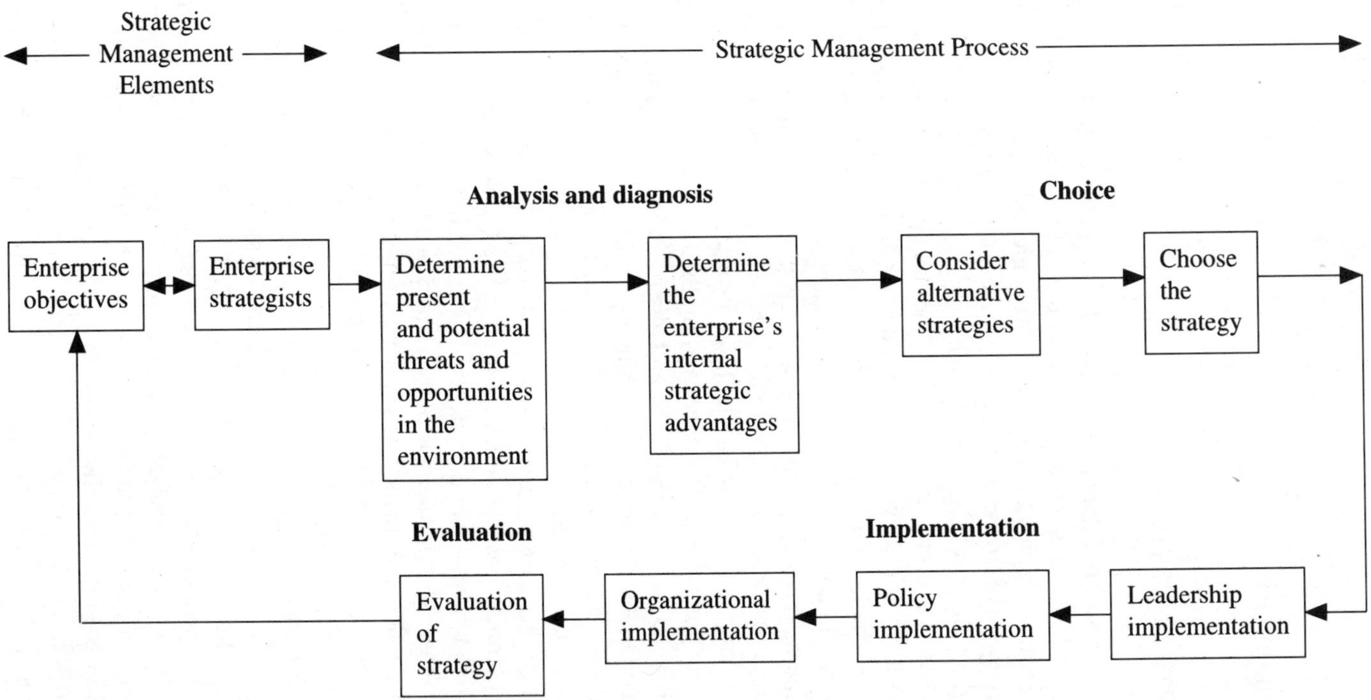

Strategic
— Management —— Strategic Management Process ——
Elements

Analysis and diagnosis

Choice

Implementation

Evaluation

Enterprise objectives

Enterprise strategists

Determine present and potential threats and opportunities in the environment

Determine the enterprise's internal strategic advantages

Consider alternative strategies

Choose the strategy

Organizational implementation

Policy implementation

Leadership implementation

Evaluation of strategy

(Adapted from C12, P7)

112

sequencing should become the analyst's first step in this part of the analysis process.

6.2   ELEMENTS

The elements of the strategic planning process include the objectives and the strategists. Both are important in understanding the strategic planning process. Objectives define the direction that the firm is taking. The strategists are the people who interpret information and actually set the course for the firm. Without an appreciation for both of these important components of the strategic process, an analysis of the process would be hard to accomplish.

Objectives

Objectives are what "the organization seeks to achieve by its existence and operation" (C12, p. 35). There are a variety of different objectives that an organization might pursue. Some examples are:

- Profitability
- Efficiency
- Employee satisfaction
- Quality
- Good corporate citizenship
- Social responsibility
- Market leadership
- Maximization of dividends
- Maximization of stockholder's wealth
- Survival
- Adaptability
- Service to society (C12, p. 35)

Most organizations have more than one objective. Just as you cannot ask for directions for a car trip before you know where you are going, it is equally true that you cannot really talk about marketing or operating plans without first knowing where the business is going. Where it is going is in fact defined by its objectives.

Determining the relative importance of the various objectives and the proper weight to be assigned to each obviously creates some challenges. It is essential to accommodate all of the stated objectives of the organization. A question arises as to whether the objectives that have been stated are in fact the objectives that the firm is pursuing. Additionally, sometimes a firm's objectives do not seem to be reflected in its operating plans, because the resources have not been made available to assist in the realistic achievement of its objectives. Therefore, it is necessary to distinguish between a firm's objectives—reflected in its strategic planning—and its actual business or operating plans.

Strategists

Strategic planning is often the domain of a number of different groups within the business environment. They can include:

- Board of directors
- Top management
- Special corporate planning staff
- Consultants (C12, p. 44)

An important component of analyzing prospective financials is knowing and understanding who was responsible for the strategic planning process. This becomes a part of understanding the context in which the strategic plans were developed. For example, there is usually a substantive difference between a plan involving an entrepreneur who is involved in a business start-up and a plan developed for an already successful business. The important thing to remember is that a full appreciation of the financial information presented requires an understanding of *who* and *why*. Who developed the strategic plans? Why were they developed? What were the developer's immediate and personal goals?

6.3 PROCESS

The process of strategic planning consists of four major steps.

1. Analysis and diagnosis
2. Choice

3. Implementation

4. Evaluation

Each of these steps is an important component of the strategic planning process. An appreciation for how they were performed and the results of the strategic planning analysis will greatly add to the efficacy of any efforts to analyze the prospective financial statements that evolved as a consequence of this process.

Analysis and Diagnosis

The process of analysis and diagnosis concerns itself with addressing threats and opportunities that the firm is confronting and with matching these with the firm's strengths (C 12, p. 155). Some call this process "scanning the environment." It should be a continuous and ongoing process. Most firms will find that it is easier to perform analysis and diagnosis continually than to do so periodically.

Firms often appear to have made their decisions in a vacuum. Those firms have not addressed the analysis and diagnosis step in the strategic planning process. Analysis and diagnosis are essential to developing a foundation upon which any type of future planning will be built. Without thorough and appropriate analysis and diagnosis the plans are likely to omit very important information that is essential to success. In the analysis of prospective financial information it is important not only to understand the process that the firm used, but also to consider whether or not the process was pursued appropriately and focused on a correct matching of strengths and weaknesses.

Most firms are weak in this area. Careful attention and scrutiny needs to be applied in assessing how the firm approached this important component in the evolution of its plans. The overall result of this step in the planning process is to yield clues about issues that are important to the firm. Specific people must be assigned responsibility for looking for specific types of clues. After they are gathered these clues must be translated into a form that the firm can use and then the firm must take appropriate actions through the implementation process.

At the heart of the analysis and diagnosis process is the need to recognize the importance to the firm of responding to change in a timely fashion.

There are two types of analysis and diagnosis, *environmental* and *strategic advantage*. The first is concerned with the external environment, the second with the internal environment.

Environmental Analysis and Diagnosis

The first type of analysis and diagnosis requires an examination of the environment.

Environmental analysis is the process by which strategists monitor the economic, governmental/legal, market/competitive, supplier/technological, geographic, and social settings to determine the opportunities and threats to their firms.

Environmental diagnosis consists of managerial decisions made by assessing the significance of the data (opportunities and threats) of the environmental analysis (C12, p. 88).

What role does environmental analysis and diagnosis play in the analysis of prospective financial statements? Success in business requires a sensitivity to change. Changes, especially in the external environment, are important because anticipating them in a timely fashion can determine the success or failure of a business. Often people involved in forecasting and strategic planning focus on technological solutions for their needs, such as expensive software to assist in the forecasting process. In fact a sensitivity to and monitoring of the many existing sources of information concerning the external environment would often prove far more cost-effective and valuable in the forecasting process.

As the environment changes, so too does the whole context in which a business is conducted. Therefore, many of the numbers in the prospective financial statements also change.

Managers have to search the environment and find:

- Which factors pose the greatest threats to their business, and
- Which factors propose the greatest opportunities (C12, p. 89)

Some of the factors that should be monitored include:

- Economic factors
- Governmental/legal factors
- Market/competitive factors
- Supplier/technological factors
- Geographical factors
- Social and other factors (C12, p. 93–104)

After the environmental analysis is complete the environmental diagnosis should be performed. This is the process whereby managers "assess the significance of the opportunities and threats discovered by the analysis" (C 12, p. 109). Diagnosis is a complicated process. Something that looks like an opportunity to one person might be perceived as a threat by another. There are a number of important considerations related to managers' styles that often will dictate the resulting constraints on the diagnosis. Some of these considerations are:

- Experience and age
- Motivation/aspiration level
- Willingness to take risks
- Psychological mood (C12, p. 110–111)

Strategic Advantage Analysis and Diagnosis
The previous section dealt only with the external environment, but the internal environment, too, has to be carefully examined.

> Strategic advantage analysis and diagnosis is a process by which the strategists examines the firm's finance/accounting, marketing/distribution, production/operations, personnel/labor relations, and corporate resources/factors to determine whether the firm has significant strengths (and weaknesses) so it can most effectively exploit the opportunities and meet the threat the environment is presenting the firm. (C 12, p. 154)

A list of those factors that are most important to this process includes:

- Finance/accounting
- Marketing/distribution
- Production/operations
- Management/labor relations
- Corporate resources/factors (C12, p. 158–162)

All of these factors must be examined in light of where the business is purportedly going. There are a number of approaches that may be used when performing this analysis. The Boston Consulting Group developed a method for business portfolio analysis that used a series of matrices to analyze multiproduct companies (C 12, p. 162). Firms were graded on two axes. One was the firm's growth rate and the other was its relative competitive position or market share. Each axis had either a high or a low rating. When the process was complete, each division was graded and labeled as a dog, a cash cow, a star, or a question mark, depending upon where they fit into the matrix.

As with environmental diagnosis, a large part of the analysis process and the ultimate diagnosis itself is determined by the values of the managers who make the decisions.

Choice

After conducting the environmental and strategic advantage analysis and diagnosis, it is necessary to make a decision. The first step in that decision is to consider the various alternatives available. Then the choice of the best strategy must be made to "fill the gap or exploit the opportunity" (C 12, p. 197).

It is interesting to note that in fact many plans evolve more out of choices that were made prior to the planning process than from choices formally made as part of the process. Also, some firms make a multiplicity of choices, which may or may not be mutually exclusive. On paper firms often appear to make progress, when in fact they are deferring making real decisions. The trade-offs and cost-benefit implications of a choice have to be fully appreciated and have to clearly come out of the stated strategy. Otherwise, firms can end up like the federal government, with a lot of nice-sounding platitudes for plans but with a shortage of resources with which to achieve their rhetorical goals.

Considering Strategic Alternatives
There are some alternatives that strategists should always consider. They include:

1.   What is our business? What business should we be in five years from now? Ten years?
2.   Should we stay in the same business(es?)
3.   Should we get out of this business entirely or subparts of it by merging, liquidating, or selling off a part of it?
4.   Should we do a more efficient or effective job in the business we are in in a slim down way?
5.   Should we try to grow in this business by:
      (a) Increasing our present business?
      (b) Acquiring similar businesses?
6.   Should we try to grow primarily in other businesses?
7.   Should we do alternatives 3 and 5a? (C12, p. 199)

There is often a need to weigh the various factors examined in the environmental and strategic advantage analysis and diagnosis phase. This process is based on the strategist's predispositions and assessment of relevant factors. Some of the standard types of strategies that usually evolve are:

- A stable growth strategy
- Growth strategies
- Retrenchment and turnaround strategies
- Combination strategies (C12, pp. 204–230)

Within each of these main headings there are a number of possible substrategies. What is needed in the analysis of the prospective financial statements is to clearly identify which strategy and substrategy has been chosen or taken and to assess this strategy and the firm's analysis and diagnosis of its environment.

Strategic Choice
Once various alternatives have been considered, a decision must be made.

> Strategic choice is the decision which selects from among the alternative grand strategies considered the strategy which will best meet the enterprise's objectives. The choice involves consideration of selection factors, evaluation of alternatives against these criteria, and the actual choice. (C12, p. 279)

As discussed earlier, the ultimate challenge—which can only be undertaken after the analysis and diagnosis are made and various strategic alternatives have been considered—is to make a decision. This is made in light of four selection factors:

1. Managerial perception of external dependence
2. Managerial attitudes toward risk
3. Managerial awareness of past enterprise strategies
4. Managerial power relationships and organizational structure (C12, p. 281)

The ultimate choice is made in the context of these four subjective factors. Like all decisions it is done in the context of the specific strategists, firm, and environment.

Implementation

After management chooses a strategy it must be implemented.

> Strategic implementation is the assignment or reassignment of corporate and
> SBU (strategic business unit) leaders to match the strategy. The leaders will
> communicate the strategy to the employees. Implementation also involves
> the development of functional policies in organization structure and climate
> to support the strategy and help achieve organizational objectives (C12, p.
> 305).

The main method of implementing strategy is through the budget. After
scanning, establishing long-term strategy, and creating capital budgets,
specific actions must be assigned to projected short-term schedules. These
actions, when taken as a whole, are the operating budgets, which are used
to break up the strategic plan into shorter segments, sometimes as short as
a single month. In order to pursue this process it is necessary to recognize
that each element has a unique role. All the elements should fit together
when the organization is viewed as a system.

The question of what resources are required to accomplish the firm's
goals is an important one. Equally important is the need to establish how
the firm will measure progress toward its goals. How will it judge how well
it is using its resources to accomplish its goals?

The firm's resources (both quantitative and qualitative) have to be reviewed as a set, which is a group of related elements. If any one element
in the set changes, you have an entirely new set. Each short-term budget
thereby becomes a step toward the long-term budget. By viewing the firm's
resources as a set it is easier to see budgeting as a process that does not
necessarily only include cash. The proper management of all the firm's resources is necessary in order to accomplish the firm's strategic plans and
goals. These goals in turn become the future resources available for the ac-
complishment of yet another generation of future goals (F54, pp. 5–8).

If implementation has already been started, the analyst can find a wealth
of information in this step of the strategic planning process. Plans can
often be misleading or too general for detailed analysis. The implementation process requires the firm to very specifically articulate their interpretation of the overall plan. This process is not only academic—it also affects
their checkbook. The firm's willingness to commit its funds is usually a
good indication of its sincerity of purpose.

Leadership Implementation

Probably one of the more important aspects of the implementation process is ensuring that the right leadership is in place. This is often done in several ways.

1. Changes in current leadership at appropriate levels
2. Reinforcement of manager's motivation through financial incentives, etc.
3. Involvement in career development for future strategists. (C12, p. 306)

Because getting the right people in place is probably the most important component of the implementation process, the analysis of prospective financial information must carefully examine this step.

In practice it is common to find companies that have wonderful plans on paper but that have failed to get a management team in place that can carry out its plans. The implementation process requires a realistic assessment of the skills and abilities of the staff. Some managers might function exceptionally well in static environments but can never do as well in entrepreneurial environments. Putting the wrong person into the wrong position will lead to failure and the possible loss of a very good manager. In fact, the mistake is not that manager's but the decision to put someone into a role for which he or she is not well suited. This problem often derives from the fact that most companies do not have an appreciation for the nature of their human resources. The reality is that it is people who make for success, a point that is all too often missed by many managers, analysts, and accountants alike.

Functional Policy Implementation

Another important area is functional policy implementation. It is common to find many policies on paper, but functional policy implementation goes beyond that. The need for policies has to be analyzed, engineered, and implemented. Too often one of the problems encountered in a firm is a lack of appreciation for the interrelatedness of various policies. It is essential to examine the consistency between needs and the policies that supposedly fulfill them. There is often a vast disparity between them.

Functional policy implementation involves two processes: resource deployment and, development of policies which operationalize the strategy (C12, p. 310).

Resources must be appropriately deployed, and they must be consistent with the strategies developed. Businesses often talk about what they would like to do but often they do not provide the necessary resources. The development of policies is also important in order to let people know exactly how the strategy will be implemented. This will allow subordinate managers to:

- Know what they are supposed to do
- Willingly implement the decision (C12, p. 311)

Obviously, policies must cover the key functional decisions in such areas as

1. Finance/accounting,
2. Marketing,
3. Production/operations management,
4. Research and development,
5. Personnel, and
6. Logistics (C12, p. 312)

Detailed operational planning, using very specific planning and control techniques, is essential if the policy implementation phase is to be successful.

Organizational Implementation
Organizational implementation has to address whether the firm has the right organizational structure for its strategy. The various functional areas work together based on an organizational philosophy. It might be very loosely structured, as in an entrepreneurial organization, or it might be highly centralized. There is a continuum of differing organizational structures and styles. The analysis of prospective financial information requires an appreciation for the specific type of organizational structure that the plan has called for and/or requires.

Additionally it is essential that there be consistency between the management, its policies, its leadership, and the organization that is set up to utilize these resources. It is not uncommon to find inconsistencies between some of these elements. Quality circles often appear on paper, but in reality hyper-autocratic management styles do not fit in well with the rhetoric that many organizations like to promulgate. The analyst has to be sensitive to the inconsistencies in these important components of the planning process.

Evaluation

The last component of the strategic planning process is the evaluation stage. It is important for two reasons. First, because evaluation in and of itself is important. Second, because it is equally important to see how it was addressed in the planning process by those who developed the strategic plan. Failure to consider the need for evaluation could be indicative of some strong management weaknesses. The need for ongoing evaluation is incumbent on any successful organization.

> Evaluation of strategy is that phase of the management process in which the top managers determine whether their strategic choice as implemented is meeting the objectives of the enterprise. (C12, p. 348)

It is necessary that the firm assess whether it is achieving the objectives it set. Various specific methods for evaluation will be discussed in the latter part of this book.

6.4 REALITY

The model presented in the strategic planning process section is basically straightforward and linear. In reality this basic model is seldom followed formally. Usually a nonlinear iterative process in which new strategies arise concurrently with formally planned strategies is used. In this process, strategies merge and a synthesis strategy evolves.

Many strategists address the concept of "crafting strategy" rather than using the linear mechanical approach that I presented earlier. In fact, when crafting strategy a whole different image evolves than when using the more traditional linear model. Crafting evokes a number of images, including traditional skills, dedication, and perfection through mastery of detail. What crafting really focuses on, more than the purely rational and logical, is a feeling of involvement and harmony with the process itself. Through the use of a crafting paradigm "formulation and implementation merge into a fluid process of learning through which creative energies evolve" (C29, p. 105).

For many businesspeople, the concept of formal planning has evolved from a very dated, mechanistic view of management. In reality, strategy evolves. Part of this evolution is based on reflecting on patterns from the past. Another part of the evolution focuses on formal plans for the future. The strategies that evolve need not necessarily be deliberate. They usually emerge. The linear planning model is helpful for understanding some of the important components of strategic planning but it does not necessarily reflect the actual process (C29, pp. 105–110).

In fact, much of what happens to affect strategic planning in a firm happens in discontinuous quantum leaps. Clear periods of stability are followed by periods in which radical and substantial changes occur. Therefore, the strategic planning process has to be able to address "thought and action, control and learning, stability and change" (C29, p. 114).

The point is the need for the analyst to appreciate that in spite of the somewhat linear model discussed above, the strategic planning process is an evolutionary and dynamic one. Planners or plans that are totally linear might run into some substantive problems. Firms must be able to address the dynamic realities of the business environment with which they are guaranteed to be confronted.

6.5   STRATEGIC PLANNING AND BUSINESS PLANS

Consistency with Operating Plans

Very detailed operating or business plans are usually created to help in the implementation phase of the strategic planning process. These detailed operating plans usually drive a financial model (projection) that has the following elements:

- Assumptions
- Income statements
- Cash flows
- Balance sheets

These elements must cover the entire period presented. The first year is often presented on a monthly basis, the next two years on a quarterly basis, and the last two years of a five-year operating plan are presented using annualized data. A challenge for the analyst in the analysis of prospective financial statements is to determine the consistency between operating plans and the strategic plans.

General, nondetailed business plans often mask the fact that there is potential for some very substantial inconsistencies between the strategic and operating plans. Resources are often not allocated in the amounts necessary or they are not timely enough to support the plans as presented. For example, a highly skilled workforce might appear in the financials without the expected costs for start-up or training. If inconsistencies start to turn up, they could be symptomatic of more substantial problems with the overall planning process.

Another problem area is the stipulation of qualitative objectives for the firm such as—improved relations with the community, improved employee morale or product quality, and environmental sensitivity. These goals, if they are in fact substantive, necessarily must have resources allocated to them if they are to be achieved. What often happens is that the goals are promulgated but resources are not specifically allocated within the plan to ensure their achievement. To a degree most firms participate in this type of propagandizing, but it is necessary to appreciate if these goals are material to the outcome of the overall plans.

Investors

How Is a Plan Read?
For the most part, prospective financial information is prepared for and presented to present and potential investors. This has an impact on the analyst. Sophisticated preparers of business plans understand that the typical reading process involves about six steps. These six steps usually take a total of about five minutes to complete. The six steps in the process are:

1.   Determining the characteristics of the company and the industry
2.   Determining the terms of the deal
3.   Reading the latest balance sheet
4.   Determining the caliber of the people in the deal
5.   Determining what is different about the deal
6.   Giving the plan a once-over lightly (C26, p. 14).

The point is that the emphasis of the plan and the accompanying financial statements is often on hooking the reader. Less than a minute usually is allocated to each of the six steps. Therefore, the plan and the prospective financials have to be able to create an immediate interest on the part of the reader. For this reason, prospective financials often attempt to project overly favorable results. The analyst has to be careful to fully appreciate how much of the plan as presented is simply marketing.

Because of these realities, the analyst has to be very careful in assessing all the information contained in business plans. Most entrepreneurs really believe in what they are doing. This faith is contagious, and the overoptimism often is inadvertently incorporated into prospective financial statements. This is particularly true with the issues of sales volumes and prices. The marketing plans in many prospective financial statements have a tendency to be overoptimistic while the cost figures usually are projected to be lower than they actually will be. These deviations can be understood in light of the people writing the plans and their personal goals, objectives, and needs. The analyst has to be sensitive to these issues and carefully consider all the motivations, conscious and unconscious, in the information presented for analysis.

The Life Cycle for Entrepreneurs
The typical entrepreneur follows a life cycle of seven stages:

1. Early development
2. Idea stage
3. Start-up problem
4. Venture financing
5. Growth crisis
6. Maturity crisis
7. Impossible transition (C26, p. 40)

Once again we are confronted with the importance of the context in which business plans usually develop. Often business plans and their related prospective financial statements are presented somewhere between Stages 3 and 5, when substantial financing is needed. The figures presented in the prospective financials are usually aggressive and optimistic. The reason for this is that without financing the venture will die. At this time extensive modeling is usually pursued and prospective financial statements are developed. There is a need for the analyst to appreciate this tendency toward overoptimism in most business plans.

In a number of the stages of the entrepreneur's life cycle there is the recurring problem of a shortage of cash. In Stages 1 and 2 the entrepreneur is usually bootstrapping, trying to make do with almost nothing. At Stage 3, the start-up, as "the idea" evolves, major cash shortages also develop. It is this cash shortage that precipitates Stage 4, which is venture financing. Then the entrepreneur usually encounters a growth crisis (Stage 5) and a maturity crisis (Stage 6). Although they are not all entirely cash-oriented, many of these stages reflect problems often perceived to result from the need for more cash. This is usually not the real problem at all, but only a symptom of other problems. The perceived need to obtain more funds often is not only a stopgap solution for other problems, but also causes many companies to be overoptimistic in their projections.

Capital
There are five questions that an investor should want answered before investing. They are:

1. How much can I make?
2. How much can I lose?
3. How can I get out of the deal?
4. Who is in the deal?
5. Who says the product and the people are good? (C26, p. 53)

Once again, the analyst is confronted with the importance of being alert to the tendency to exaggerate. The decision to invest comes out of the answer to the primary question, "How much can I make?" Therefore, there is often a tendency to exaggerate. There is also a strong tendency for entrepreneurs to put together numbers that are marketing and selling oriented when they are raising money. The analyst has to be very careful with the figures as presented (C26, p. 64).

Because of the tendency for investors to focus on how much they are going to get out of a deal, and the related tendency of the preparers of projections toward the overoptimistic, projections are often more wishful thinking than actual prospective financial statements. This is not a major problem if the assumptions underlying those figures are clearly defined and fully appreciated. A problem may arise, however, because many people—even venture capitalists—have a tendency to be optimistic on the front end of a deal when they begin to review information. But down the road, when problems arise, the tendency is to look for someone to blame. This usually ends up being the financial analyst, who is left to justify, explain, and be responsible for the optimism. That's when the lawyers enter the picture.

6.6 SUMMARY

The heart of the analysis process for prospective financial information are the strategic planning and business planning processes. These both must be appreciated and understood if the analyst is going to be effective in conducting an analysis.

Without a clear understanding of the context in which the projections are structured and presented, it is almost impossible to analyze them. By no means will an appreciation of the strategic and business planning processes provide all the information an analyst will need, but it will provide some important background information essential to this analysis and it will also provide some very important insights into the character of the people who have done the planning. Both of these are essential in the analysis of prospective financial statements.

This understanding can be the most important in the analysis process, yet, as we discussed earlier, it is often ignored.

The proper understanding of the context in which a business functions, especially in its strategic and operating plans, should provide a window into the very soul of the business. As with people, the view through this window is sometimes a bit inconsistent and confused, but it is a source of information that the analyst cannot afford to overlook.

CHAPTER SEVEN

Systems—The Reality

CHAPTER OUTLINE

7.1　INTRODUCTION

A system is a "series of elements which are linked together to achieve a purpose" (H21, p. 1). The importance of systems is due primarily to the analyst's need to understand how all the parts of a firm work together to affect the successful operation of a business. But additionally, it is important to the analysis process itself, which needs to be approached from the systems perspective.

All organizations are open systems. Therefore, it is not possible to study or analyze organizations without understanding systems. In open systems it is necessary to "consider all possible effects of the environment on the system, and vice versa" (H3, p. 21). If they are to succeed, businesses cannot ignore the environment(s) in which they exist—for example, owners of car dealerships must be aware of shifts in the U.S. auto industry.

The systems approach has to do with perspective. For years Western society has been obsessed with the process of fragmenting, intellectually breaking down and separating. The early scientific revolution in the late Middle Ages rested on a philosophical base that "believed in the concept of the uniformity of natural causes in open systems. . . . The shift to the truly modern science was a shift from the concept of the uniformity of natural causes in an open system to the concept of the uniformity of natural causes in a closed system" (J17, p. 144), where no interaction with the environment is considered. The use of a closed systems model leads to a very unrealistic and limited view of any system under investigation. Although the closed systems paradigm worked for a time during relatively stable times, most businesses are now realizing that an open systems view must be taken when trying to understand how a business really functions and prospers.

The systems perspective appreciates and emphasizes interrelationships. Rather than fragmenting, the systems approach relies on analyzing the interrelationships among all the elements of a system.

A key feature of the systems approach is its critical emphasis on analyzing the interrelationships among system elements. Rather than dividing the system into smaller and more manageable components prior to analysis, the elements are brought together and kept together for analysis and management. Only in this way can total system performance be estimated and measured. The systems approach thus provides the only means of determining the influence of each element on the characteristics of the total system as well as the effects that any set of decisions or operating conditions will have on characteristics of the system. (H25, pp. 8–4)

The systems approach focuses on three specific areas:

1.   Systems analysis
2.   Systems engineering
3.   Systems management (H25, pp. 4–5)

Systems analysis deals with the investigation of the objectives and the criteria for evaluating solutions. Systems engineering is concerned with the development or major modification of the systems to support the plans and tasks of an organization. Systems management is concerned with the development of procedures and organizational structure to maintain the organization once it has been developed (H25, pp. 8–4 to 8–5).

The systems perspective is essential in the analysis process. Without it various elements are viewed in a relative vacuum. Only by understanding their interrelatedness can their true importance be fully appreciated. Herein lies the real importance of this topic to the analysis of prospective financial information.

7.2   THE SYSTEMS VIEW OF THE FIRM

A major theme of the process model presented in Chapter 2 is the need for a systems perspective throughout. This applies not only to the process model, but also to the firm under investigation as well as to the prospective financial statements themselves.

Although much has been written about systems in the last fifty years, most of this work focuses only on systematic and orderly approaches to very limited closed systems situations. The systems view of the firm is an open systems view in which the firm is seen as a system of interrelated subsystems that together must also be viewed in their interrelatedness to the environment. The firm (system) itself is seen as really being only a subsystem of ever larger and larger systems found in the environment. These larger systems are to be found outside the immediate perimeter of the specific business, and could include economic, governmental, markets, technological, geographical, and social systems.

However, the systems view of the firm is not concerned only with the interaction of the firm as an open system within the environment, but also with the need to fully appreciate the total interrelatedness of all of the subsystems within the firm itself. There are an infinite number of subsystems that can exist within the firm, including such areas as accounting, finance, operations, human resources, strategic planning, modeling, and forecasting. This book can be viewed as addressing various important subsystems of the firm. Figure 7–1 depicts the systems view of the firm in a three-dimensional form—an octahedron.

The most important point to be derived from a first look at Figure 7-1 is the organic interrelatedness of all the elements within the firm. The central plane of the octahedron has as its four vertices four of the basic Leadership Outputs essential to the firm. The top and bottom vertices of the octahedron together provide the fifth Leadership Output. These Leadership Outputs are the real functions of management

1. The search for new profit opportunities
2. The achievement of measurable progress
3. The creation and apportionment of resources
4. The creative employment and utilization of resources
5. The application of risk taking in uncertainty

Most businesses completely ignore the Leadership Outputs and focus on the Business and Management Function Inputs. The inputs in Figure 7-1 are the traditional ones found in almost all business texts.

Although one may find more exhaustive lists, these inputs are considered by many to be the most basic and important ones.

In Figure 7-1 the basic Business Function Inputs are shown on the top four faces of the octahedron:

a. Marketing
b. Operations
c. Finance
d. Development

The basic Management Function Inputs are shown on the bottom four faces:

e. Planning
f. Organizing
g. Directing
h. Controlling

Figure 7-1 The Systems View of the Firm

KEY TO DIAGRAM:

Business Function Inputs (4 Top Faces)

a. Marketing
b. Operations
c. Finance
d. Development

Leadership Outputs (Vertices)

1. Search for new profit opportunites
2. Creation and apportionment of resources
3. Creative employment and utilization of resources
4. Achievement of measurable progress
5. Application of risk taking in uncertainty

Management Function Inputs (4 Bottom Faces)

e. Planning
f. Organizing
g. Directing
h. Controlling

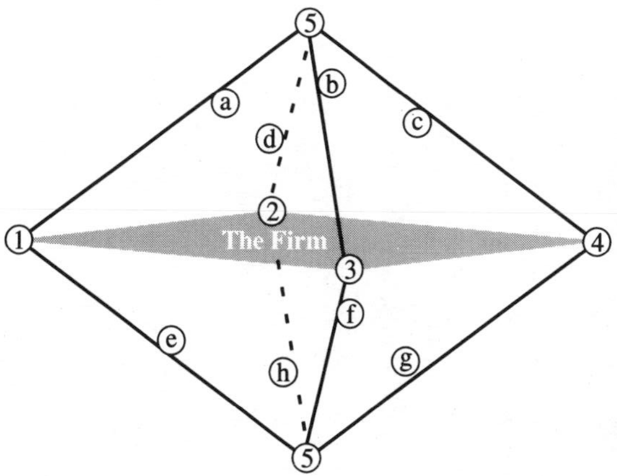

© BPA, 1994

CHARACTERISTICS:

Input Characteristics

Classic Academic View
Theoretical
Logical
Linear
Bureaucratic
Efficient
Deterministic
Tools Oriented

Output Characteristics

Action Oriented View
Practical
Intuitive
Non linear
Dynamic
Effective
Probabilistic
Results Oriented

The systems view of the firm in Figure 7-1 contrasts the inputs and outputs.

The Input Characteristics, which reflect a classic academic view, are:

- Theoretical
- Logical
- Linear
- Bureaucratic
- Efficient
- Deterministic
- Tools oriented

The Output Characteristics, which reflect an action oriented view, are:

- Practical
- Intuitive
- Nonlinear
- Dynamic
- Effective
- Probablistic
- Results oriented

Most entrepreneurial firms focus on the outputs, shown at the vertices of the octahedron, while ignoring the basic discipline inherent in the inputs. Most process-oriented organizations focus on the inputs (both business function and management function) shown on the eight upper and lower faces of the octahedron, while ignoring the need to achieve results and add real value to the firm.

Figure 7-1 also shows an important problem found in most firms. All the inputs and outputs are essential and all of them are interrelated. You cannot have only part of the octahedron operating in the successful firm. All of the parts are important; all are organically interrelated.

The entire octahedron shown in the figure is bounded by risk and uncertainty, two pervasive constraints found in the real world. The upper and lower vertices of the octahedron, labeled 5, jointly depict this fifth Leadership Output, the application of risk taking in uncertainty. All decisions made and all actions taken in the real world must necessarily apply risk taking in uncertainty. Risk is an estimate of the probabilities associated with the various outcomes expected by pursuing a course of action. Uncertainty exists whenever there is less than a 100% probability of an outcome occurring.

The figure represents the systems view of the firm, showing the firm as a system with subsystems. But if this system were tied into a lattice of other octahedrons, each representing other firms, then each firm would become a subsystem of the larger system—the economy of a country. This system—the economy of a country—in turn becomes a subsystem of the larger environment. This is what is meant by open systems and why it is so very important to understand the systems view of the firm. When all levels of interrelatedness are considered, innumerable interactions can and might occur. The total organic interdependency of all possible elements and their interactions must be considered by the analyst if proper analysis is to take place.

7.3   THE ELEMENTS OF SYSTEMS

This section will discuss some of the elements in the systems perspective. There are three that will be considered:

1. Organization
2. Control
3. The environment

These elements form the foundation on which the systems approach is predicated.

Organizations

Three topics will be addressed concerning organizations:

1. Goals and culture
2. Structure
3. Environment and technology

These three elements of the organization are important in order to understand how organizations are viewed in the systems perspective.

Goals and Culture

A problem often encountered in any type of analysis process is that analysis is often fragmented to incorporate only some limited and isolated dimensions of the problem. When this happens more salient and important elements for analysis often are overlooked. Moreover, this viewpoint is myopic in that it fails to address the impact of each element on the system as a whole. Ignoring goals and culture can present such problems in the analysis of financial statements, whether historical or prospective.

To understand an organization, it is necessary to understand that organization's goals. Without this understanding the analyst is like an observer watching a car move down the highway, focusing only on speed, acceleration, and other characteristics, and never asking where the car is going. The starting point of any analysis must be a clear understanding of the goals of that particular firm, whether formal, as in the strategic process discussed in Chapter 6, or informal. But an effort to understand both is essential for any type of substantive analysis of the financial statements.

Another often-overlooked component of an organization is its culture. All organizations contain various cultures within them. Any substantive analysis must focus on the importance of "the role that cultural environment plays in the lives of people" (J1, p. 2). The concept of culture is quite broad, including "any group of people who identify or associate with one another on the basis of some common purpose, need, or similarity of background" (J1, p. 2). A culture may be defined as "the total personality of a group that emerges from its members' interpersonal transactions" (J1, p. 3). Culture defines the rules of behavior that govern action. Cultures usually have a unique language. There are various ideas and concepts as to what a culture is. An alternative to focusing on a specific definition of culture is to take a look at culture based upon some of its important dimensions. Some of these dimensions include:

- Social structure
- Kinship systems
- Personality
- Psychological adjustment
- Ethnic diversity
- Socioeconomic status (J1, pp. 3–5)

Cultures and cultural systems develop to meet the needs of people. It is "the process that a group of people have developed for satisfying needs, for solving problems, and for adjusting both to the external environment and to each other" (J1, p. 7). An important part of cultural analysis is the study of the interdisciplinary and integrative aspect of the various themes that underpin culture (J1, p. vii).

But what does this culture have to do with accounting and finance? What does it have to do with the analysis of prospective financial statements? The heart of financial statements is communication. The heart of communication is the transmission of information that has the ability to influence decisions. The process of accounting cannot be viewed as a mechanical function. Rather, it is necessary to see accounting and finance in their role in the communication of information. To fully appreciate the various important aspects of communication discussed in Chapter 3 it is important to understand the culture of the people in the process.

Structure

Another important aspect of organizations is structure. Our understanding of structure has evolved over the last seventy years. There are various classifications for structure and they provide an important background for understanding systems. These classifications include:

- Classical theory
- Neo-classical theory
- Behavioral science theory
- Systems theory

Classical Theory. The classical view of management evolved through the work of various business theorists. Frederick Taylor drew upon the scientific approach for defining rules (H21, p. 85). Following on Taylor's efforts was Henri Fayol, whose influential principles include

1. *Division of Work*—The principle of specialization of labor to gain efficiency.
2. *Authority and Responsibility*—Authority is the right to give orders and the power to exact obedience.
3. *Discipline*—Discipline is absolutely necessary for the smooth running of business, and without it no enterprise could prosper.
4. *Unity of Command*—An employee should receive orders from one superior only.

5. *Unity of Direction*—A group of activities having the same objectives should have one head and one plan.

6. *Subordination of Individual Interests to General Interests*—The interests of one employee or group should not prevail over those of the organization.

7. *Remuneration of Personnel*—Compensation should be fair and, as far as possible, afford satisfaction to both employees and the firm.

8. *Centralization*—Centralization is essential to the organization and is a natural consequence of organizing.

9. *Scalar Chain*—The scalar chain is the chain of superiors ranging from the ultimate authority to the lowest-ranking worker.

10. *Order*—The organization should provide an orderly place for every individual. There should be a place for everyone and everyone in his or her place.

11. *Equity*—Equity and a sense of justice should pervade the organization.

12. *Stability of Tenure and Personnel*—Time is needed for the employee to adapt to his or her work and to perform it effectively.

13. *Initiative*—At all levels of the organizational ladder zeal and energy are augmented by initiative.

14. *Esprit de Corps*—This principle emphasizes the need for teamwork and the maintenance of interpersonal relationships. (H21, pp. 85–86)

After Fayol there were a number of other important management thinkers. The trend in the classical approach was toward the establishment of rules that viewed businesses and organizations as machines. These rules were supposed to be the guiding principles that would help to sustain those organizations. Mooney and Riley developed four major principles that sought to clearly define the running of these highly structured machines. They were:

1. *The coordinate principle,* which provided for a unity of action in the pursuit of a common objective.

2. *The scalar principle,* which emphasized the hierarchical organization's form and authority.

3. *The functional principle,* which organized tasks into departmental units.

4.   *The staff principle,* which recognized the role of management in the exercise of authority but provided a staff to give advice and information. (H21, p. 86)

The entire classical view of management sought to run an organization by clear concise rules. The more rational and mechanistic these rules were the better the organization was supposed to run. The culmination of this philosophy was the assembly line approach to management, which seemed to serve organizations well—for a time. But problems developed and some of the limitations of the classical approach soon became apparent, and that led to the neoclassical form of organization.

Neoclassical Theory.   The neoclassical school basically drew on the classical traditions and rules, but perceived that the rules were incomplete. "The element of the human being in the organization was now to be considered" (H21, p. 87). The neoclassical was basically the classical with some concern for people. The addition of new inputs, in particular the human aspect, basically focused the rules of classical structure in order to address a concern for "the motivation of the employee" (H21, p. 87).

   The employee was no longer perceived solely as an inert tool. Rather, an attempt was made to incorporate an appreciation for the multifaceted aspects of the individual into the equation. But the employee still remained a tool—a human tool. Out of this school evolved human engineering and the sensitivity for the peculiar needs of what was called the human machine. The theory helped the evolution of classical organizational theory very little, and made only minor modifications to the concept of organizations.

Behavioral Science Organizational Theory.   The emphasis of the behavioral science approach to organizational theory focused on a perception of the organization as a subsystem of a large social system. The ultimate controlling needs of the members became the determinants of the organization's structure. The firm was seen as a cooperating system of physical, logical, personal, and Social components (H21, p. 88).

   The structure of the organization sought to meet these competing needs and to balance them. The function of organizations was defined in the context of this process. "Shared goals allow the firm to exist; cooperation is the mechanism for success" (H21, p. 88). The behavioral science organizational theory approach was a substantive change from the classical perspective, but it too had its shortcomings. It still viewed the problem in organizations as related to "the need of some kind of structure in attaining objectives" (H21, p. 89).

Systems Theory. The next stage in the development of organizational theory, the systems stage, viewed the entire organization as a subpart of a larger system, not just a larger social system as was the case in the behavioral science approach.

> A systems approach to organizational theory attempts to interrelate key elements of the perceived parts into an integrated whole. If the organization is seen as an open system, the effect of the environment on the organization is extremely important. In fact, a key consideration of an open system is its response mechanism, since the way it relates to its controlling environment may well be the key to success or failure. (H21, p. 89)

As can be seen, the emphasis in a systems approach is on interrelating key elements into a whole. In fact, if this becomes the guiding aspect of management structure, then the focus is on an appreciation of all the elements in that system and the dynamics of the real world where the relative importance of each element might be constantly shifting. Organizational theory has been described as:

> the study of the structure and functioning of organizations and the behavior of groups and individuals within them. It is an emerging interdisciplinary quasi-science, drawing primarily on the disciplines of sociology and psychology, but also on economics and, to a lesser extent, on production engineering. (H21, p. 89)

In this view of organizational theory the emphasis is on people (H21, p. 89). The important point is understanding the need to interrelate various elements and components of the organization and the fact that the organization is viewed primarily from the sociological context. This view has peculiar importance in the information age, especially as it relates to the communication of financial information. It sees that financial information should not be isolated and studied out of context. Rather, it can only be fully appreciated with an understanding of the people and systems involved.

Environment and Technology
Environment and technology are also important to the organization. "Change is the nature of the game" (H 21, p. 90). The ability to respond to change is the ability to succeed. This is clear to observers who look at the role that technology is playing in the current business environment. The ability to deal with technology is also the ability to deal with change. Because its rate is increasing, change is less and less controllable—it is like a mighty river, pushing along and destroying anything that is unable to navigate its mighty force. This becomes important in understanding and developing processes for the analysis of prospective financial statements. A fuller discussion of important environmental factors is pursued latter in this chapter in the section called *Environment*.

Control

Control is the function within an organization that seeks to guarantee that things operate as they were designed. As with the other aspects of management theory discussed in the previous sections, control will vary with the type of organizational structure in place. There are a number of different components of the control structure, which to a large extent are predicated on the world view of management in the particular organization.

Open Systems Needs
The concept of organization viewed from an open systems perspective presents some important differences that affect control. There are various open system needs, some of which are:

1. The input of energy from the environment.
2. The transformation of the input into some product form.
3. The exporting of the product back into the environment.
4. A re-energizing of the system from sources in the environment.
5. The importing of more energy from the environment than is expended, which helps the system survive.
6. The feedback of information which helps the system maintain homeostasis.
7. The tendency for differentiation and elaboration because of subsystem dynamics and the relationship between growth and survival.

8.   The ability of the system to reach the same final state from different initial conditions and by different paths of development. (H 21, p. 105)

Control and feedback in an open system cannot be based upon inflexible and unyielding rules and procedures. Rather, the feedback mechanisms have to be tailored to the individual characteristics of the organization. The specific types of feedback mechanisms will be determined by the state of the environment. In relatively stable environments the feedback and control mechanisms can afford to be less responsive to dynamics. But as the environment becomes less stable, it becomes more important to have feedback mechanisms that are responsive to the demands of the environment.

Rather than the structure driving the organization, it is imperative that the organization and structure respond to the realities of the environment.

Traditional Accounting Control Process
Before proceeding further, a short discussion of some of the elements in the traditional accounting control process would be appropriate. Some of the basic elements include:

1.   Defining the goal of the subunit (e.g., a division of a company or a functional activity within a governmental unit).
2.   Delineating the performance indicators established to ascertain whether operations have been carried out effectively (market share, rate of return on investment, or budget overruns).
3.   Establishing standards of performance.
4.   Performing the activity.
5.   Measuring the results of the operations performed.
6.   Comparing the actual results with the standards in order to measure deviations or variances in performance.
7.   Communicating the results and analyzing significant variances. (H 21, p. 106)

Behavioral Aspects of Control
Central to an understanding of control is an understanding of the behavioral issues that have to be addressed. The goals and objectives of management have to be fully appreciated not only by the managers, but also by all of the other people within the organization. Although formally pro-

mulgated goals and objectives are sometimes found, in fact many goals are neither clearly stipulated nor clearly understood.

Also there is the issue of goal congruence, which demands that the aspirations of the individuals within the organization have to be appreciated. Whether the employee's goals are consistent with the organization's becomes an important issue, which ultimately can result in the success or failure of the organization (H21, pp. 116–117).

Participation can be an important component of the behavioral aspect of an organization. The organization does not exist in isolation from group participation; instead, the organization and the group are interrelated and mutually dependent at all levels. Work quality can be greatly affected by the performance or lack of performance of employees. Issues of how standards are imposed or whether participative management is appropriate to a particular organization can contribute to its success or failure. How people perceive the various processes within an organization will determine how well they participate and the quality of information that they provide.

Goal congruence at the group level is similar to congruence with the individual. Group aspiration level is important. Minimally the goals of the group must not conflict with or oppose the goals of the organization. Many traditionalists feel that the primary driver of motivation is money, but there are many other needs that have to be satisfied as well in order to ensure full participation (H21, p. 120).

Budgets are the main aspect of control and can be a large determinant in the success or failure of an organization. Budgets can be used in a very positive way, but they can also create quite a few conflicts and many problems. Many budgetary systems encourage dysfunctional behavior, and one of the reason is the organization's failure to embrace a systems view. Without an appreciation for the systems perspective, many subsections of an organizations find themselves competing with each other and hurting the performance of the overall organization.

Another problem with budgets is the phenomenal ability of people to consistently manipulate outcomes. Budgeting cannot ignore behavioral issues. It seems that every salesperson, regardless of how nonmathematical or nonquantitative he or she might be, can figure out how to beat any compensation scheme, no matter how sophisticated it might be (H21, p. 121).

Organizational style is another important component of the behavioral aspect of control. Style varies with the type of industry as well as with the particular firm's managerial philosophy. Stable industries are able to function with relatively rigid hierarchical relationships, avoid ambiguity, and have relatively clearly defined lines of authority. In more dynamic industries, though, the same type of structure could spell failure. Dynamic industries require a greater degree of independence and tolerance for ambiguity. In general our current business environment is such that there are very few industries that can avoid being responsive to the dynamics of the global economy and environment (H21, p. 121).

Communication channels and feedback are important for the success of any control system. Feedback, especially in the form of performance reports, is essential in order to allow management to track differences between actual and budgeted results. Feedback should be a tool for positive reinforcement and motivation of employees at all levels of an organization. It should help to improve performance.

The following are relationships between accounting systems and individual performance:

1. Performance reports . . . accompanied by supportive comments generally stimulate higher performance more than a mere presentation of figures.

2. The effects of certain combinations of factors on performance (e.g., ability and self-esteem) can be enhanced through the use of supportive feedback or diminished by neutral feedback.

3. Initial budget estimates prepared by individuals holding varying levels of ability and self-esteem will be unrealistically high or low estimates of performance in (relatively) new activities. For example, moderate ability subjects tend to be unrealistically low in estimated performance while lower ability subjects tend to be unrealistically high in estimated performance, especially if coupled with high self-esteem.

4. Accounting-type feedback decreases differences between expected and actual performance (with the type of feedback in influencing actual performance). (H21, pp. 124–125)

Accounting literature has often focused on the issue of management by exception. What management by exception really means is focusing on those deviations from the norm (either above or below) that are outside a range of acceptable variance, and even this process must be viewed from the systems perspective. This method accepts a mean figure as a benchmark in order to avoid getting lost in reams of detail. Over the years it has often degenerated into a focus on substandard performance and failure to meet the budget. The concept is a solid one, but its implementation has tended to emphasize negatives while ignoring positive feedback.

Additionally, a distinction must be made in any system between controllable and noncontrollable elements. Given the dynamic nature of our economic environment, there are elements that might not be controllable at one point yet become controllable a short time later. Therefore it is necessary not only to identify those elements that are controllable or noncontrollable, but also to constantly reassess and monitor those elements.

The Environment

The creation, generation, and analysis of any type of financial information requires a sensitivity to the environment. In addition to the traditional and obvious constraints of the regulatory environment as it relates to financial accounting information, there are many other very important environmental factors that must be carefully considered when financial information is analyzed.

Information Demands
Various types of environmental information are particularly important to financial information and help define the context in which a firm should be viewed. The four types of information that should be reflected in all financial information are:

1. General economic conditions
2. Political and governmental agencies
3. Industry development
4. Competitive conditions (H21, pp. 133–134)

These concerns span economic, political, industry, and other competitive conditions. Without an appreciation for and a tracking of these factors the firm is bound to ignore important components of the information needed. Therefore, these factors are also important to the analyst.

Areas of Concern
A list of the types of specific information and data that are necessary in order to develop strategic plans is presented in Figure 7-2.

These various specific categories are all components of the environment and all must be scanned if in fact the analyst is going to be able to fully as-

Figure 7-2 Information for Strategic Planning

Category	General Content
1. Market potential	Supply and demand considerations for market areas of current or potential interest: for example, capacity, consumption, imports, exports.
2. Structural change	Mergers, acquisitions, and joint ventures involving competitors; new entries into the industry, and so forth.
3. Pricing	Effective and proposed prices for products of current and potential interest.
4. Sales negotiations	Information relating to a specific current or potential sale on contract for the firm.
5. Customers	General information about current or near-potential customers, their markets, their problems.
6. Leads for mergers, joint ventures, or acquisitions	Information concerning possibilities for the manager's own company.
7. Suppliers and raw materials	Purchasing considerations for products of current or potential interest.
8. New products, processes, and technology	Technical information relatively new and unknown to company.
9. Product problems	Problems involving existing products.
10. Costs	Costs for processing, operations, and so forth for current and potential competitors, suppliers and customers, and for proposed company activities.
11. Licensing and patents	Products and processes.
12. General conditions	Events of a general nature: political, demographic, national, and so forth.
13. Government actions and policies	Governmental decisions affecting the industry.
14. Resources available	People, land, and other resources possibly available for the company.
15. Miscellaneous	Items not elsewhere classified.

(Adapted from H21, pp. 136–137)

sess the potential ramifications of the financial information at hand. Analysts often spend their time focusing on whether the prospective financial information under investigation is arithmetically accurate and ignore other important issues. Knowledge of the issues listed in Figure 7-2 is essential for a full appreciation of the context in which the numbers are constructed. This is the context in which the firm should be viewed. It is often much easier to give the appearance of precision in the analysis process by focusing on arithmetic computations than to address those elements that are really much more relevant.

7.4 SYSTEMS PERSPECTIVE

Unity

The systems process and systems perspective are really ways of seeking and seeing unity. It has been said that "we must stop acting as though nature were organized into disciplines . . . " (H3, p. 3). This applies to the process of management, and ultimately to the analysis process itself.

To see management as a system is:

To see the process in large perspective

To understand more comprehensively its nature, its structure, and its process.

To be able to deal (within the limitations of present knowledge) with the interrelationships that characterize the operation of the whole.

To be able to serve as the architect and the engineer of the system by means of which any whole is managed. (H3, p. 3)

Specifically, when it is applied in management theory the concept of the dynamic whole is of paramount importance.

> The systems view of management is a concept of the dynamic whole based on the model of the process that is identical to that of any other system, any other whole. Management is the manipulation of levels and flow rates, through the use of decisions, based upon information and related to standards—which is to say, the operation of a system. (H3, p. 157)

What has to be appreciated is that with the systems perspective any one system can be viewed as a super or subsystem of another system. The extreme extension of this could lead to intellectual and practical impotence, but when properly appreciated it is a powerful tool. What is needed is a sensitivity for the interconnectedness of all systems to other systems. An example of a systems and subsystems hierarchy and interrelatedness is as follows:

> system- Federal Government
> subsystem- Executive Branch
> sub-subsystem- Department of Commerce
> sub-sub-subsystem- Environmental Science
> Service Administration
> sub-sub-sub-subsystem- Weather Bureau
> sub-sub-sub-sub-subsystem- Western Region
> sub-sub-sub-sub-sub-subsystem- Seattle District

(H3, p. 17)

According to Peter Drucker, one of the shortcomings in business has been the absence of a real theory of the business enterprise.

> The absence of an adequate theory of business enterprise is not just an "academic" concern; on the contrary, it underlies four major problems central to business as well as to a free enterprise society.
>
> One is the obvious inability of the layman to understand modern business as well as a free enterprise society.
>
> The second problem is the lack of any bridge of understanding between the "macroeconomics" of an economy and the "micro-economics" of the most important factor in this economy, the business enterprise.
>
> The third area . . . is that of the internal integration of the organization.
>
> The final problem . . . is of course the businessman's own attitude toward theory (when he says "this is theoretical," he means "this is irrelevant"). (H3, pp. 154–155)

The third area referred to by Drucker, the need for an internal integration of the organization, is one of the real pressing problems of current management and management theory. In order to address this deficiency there has been a good deal of research in the area of systems and systems theories, including efforts to derive certain principles from other disciplines, especially biology and the sciences.

> From now on any serious student of management will need to be aware of general systems thinking and its impact on management. (H3, p. 70)

As mentioned above, the basis for much of the theoretical work in systems theory is grounded in the study of nature.

> The renewed attention being given to the continuity of nature, particularly that between the physical, the biological, and the psycho-socio-cultural; the fully interactive nature of these various aspects (which have become so compartmentalized in the academy); and the consequent newly insistent demand for interdisciplinary integration are all leading students of management to see organizations as integrated wholes, and to use basic systems knowledge in order to manage organizations (H3, pp. 70–71).

General Systems Theory

One of the primary quests in systems has been to find a general systems theory. This is a theory that would integrate the various components of the study of nature and ultimately of all other disciplines. This approach is in direct conflict with much of the traditional research that has been done, from which manageable "units" of study or disciplines have evolved. Along with these disciplines, the specialist has also evolved. There are advantages and disadvantages to both the general and the traditional approaches.

> For centuries man has speculated about the existence of a single, all embracing science. At the same time he has chosen to study his environment by dividing it into manageable chunks such as physics, chemistry, biology, psychology, sociology, and others. Such divisions:
>
> - Promoted depth studies within branches of science;
> - Stimulated the development of specialized languages to encourage precision of expression and improve communication among the specialities;
> - Encouraged the drawing of arbitrary limits to confine within practical bounds the works of the scientific specialist—the physicist, the chemist, the biologist, and the others. (H3, p. 55)

On the negative side, these arbitrary divisions discouraged cross-disciplinary communication and discussion, a problem that was inherited by management theorists.

There have been two approaches suggested for the process of studying general systems theory. The first approach is to pick some general phenomenon from the physical world and attempt to create a theoretical foundation for all the samples observed. The second is to arrange various classes of observed systems in a hierarchical format and attempt to draw conclusions about them. In the first approach one would look at common characteristics such as:

- Populations (aggregates of individuals)
- Behavior of units within populations
- Growth at low levels, where relatively simple population models suffice
- Communication patterns (H3, pp. 65–66)

Using the second approach, the following hierarchy has been proposed:

- Static structures
- Clock works
- Control mechanisms
- Open systems
- Lower organisms
- Animals
- Human beings
- Sociocultural systems
- Symbolic systems (H3, pp. 67–68)

This listing was an attempt to create a hierarchy of systems from an intuitive and impressionistic rather than a logical perspective. It was an important step in the process of refining the concept of a general systems theory.

For businesses, the general conclusion reached by general systems theory is that businesses do not exist in a vacuum but are really only a part of many other interrelated systems. This view of the organization leads to the radically different emphasis placed on most of the topics discussed in this book. The open systems view, or, if I may qualify this term, the relatively open systems view, attempts to "consider all possible effects of the environment on the system, and vice versa" (H3, p. 21). This view, which has been lacking in management theory, is the one that this text embraces. The important point is that businesses must be viewed in the context of the environments in which they exist. Failure to do so invites failure, and the analyst must be aware of this.

7.5   SYSTEMS DESIGN PROCESS

This section briefly discusses the systems design process as it applies to financial information, although the concepts addressed apply equally to the other systems within the organization. Financial information and the systems that support it evolve out of the needs of both the users and the generators of that information. A sensitivity to these needs is essential to understanding and analyzing prospective financial information. There is no simple formula for perfect prospective financial information. Each system is unique, based on the peculiar needs and demands of each particular organization. The analyst must have a sensitivity for the basic underlying principles that can be used to satisfy these needs.

One common misconception has to do with appearances. Systems that on the surface appear to be efficient in reality often are not (H21, p. 269). This is because many systems that appear on the surface to be complete, comprehensive, and orderly have some major structural deficiencies. These deficiencies often revolve around issues of flexibility or responsiveness to the needs of the users of information. Often systems serve the needs of the generators rather than the users of information.

The real test of a well-designed system for financial information is whether it operates successfully. This is the ultimate criteria of its acceptability or nonacceptability. Success must be defined based solely on fulfilling the needs of the primary users of this information (H21, p. 269). The analyst must have a thorough understanding of the organization in order to address the specific information needs that must be met (H21, p. 270).

There are some basic principles that should be used in the design of the accounting information system. These principles reflect the discussions in the previous sections of this text and include:

1.   The design of the system should be requested by the users.
2.   The organization should be understood by the designer.
3.   The users of the system should be involved and their needs should be understood by the designer.
4.   The critical elements should be identified.
5.   The information needs should be identified.
6.   The technology should be determined by the information needs.
7.   The system should be designed in modules.

8.   The design process and the system should be documented.

9.   The control of the system should be built into the system. (H21, p. 270)

7.6 SUMMARY

Some of the important elements of systems have been discussed in this chapter. It is always interesting to see the many efforts to constantly fragment the various components of a business, both in the academic environment and in the real world. The interrelatedness of all the systems within business and society is an unavoidable reality. It is incumbent on the analyst to fully appreciate the importance of this interrelatedness.

Even the smallest business must consider in its planning the reality that it is part of a global economy. Without doing this, any business, no matter its size or market, eventually will fail. The reason is that businesses are in fact part of a larger whole. Refusal to acknowledge this reality will not change the fact that businesses must operate in a dynamic interdependence with many other systems, which can ultimately determine the firm's success or failure.

Finally, the various topics addressed within this book must be viewed as parts of a system, not in isolation. They all are integral parts of the firm, and must be seen as such if proper analysis of prospective financial statements is to take place.

CHAPTER EIGHT

Modeling, Forecasting, and Sensitivity Analysis— Some Tools

CHAPTER OUTLINE

8.1 MODELING

Introduction

This section discusses some of the basic concepts and principles of computer modeling. These are important because modeling is usually a basic tool used in developing prospective financial statements and should be understood in order to effectively conduct any analysis.

All models have various characteristics. The objectives or purposes for a specific model will determine which of these characteristics becomes relatively more important. Some of the characteristics that are commonly found desirable include:

• Insight-generating capacity
• Descriptive realism
• Mode reproduction ability
• Transparency
• Relevance
• Ease of enrichment
• Fertility

- Formal correspondence with data
- Point predictive ability (H37, p. xix)

As stated earlier, depending on the objectives and purposes, certain characteristics will be more important than others.

Types of Models

There are a variety of different ways to categorize models. One way is to differentiate whether the model is physical or symbolic. A physical model focuses on replicating the actual characteristics of the system. In fact, physical models are actually physical representations of the systems under investigation. The other major class of models is the symbolic. These may be either verbal or mathematical. The thrust of most of what we will be discussing and pursuing will focus on various types of symbolic mathematical models.

Mathematical models may be characterized according to their technical characteristics. Four of these major characteristics are:

1. Purpose
2. Mode of analysis
3. Treatment of randomness
4. Generality of application (I20, p. 5)

A discussion of the *purposes* of a model usually includes two general purposes—optimization and description. An optimization model seeks to find points of either maximization or minimization. A descriptive model seeks to describe the behavior of a system. The *mode of analysis* is usually subdivided into either analytic or numeric. The analytic mode seeks to take traditional mathematical and statistical techniques and incorporate them into the analysis. Numerical analysis uses a series of relatively simple arithmetic computations. The *treatment of randomness* is usually broken into the deterministic or the probabilistic. Deterministic models use a single-valued estimate for the variables in the model and usually generate a single-valued output. A probabilistic model attempts to deal with the random nature of the system and usually has probabilistic data for inputs and probability distributions for outputs. The *generality of application* implies that the model is either ready-built or custom-built.

Although not intended as a comprehensive discussion of these topics, the various technical characteristics do give a good starting point towards an understanding of the various types of models. Most of the models that the analyst encounters are mathematical. The variety of technical characteristics presented help demonstrate that there is no one ideal approach for either modeling or analysis. In fact, the analysis approach that should be followed could include various combinations of all the various options presented in the technical characteristics listed above.

An outline of the various types of models is presented below (I20, pp. 3–6).

1. Physical
    a. Iconic
    b. Analog
2. Symbolic
    a. Verbal
    b. Mathematical
        (i)   Purpose
              (a) Optimization
              (b) Description
        (ii) Mode of Analysis
              (a) Analytic
              (b) Numeric
        (iii) Treatment of randomness
              (a) Deterministic
              (b) Probabilistic
        (iv) Generality of application
              (a) Ready built
              (b) Custom built

Model Development

Process
There is no shortage of approaches to the process used in the development of a model. A standard format for the overall basic process is:

1.   Problem and/or information identification
2.   Data collection
3.   Model building
4.   Model validation
5.   Model implementation
6.   Model operation (I20, p. 13)

The overall process is more than basic model building. It is a development process that emphasizes the order of the steps. The first need is to clearly identify the problem and the information necessary to develop the model. The second step involves identifying and collecting the specific data that is necessary in order to drive the model. Only then can you start the third step, which is model building itself. After the model is built it must be validated. Then comes implementation, which consists of actually introducing the model into the organization and beginning to use it. The model operation step addresses the model's ongoing and continued use after a successful initial implementation.

Format
Although there are a number of different formats for the presentation of financial information in models addressing prospective financial statements, one standard format including the following sequential steps:

- Assumptions
- Income statements
- Cash flows
- Balance sheets
- Proofs

Assumptions.   The assumptions section should contain a clear description of all the input drivers that are relevant to the model. Of course, more detailed assumptions will lead to more detailed models.

There are two general approaches taken in incorporating assumptions. They are the micro and the macro approaches. The macro approach takes certain drivers (for instance, the cost of goods sold) and sets them at a certain level (for example, 66% of sales). This would then drive the gross profit and ultimately the net income. The 66% figure would reflect both fixed and variable components in the cost of goods. This presents some problems because if the level of activity varies substantially, although the variable component might be correctly reflected, the fixed component would only be correct near the level of activity initially reflected in the model. If the actual activity varies substantially then the joint fixed and variable percentage of 66% would necessarily become inaccurate. If the activity level goes much higher the percentage would be overstated. If the activity level is reduced substantially the actual 66% for cost of goods sold would in fact be understated. Additionally, the macro approach usually assumes that the average historical figures apply. The purpose of most prospective financial statements is to anticipate and understand change, and so these historical figures are often inappropriate and inaccurate.

The micro approach, however, uses detailed schedules to clearly specify all the components of the model. Instead of using a single figure for cost of goods sold, this approach would present the labor, materials and overhead reflected in the cost of goods sold figures in detailed schedules. The cost of goods sold figure presented can then easily be broken down into its parts, and a thorough going analysis conducted on each component individually.

Income Statements and Cash Flows.   The income statement is driven primarily from the assumptions section. Most of the elements in the income statement merely refer directly to the various assumptions contained in the assumptions section of the model. These in turn were derived from specific projected activity as well as from the general assumptions governing GAAP discussed in Chapter 4. The cash flow statements are simultaneously derived from figures from both the assumptions section and the income statements.

Balance Sheets.   When they are dealing with a fully integrated set of income statements, the balance sheets will be derived primarily from the previous three sections—assumptions, income statements, and cash flows.

Proofs.   A set of proofs is sometimes included as a last section so that various arithmetical checks can be incorporated directly into the model to ensure arithmetical accuracy. The proof section can be set up to reflect a series of zeroes if everything is correct. If it is not full of zeroes, then something is wrong. One check is, of course, the balance sheets, where the assets must equal the liabilities and ownership equities. Additionally, each detailed schedule within the model can be footed and crossfooted, and the two figures (the foot and the crossfoot) subtracted one from another to yield a zero figure. All of the differences for all of the foots and crossfoots for each of the schedules in the model can be added together. If there are no arithmetical errors then the sum total of all these differences is equal to zero. Any loan covenants can also be checked against constraints and proved in this section of the model.

The modeling approach described flows from an appreciation for the accounting equation—assets equal liabilities plus ownership equity. There are numerous other approaches to modeling. Many do not use the accounting approach described above. Instead, they project the levels for the various elements of the financial statements to a point in the future. These projected elements are then reconciled through the statement of cash flows. Both methods are widely used and the analyst must be conversant with each.

Benefits

Although any decision making process is in effect a model, there are a number of benefits that accrue as a consequence of using computer models in the decision making process. Some of these benefits relate to personnel considerations, and some relate to the use of the actual models themselves. The benefits related to *personnel* include:

1. Freeing personnel for other activities.
2. Saving time spent on the decision-making activity.
3. Saving money spent on the decision-making activity.
4. Providing decision-making skills that are in short supply.
5. Moving toward more nearly optimal decision-making.
6. Increasing decision-making consistency.
7. Providing a model for training new personnel in decision-making.
8. Providing a standard of performance for control. (I20, p. 218)

There are also a number of general benefits associated with the use of computers in modeling. They include:

1. Models can be large enough to include as many variables and relationships as usually need to be handled.

2.   They can handle various complex, probabilistic and other relationships which are difficult or impossible to deal with by formal analysis.

3.   They can be run successively to reveal how sensitive a result is to specific ranges of variation in input data, or in the coefficients and constants defining the relationships between variables.

4.   Models can be used to portray the dynamic and static relationships and reveal the real world and the affects which occur when conditions change.

5.   Mathematical models, as compared with purely verbal description and analysis, force the clear and precise stipulation of the assumptions that underpin the model. (K13, p. 29)

There are also a number of disadvantages associated with using computers in the modeling process:

1.   Even the most complex model is a gross simplification of reality and we can never be certain that every important factor has been included and given its proper weight.

2.   By producing detailed results models help to foster the delusions of precision and certainty. When data are imperfect and assumptions are uncertain we can be just as wrong with a computer model as without one.

3.   It is impossible to check a model that projects future activity by comparison to actual results until some point in the future.

4.   Goals and priorities change continually so that future human behavior will diverge more or less rapidly from the past on which the design of the model was based.

5.   Models appeal to theoreticians, but their combination of complexity with mathematics can confuse or repel those who are less academically minded, and thus reduce their practical value for business managers and government administrators.

6.   Models rarely include all the circumstances and variables that could have an impact on the ultimate results that are being studied. (K13, p. 30)

Simulating Decision Making

The discussion above presented some of the general steps in the modeling process. That process, if specifically related to the decision making process, would be refined to include the following eight steps:

1. Gain an understanding of the information flows and the decisions that are made.

2. Generate a list of variables that are possibly used in the decision-making process.

3. Analyze the decision-making process.

4. Collect appropriate data for developing the model.

5. Develop the model for the decision-making process.

6. Test the model that has been built.

7. Iterate steps 3 to 6 until an appropriate model is developed.

8. Implement the model in the organization. (I20, p. 219)

These steps in the process for simulating decision making are presented for several reasons. They emphasize the importance of gaining an understanding of information flows and what decisions are being made with the information that will be generated. A very important issue is that most decisions made in an organization use information generated in various models, and in particular in financial models.

Problems at one level in the generation of the projected information affect other levels of the organizational decision making process. It is important to appreciate that the output of a financial model might become the input of a decision making model. It is easy to see how an error at one level can be multiplied in its impact at multiple other levels within the organization. Also, in a dynamic feedback driven decision making system, the errors sent out of one subsystem affect the feedback that is later received by that subsystem. Because of this the original error and its impact are directly compounded in that specific subsystem, as well as throughout the entire organization.

Financial Modeling and Qualitative Elements of Business Plans

One shortcoming of most financial modeling is that it does not address many of the qualitative elements in a business plan. Often there are a variety of different stated objectives, such as improved community relations, improved local environment, or increased employee morale. Although they are part of the strategic plan, these objectives seldom are reflected in the detailed business plans or the prospective financial statements. This means that the resources necessary to achieve these goals are not addressed or reflected in the models.

In the contemporary business world it is necessary to pay attention to many qualitative issues. In fact, many of these issues probably are as important as the more quantifiable issues. The resources needed to achieve these various goals must be reflected clearly in the financial model if that model is going to accurately describe the real business plans. Unfortunately, in practice many qualitative components of business plans are added as boilerplate, and the businesses have no intention of allocating any substantial resources to these goals. But the goals do sound nice and look good in the annual reports of the corporations.

Regardless of the reasons, qualitative goals are seldom reflected in prospective financial statements. An analyst, when presented with prospective financial statements, must determine if the qualitative goals are secondary or really important to the business plan. If they are important, then the resources associated with the achievement of these goals must necessarily be reflected in the model.

Although beyond the scope of this section of this book, a methodology for addressing and handling qualitative information in models is presented in Section 2.5.

Model Integrity and Documentation

From a mechanical point of view, there are a number of potential problems with the development of models. The well-being of a company may depend on the accuracy of these figures. An appreciation for the types of errors that can occur in the spreadsheets helps with the maintenance of model integrity. Some of the typical errors include:

- Wrong data
- Erroneous formulas
- Logically incorrect formulas
- Wrong version
- Wrong template/application
- Data overriding formulas (I10, p. 31)

In the model development process discussed above, specific steps for the general development of any model were outlined. An important part of the model implementation step includes the documentation of that model. Documentation allows a clear trail tracing the particular bits of real data that are used to produce a specific version of a model (I 10, p. 32). It also allows for a clear explanation, description, and understanding of how the model is supposed to work.

What usually happens is that the modeler creates a generalized version of the model, which is called a template. This general version of the model then usually undergoes several runs, each of which incorporates specific real data. This particular data is associated with a different set of specific assumptions for each of the separate runs. Often, modelers choose not to present a single-run output for the model; instead, they show several runs—a base case, a median, and an optimistic scenario—which are used to depict the range of possible outcomes resulting from varying certain important assumptions. However, this approach presents some real challenges. Multiple runs make it difficult to identify and articulate the particular assumptions used in a specific run. In order to clearly identify the elements included within a specific run, and to confirm that they in fact are incorporated and reflected in that run, certain documentation guidelines are helpful. *Spreadsheet documentation* should consist of the following:

1. Change log
2. Description/purpose of the spreadsheet
3. Explanation of how it works/normal processing sequence
4. Description of how data are entered
5. Sample output
6. List of formulas/cell contents
7. Special considerations for making computations
8. Security considerations
9. System diagram
10. Audit reports (I10, p. 32)

The change log records information about the various revisions. It details when, why, and what was changed between the various runs. The description/purpose of the spreadsheet presents a general overview of how the spreadsheet is set up and what goals it is supposed to be meeting. The explanation of how it works and the normal processing sequence is important to help users know how to execute the actual spreadsheet. The description of how data are entered helps to define exactly what data can be changed and how to go about changing it. In most models not all the elements of the model are intended to be changed. Additionally, the method used to change a certain cell often is not to touch that particular cell, but rather to change an input cell to that cell. This input cell might be found in a totally different section of the spreadsheet—for example, in the assumptions section for a cell being examined in the income statement.

Sample output is helpful for developing a sense of what the hardcopy results should look like. The list of formulas and cell contents is an important part of the documentation. Many modelers do not in fact provide a detailed list of all the formulas in the cells in their documentation, yet if the documentation process is to be complete this is a very important component. There are often special considerations for making modifications that could include the use of certain macros. This information also must be clearly stipulated. Certain security issues and considerations are important, including passwords for various levels of entry, modification, or self-protection, and these issues all should be stipulated clearly.

A systems diagram should be included in the documentation in order to clarify the flow of data among the various sections of a spreadsheet and between multiple spreadsheets, if they are linked. An audit report should be included to provide information on various basic issues, such as range names, functions, and so forth (I10, p. 32). One method of creating and storing documentation is to use a notebook with sections divided into these ten major subheadings. This allows easy updating as appropriate.

There are a number of auditing packages that can assist with some of these functions. There are also functions within the LOTUS program itself that will allow the display of the contents of the various cells. Other specialized packages, such as the Spreadsheet Auditor, can also be helpful. Some spreadsheets such as Excel have many of these features built in. Excel also allows the display of precedent and dependent cells, which is helpful not only in documentation but also in troubleshooting the model (I10, p. 33). No matter what approach is taken it is important to document your model. This tool can provide a great degree of information for the analyst.

Summary

An understanding of the modeling process is essential to a clear understanding of the analysis of prospective financial information. The creation and use of models is a reflection of the ideas incorporated into them. It is interesting to note that the AICPA Guidelines presented in Chapter 5 do not emphasize the use of the computer model in the analysis process. In spite of AICPA's Report stipulating that in fact the projected results will not be achieved, their analysis process proceeds with a basic focus on these "incorrect" numbers, rather than a focus on the range of probable outcomes, which could be pursued if the model used in developing the prospective financial statements is also used in the analysis process.

8.2 FORECASTING

Introduction

Understanding forecasting is important to the analysis process because the forecast of specific data is often an integral part of the complete forecasted or projected financial statements. This important tool will only be discussed briefly here. Too often people associate forecasting with sophisticated high tech equipment, including computer hardware and software, or with highly trained personnel. This is not really what forecasting is about. Forecasting is concerned with the methods used to predict the future. The methods can vary widely and do not necessarily have to use sophisticated technology or highly paid specialists. What is important is whether the forecasting method chosen meets a firm's specific needs in a cost-effective fashion.

Systems Approach to Structuring Forecasting Problems

The systems approach to structuring forecasting problems consists of a four-step method:

1. Identify objectives
2. Develop indicators of success
3. Generate alternative strategies
4. Develop and select programs (I2, p. 20)

Like any other problem there is a systematic method for approaching this one.

The systems approach suggests that there is no single method for structuring forecasting problems; rather, the method chosen will be a function of specific goals and objectives, limited by the constraints of specific resources. In addition to focusing on specific objectives, certain indicators of success are necessary. What type of output is needed? Alternative strategies must be considered. Once the constraints of limited resources have been appreciated, objectives the success indicators have been established, and various alternative strategies have been examined, then and only then should a specific program for forecasting needs be embraced.

There is no ideal or optimal forecasting system. Rather, the ability to meet specific needs in a cost-effective fashion is the prime determinant of value. Whether the system is well used and helpful in meeting the firm's requirements determines whether or not it is successful.

Classification of Forecasting Methodologies

There is a wide variety of forecasting methodologies available. The two primary categories are subjective or objective. There is some crossover. A brief outline of some of the methodologies available includes:

1. Subjective
    a. Judgmental
    b. Bootstrapping
2. Objective
    a. Naive (Extrapolation)
    b. Causal
        (i)   Linear (Econometric)
        (ii) Classification (Segmentation) (I2, p. 71)

The judgmental and econometric methods are used for forecasting shorter time frames and estimating current status. The judgmental and extrapolation methods can be used along with econometric methods for middle-range forecasts. Long-range forecasts usually use econometric and segmentation forecasting (I2, p. 250).

The subjective methods are not to be discounted for apparent lack of rigor. Much of what is done in business proceeds from judgmental forecasts and these are often effective.

The objective method is divided into two primary groups: the naive and the causal. The naive is primarily concerned with extrapolation, or what many people would call the establishment of correlation. The causal seeks to establish a cause-and-effect relationship between inputs and outputs and is usually divided into linear and classification methods.

The real question is how to decide which methods will be most beneficial for your specific needs.

Trends and Tradeoffs

The whole process of forecasting requires a sensitivity to the costs and benefits associated with the forecasting function. Most small to medium size companies or divisions within large companies cannot support a sophisticated and expensive forecasting function, but forecasting still remains an important and essential component of running their business. Therefore, the forecasting methods available to small and medium sized businesses are usually subjective and less expensive. This is not to say that they are less accurate or less valuable. There is an abundance of industry and product information available from various sources. An example of this is *Predicasts*. These resources are available at most good libraries. The only cost to the business is their employees' time.

There are three classes of environments into which all forecasting situations fall.

1. Static
2. Dynamic
3. Chaotic or volatile (C24, p. 1)

The static environment does not present much of a challenge for forecasting. In the dynamic situation there is change, but a reasonably predictable future. The third case presents the real challenge for forecasters and for business people alike. An apparently unpredictable environment causes many forecasters and business people to shake their heads and avoid the whole process. This is hardly advisable. A vast storehouse of data is stored in the minds of the people within any business. This can be used to great advantage, when coupled with other cost effective sources of information.

Viable forecasting systems can be inexpensive. A basic format for a simple *qualitative system* is as follows.

Forecasting consists of recognizing relevant clues in the environment and then translating them. This can be done with reasonable success in any of those conditions if it is done right. The process is as follows:

1. Establish the significant areas of the environment to be scanned:
   a. The economic at all levels
   b. All significant legal implications

  c. Technological changes, and

  d. Social attitudes

2. Assign competent people to monitor, on a continuous basis, each of the above areas.

3. See that all significant information is made available to the proper people at the proper time and in the proper form.

4. Prepare, in advance, the basic frameworks of the potential decisions.

5. See that all these steps are monitored constantly to make sure they are consistent with the prevailing conditions and possibilities. (C24, pp. 1–2)

The trend in larger businesses is from subjective to the objective methodologies, in spite of the fact that these forecasting systems often are unresponsive to the immediate information needs of the business (I2, p. 395). However, small businesses can have cost-effective forecasting systems if they follow the approach outlined above.

  The analyst may need to use a specialist in assessing certain forecasts. In these cases *SAS 11* should be consulted.

Summary

The variety of different methods available for forecasting provides a bit of flexibility in the forecasting function. Full understanding of the process whereby forecasts are developed is important to the analyst. Probably the most cost-effective method for most businesses is using research readily available outside of the firm. The analyst needs to fully understand how the various forecasts reflected within the prospective financial statements were derived, and how the forecasting systems operate.

8.3 SENSITIVITY ANALYSIS

Introduction

Any realistic effort at evaluating financial statements or a model relating to them will require sensitivity analysis. This process emphasizes a study of the effects of uncertainty on the model. How does the model respond to change (H37, p. 187)?

Decisions always involve inputs such as assumptions, estimates, and simplifications, all of which are prone to error in varying degrees. Two common questions regarding inputs are:

- Which inputs are the most important? and
- How confident can management feel about the values of particular inputs being used?

The answers to questions like these are most meaningfully addressed by examining the implications that changes in inputs have for the analyses in which they are used. Examinations of this type are based on the response-to-change concept. (I16, p. 1)

The propensity to error in varying degrees raises the question of uncertainty.

Uncertainty is the lack of confidence that you have regarding any input or output in a decision-making process. Risk, on the other hand, is what you undertake when you act in the face of uncertainty. Uncertainty is the cause of risk, and the greater the uncertainty, the greater the risk you take in using that about which you are uncertain. (I16, p. 3)

The question that actually is addressed is how much reliance you can put on something that is in itself uncertain. These definitions of risk and uncertainty vary somewhat from the more technical definitions used in decision making under uncertainty, but they are helpful for the immediate discussion at hand (I4).

Sensitivity analysis seeks to assist in evaluating the significance of responses to change. It involves three related considerations:

1. The type of output
2. The context of the output
3. The risk the user takes in relying on input (I16, p. 4)

The issue of risk due to relying on various inputs was discussed in Chapter 4 in the discussion on the qualitative characteristic of financial information called reliability. How much can things change before a different decision is reached?

A number of techniques have been developed to deal with sensitivities. One is the decision tree. This is usually helpful in situations with a limited number of inputs. Another method often used is the Monte Carlo simulation. "However, simulation results do not provide any information regarding the response of the output to changes in specific inputs" (I16, p. 10). Additionally, the Monte Carlo simulation usually requires the creation of subjective probability distributions that themselves are subject to uncertainty. Hence, "It can be seen, therefore, that Monte Carlo simulation, rather than being an alternative to sensitivity analysis, is actually a subject for its application" (I16, p. 10).

Objectives

The primary objectives of sensitivity analysis of a model are:

- To test the effects of uncertainties on parameter values
- To generate insight about structure, behavior and the real world
- To direct further work on parameters and structure (H37, pp. 188–190)

An important consideration in any sensitivity analysis is that it has to be "related to the purpose of the model under investigation" (H37, p. 188).

Testing Effects of Uncertainties in Parameter Values

A parameter "is always a constant whose value is not determined by the rest of the system" (H37, p. 235). In most basic financial models, parameters are the coefficients found in many of the equations. For example, in the equation

$$CGS = 66\% \text{ Sales}$$

the 66% figure is a parameter. Additionally, most basic inputs are also parameters. A starting figure in year 1 for labor cost per hour would also be a parameter.

One of the objectives in sensitivity analysis is to test the effects of the uncertainties on parameter values. This is done by varying certain parameters and seeing the results on the output. Most models are not overly sensitive to these types of changes within a realistic range. When particularly sensitive parameters are identified, a determination must be made as to whether or not they are accurate. An alternative may be to reformulate the model (H37, p. 188), which is discussed below in "Insights on Structure and Behavior."

Generating Insight

There are two types of insights that are generated through sensitivity analysis.

1. The relation between the structure and the behavior
2. Increased understanding of the real world (H37, p. 189)

Insights on Structure and Behavior. Some of the detailed objectives related to gaining insights on structure and behavior are:

- To discover which behavior modes the model can generate.
- To identify the model changes which can shift the model from one behavior mode to another. This identification helps to sort out the parameters and structural relationships whose precise values are of critical importance for model behavior, thereby establishing which aspects a more comprehensive study should focus on. Furthermore, the modeler discovers where to allocate limited resources. Finally, such identification helps to locate appropriate levers for efficient and robust policy.
- To identify the active and dormant parts of the model structure. This procedure establishes a basis for finding the simplest recognizable structure that can generate the reference mode. To find such a simple model structure is often a goal in system dynamics modeling because it will indicate the most fundamental processes at work within the system. Moreover, as a forum for discussing the problem under study, a simple model is preferable.
- To evaluate whether the dynamic behavior in models with exogenous inputs is generated by external or internal forces. (H37, p. 189)

Insights About Real World. In addition to insights about structure and behavior, sensitivity analysis should generate insights about the real world. The operation of the model must be examined under both normal and extreme conditions to see the results on the model and the output. There are a number of important questions that should be addressed. Some of these questions are:

- Are the behavior modes produced by the model realistic?
- Does the model's sensitivity (or robustness) accord with human knowledge of the real-world system?

- Is the model (in)sensitive to the same perturbations as the real system? (H37, p. 190)

Directing Further Work on the Model
The sensitivity analysis process often results in refinements in the model itself. This is itself sometimes an approach used in modeling. Rather than having as an objective the developing of a final version of the model, some see the entire development process as an iterative one, with each preceding generation giving rise to a new generation, if so indicated (H37, pp. 190–191).

Kinds of Sensitivity

In general, models have sensitivity that can be classified into a hierarchy of three different types:

1. Numerical sensitivity
2. Behavioral sensitivity
3. Policy sensitivity (H38, p. 278)

"A model is numerically sensitive if a parameter or structural change results in changes in numerical values computed in the course of the simulation" (H38, p. 278). All financial and quantitative models exhibit numerical sensitivity. "Behavioral sensitivity is a concern for dynamic simulation models. It refers to the degree to which the behavior exhibited by the model changes when a parameter value is changed or an alternative formulation is used" (H38, p. 278). Policy sensitivity is concerned with "whether model-based policy conclusions change with reasonable changes in the model." (H38, p. 278).

Types of Model Changes in Sensitivity Analysis

In order to examine changes within the system, they are usually classified into the following categories:

- Parameter changes,
- Structural changes, or
- A combination of these two (H37, p. 191)

Parameter Changes
Parameter changes refer to changes in constants (including initial values) (H37, p. 191). The effects of parameter changes on output are usually the most basic and most common form of changes examined in sensitivity analysis, and the easiest to envision from the perspectives of both inputs and outputs (H37, p. 191).

Structural Changes
A structural change is an alteration of a basic relationship in the model (H37, p. 192). The impact and results of changes in structure and various assumptions governing structure are important components of the analysis process (H37, p. 192). This is a more advanced form of analysis than parameter changes. A full understanding of the construction of the model itself is needed. This approach can provide some very important insights for the analysis process.

Parameter and Structural Changes
The combination of parameter and structural changes can produce results quite different than those obtained when each is considered individually (H37, p. 193). If appropriate, this can be an acceptable approach to the analysis process. However, some analysts prefer to isolate the effects of parameter changes from the effects of structural changes before examining their joint impact.

Reasonable Versus Unreasonable Changes
It is important to understand the difference between reasonable and unreasonable change. This must come from experience in modeling and an understanding of the industry under examination. The objective of modeling is to see how well the model can duplicate the real world. Changes conducted on the model need to be consistent with the real-world context in which the particular business exists (H37, pp. 194–195).

Interpretation

The question of interpretation revolves around how much change in model behavior is acceptable before it becomes necessary to increase the precision in the underlying parameters (or structure) (H37, pp. 195–196). This question can only be and *must* be answered by the analyst.

Sensitivity Analysis During Modeling

Model Experimentation
A point that is often overlooked is that a good modeler usually will conduct experiments and test the model during the construction phase itself.

> Policy analysis can also be viewed as a limited sensitivity test. A policy test is nothing but a change in model structure and/or a change of parameters— a change that is feasible in the actual system, and to which model behavior may be sensitive. Moreover, an important part of policy analysis is testing the robustness of recommended policies with relation to uncertainties in model parameters and structure. (H37, p. 196)

Generating New Hypotheses
Sometimes a modeler or analyst will notice that preliminary results do not seem appropriate even before the modeling process itself has ended. The modeler might want to test new hypotheses in order to investigate how realistic the original representations might be (H37, p. 196).

Summary

Sensitivity analysis is important both to business modeling and to the analysis of prospective financial information. There is no approved solution for the process. Rather, an appreciation for the need to dynamically test any model under investigation is the only hard and fast conclusion that can be drawn.

8.4 SUMMARY

The tools that we have discussed—modeling, forecasting, and sensitivity analysis—are three important components of both the creation and the analysis of prospective financial statements. Without a solid understanding of these tools and proficiency in their use, the analyst will not be successful.

CHAPTER NINE

Financial Analysis— The Basics

CHAPTER OUTLINE

9.1 INTRODUCTION

This chapter discusses the basic techniques used in traditional financial
analysis for historical financial information, which is an important subsystem of the firm. Traditional financial analysis is employed both by
firms themselves and by outside analysts. It provides some tools that can
also be used in the analysis of prospective financial statements. But the
practical focus must be shifted from the historical to the prospective if the
processes are to be of any value in the analysis. Sometimes these shifts are
obvious; sometimes there are important subtleties that need to be appreciated. These subtleties will be discussed in this chapter, along with the
shifting and refocusing needed for the various techniques in order to adapt
them to the analysis of prospective financial information.

All financial analysis, both historical and prospective, is concerned in one
way or another with an effort to make inferences about the future. These inferences must consider a number of different factors, including the goals and
objectives of the organization, the specific environment, and even the goals
and objectives of the person or people conducting the financial analysis.

Financial statement analysis is an application of the scientific method
in the business environment. There are a number of sequential steps that
are usually involved in the application of the *scientific method.* These include:

1.   Assessment of relevant existing knowledge

2.   Formulation of concepts and propositions

3.   Statement of hypotheses

4. Design of the research to test the hypotheses

5. Acquisition of meaningful empirical data

6. Analysis and evaluation of data

7. Explanation and new problems statement (I21, p. 28)

The scientific method presents an overview of the context for financial analysis, whether historical or prospective. Financial analysis involves much more than just looking at ratios or comparing figures from one year to another. It is an effort to gain an understanding about a business. This chapter will address some of the basics that are usually considered in the process of financial analysis.

9.2 PURPOSE

Objectives

There is no one way to correctly answer the question of how to conduct an analysis of financial information. Without an appreciation for the reasons for the financial analysis, there can be no answer. There is a variety of possible reasons, some of which include:

- Equity investment
- Credit extension
- Supplier health
- Customer health
- Employer health
- Antitrust regulation
- Internal operations
- Competitor analysis
- Going concern judgment by auditors
- Damage valuation
- Valuation of acquisition candidate (E33, pp. 2–4).

This is just a partial list. The point is that the specific objective(s) for the analysis must be understood before a specific design for the analysis can be planned. Without a knowledge of the purpose for the analysis there is no appropriate technique or methodology that can be applied.

Benchmarks and Comparisons

Financial analysis often uses various figures and ratios. These numbers by themselves are close to meaningless—they must be compared to some other reference figures. These reference figures (for comparison purposes) usually fall into one of three categories:

1. Previous years' results
2. Industry norms
3. Budgets

There are potential benefits as well as pitfalls in using figures from any of these three groups. When using previous years' results there is no assurance that the firm under investigation was performing at an appropriate level during that time. Even a substantial improvement over a previous year's figures might still leave the firm in dire straits. The advantage of using a previous year's figures is that it is possible to see whether current figures have improved relative to previous years'.

Industry norms are probably the most widely used of the three categories. The benefit of using industry norms is the ability to compare performance to other firms in the same industry. But there is a problem with using industry norms. The companies reflected in the statistical information available do not always parallel the specific company under investigation. Information is sometimes presented at levels of aggregation for Standard Industrial Codes (SICs) that includes firms not in exactly the same industry as the firm under investigation.

The benefit of using industry norms is that you do get an outside reference of statistically compiled and objective information. Some of the sources for these statistics include the *Department of Commerce Financial Report, Robert Morse Associates Annual Statements Studies, Standard & Poor's Industry Surveys, The Almanac of Business and Industrial Financial Ratios,* and *Dun and Bradstreet's Industry Norms and Key Business Ratios.*

The third category of reference figures is budgets. Using budgets as benchmarks or targets can prove helpful in analysis. Sometimes the figures that a firm sets for itself are the most appropriate. A firm's ability to meet its own budgets and targets (if they are realistic and consistent with the firm's strategy) is a good indication of the firm's ability to conduct its business.

Often benchmarks are presented as absolutes. No one benchmark is appropriate or optimal for all firms. As early as 1919 a Detroit bank was using the benchmark of 2 to 1 for the current ratio (E14, p. 52). This is a good example of a benchmark that has effectively and inappropriately become an absolute. Benchmarks are guidelines, nothing more.

9.3 APPROACHES

The following discussion is an overview of the various approaches to financial analysis. There are seven different approaches that we will discuss. The first three are usually considered the traditional approaches to financial analysis.

1. Horizontal analysis
2. Vertical analysis
3. Ratio analysis
4. Discriminant (bankruptcy) analysis
5. Valuation
6. Organization and business functions analysis
7. Systems analysis

Horizontal Analysis

Horizontal analysis derives its name from the geometry of the comparisons that are made. There are two basic methods of horizontal analysis:

1. Comparative financial statements
2. Trend analysis

Comparative financial statements are obtained by presenting two (or more) years' figures for a firm side by side. These figures are then compared (year one to year two). The comparisons (increases or decreases) are made in terms of either dollar amounts or percentages. The plus or minus differences are presented in a column next to the element under examination.

The second approach to horizontal analysis, trend analysis, is very similar to the first except that the first year's figures in the comparison are set at 100%. Each year subsequent to this base year would be restated relative to the base year figure of 100% for comparison purposes. If the cash in year one was $120,000, the $120,000 would be designated as 100%. If the second year's figure for cash was $150,000, then that cash figure would be restated as 125%. By presenting the figures in this fashion it is easy to compare relative activity for as many periods as desired. The same process could also be used to track trends in financial ratios from year to year.

Vertical Analysis

Vertical analysis also takes its name from the geometry of the analysis. One tool for this type of analysis, called common size financial statements, compares figures within a single year rather than comparing multiple years as with horizontal analysis. It recasts the firm's various financial statements in terms of a key figure. In the case of the income statement, the total sales figure becomes 100%. For the balance sheet the total assets figure becomes 100%. All the other components of the financial statements are recast as a percentage of the appropriate key figure, either sales or total assets. In this fashion the financial statements become normalized and allow for easy comparison with other firms, even if they are not the exact same size. This is particularly helpful for comparison with industry statistics, for all the reporting agencies use common size financial statements in their presentations of data.

Ratio Analysis

Ratios are actually a special form of vertical analysis and are computed by taking various pairs of figures from the financial statements and showing the relationship of one to the other. There are an almost limitless number of ratios that can be created. In fact, the smart firm understands its business and creates ratios as appropriate. For example, when I worked with a retail clothing manufacturer some years ago, I used the ratio of gross margin, per department, per square foot of space allocated to that department. This ratio was examined for the previous few years' operations because the retail store in question was considering a major remodeling initiative and wanted to resize the various departments, allocating more or less space as appropriate. This ratio is not one that is tracked by the National Retail Merchant's Association, and therefore it is not one that most clothing retailers usually would consider using, but it was quite a helpful ratio for the firm given their specific needs.

There are a number of different categories into which the various ratios can be cast. One study sought to identify factors that jointly would yield the maximum information about a firm with a minimum number of computations. It resulted in the following:

- Return on investment
- Financial leverage
- Capital intensiveness
- Inventory intensiveness
- Receivables intensiveness
- Short-term liquidity
- Cash position (E 14, pp. 184–185)

The more traditional categories or groupings of ratios are usually:

- Liquidity
- Borrowing capacity
- Profitability
- Investors
- Cash flows

These are the grouping that will be used for the discussion that follows in Section 9.4.

Discriminant (Bankruptcy) Analysis

Another area of financial analysis is bankruptcy prediction. A multivariate model was built to allow researchers to study bankruptcies over a twenty-year period from 1946 to 1965. Popular ratios were used and grouped into five categories:

1. Liquidity
2. Profitability
3. Leverage
4. Solvency
5. Activity (E14, pp. 474)

One ratio from each category was chosen for a discriminant function. The five variables (ratios) were:

$X_1 =$ Working capital to total assets
$X_2 =$ Retained earnings to total assets
$X_3 =$ Earnings before interest and taxes to total assets
$X_4 =$ Market value of equity to book value of total debt
$X_5 =$ Sales to total assets (E14, p. 474).

These driver ratios were experimented with and after numerous computer runs a final discriminant function was chosen. It is equal to:

$$Z = 1.2X_1 + 1.4X_2 + 3.3X_3 + .6X_4 + 1.0X_5 \text{ (E14, pp. 474–475)}.$$

A Z score of 2.675 or less was determined to indicate a firm that either had failed or was soon to fail (E14, p. 482).

Valuation

Another method of financial analysis is valuation. A large body of research on the behavior of capital markets suggests that "stock market valuations of company shares are based on expectations of future cash flows, discounted for time and risk" (G32, p. 14).

Although there is a myriad of valuation techniques, they all are based on the fact that ultimately value is a function of anticipated future cash flows. The major weakness in using cash flows for valuation is the issue of the accuracy of the projected cash flows (G32, p. 30A). Cash flows are used by most venture capitalists in assessing the prospective activities of a potential candidate for acquisition.

Organization and Business Functions Analysis

One area that is often overlooked but may be very helpful in understanding a company is the analysis of the organization and how the business functions are performed. There is a lot of literature on the topic of operations reviews that provide guidelines and checklists to examine a company from this perspective. It is beyond the scope of this work to go into detail in this area but nonetheless organizational and functional fit need to be considered in any analysis. The discussions in Chapters 6 and 7 about different organizational structures and management styles is important and needs to be carefully considered in the context of achieving the goals that a firm has set for itself.

Systems Analysis

In Chapter 7, the systems approach, in which the elements under consideration are brought together and viewed as a composite whole rather than being fragmented into their constituent parts, was discussed. Not only is the approach useful in examining the systems and subsystems of an organization, it can also be particularly helpful in financial analysis and especially in the use of financial ratios. (The use of the systems approach in financial analysis was discussed in Chapters 2 and 7. An example of its use with ratios is return on investment and earnings per share, as can be seen in Figure 9-1 (E2, p. 243).

It should be noted that:

- The pre-interest margin, times turnover, equals return on assets to debt and equity
- Pre-interest margin, times turnover, times earnings-interest index, equals return on assets to equity
- Pre-interest margin, times turnover, times earnings interest index, times resource leverage, equals the return on stockholders' equity
- Pre-interest margin, times turnover, times earnings interest index, times resource leverage, times book value per share equals EPS. (E2, p. 243)

This process demonstrates the importance and interrelatedness of all of the components of the equation. They are all (income, revenues, assets, inter-

Figure 9-1   Earnings Per Share

EPS = Pre-Interest Margin	× Turnover	× Earnings Interest Index	× Resource Leverage	× Book-value Per Share
EPS = Net Income Plus Tax-Adjusted Interest / Revenues	× Revenues / Total Assets (average)	× Net income (After pref. Dividends) / Net income Plus Tax-Adjusted Interest	× Total Assets (average) / Stockholders' Equity (average)	× Stockholders' Equity (average) / Number of shares

(Adapted from E2, p. 243)

est, cost, equity, and shares outstanding) interrelated in the EPS and ROI calculations (E2, p. 243). Change any one of the constituents and the outcome changes.

This also serves to demonstrate the systems perspective in the use of financial ratios. Much of traditional financial analysis focuses on using various ratios in isolation. A more thorough approach for analysis capitalizes on the interrelatedness of the ratios, and the importance of viewing them only in the context of this interrelatedness. A practical example of this is included in the case study found in Section 10.6, Step 2, dealing with quantitative sensitivity analysis in the case study.

9.4   ELEMENTS AND RATIOS

The next few sections will present a number of the elements of financial statements and various ratios that are most commonly investigated in financial analysis. The ratios and elements are grouped into five categories:

1.   Liquidity
2.   Borrowing capacity
3.   Profitability
4.   Investors
5.   Cash flow

The following sections will briefly address these five categories. They will not present a detailed discussion of the ratios and the elements. A wide variety of texts are available for this purpose. The basic elements that will be presented can all be found in numerous texts. The important thing to remember is that the particular appropriate ratios or elements for consideration will vary from case to case. Only the specific objectives for the analysis can determine which are the correct items to be included.

Liquidity

The elements and ratios in this section deal with liquidity, which is the ability of a firm to "maintain its short-term debt paying ability" (E15, p. 178). These items are important because short-term survival indices not only provide a good indication of the liquidity of an organization, they also provide a sense of the organization's overall health. There are three categories under the topic of liquidity. They are:

1. Current assets, current liabilities and the operating cycle
2. Current assets compared with current liabilities
3. Other liquidity considerations (E15, pp. 177–214)

Current Assets, Current Liabilities, and the Operating Cycle
The elements and ratios in this category address the short-term debt paying ability of a firm. The primary focus is on the important components of current assets and current liabilities. The operating cycle is the time from the acquisition of inventory to the final realization of cash from the sale associated with the acquisition of that inventory. Its length has an impact on a number of elements in this category because it determines how quickly cash is received.

The receivables and inventory turnover ratios and days outstanding are standard computations that are informative. For prospective financials, if scheduled receipts are overly optimistic the analyst should carefully examine the resultant cash flows. Unrealistic planning in this area can easily jeopardize the very existence of the firm.

Another area that is often manipulated in prospective financials is the schedule of payments on payables. The figures presented are often unrealistic given a new or start-up firm. This is because creditors are usually particularly suspicious of new firms until they have an established credit history, and in fact often demand payment in cash on delivery or on very strict credit terms. A list of the elements and ratios most commonly used in the analysis of current assets, current liabilities, and the operating cycle is provided below.

1. Cash
2. Marketable securities
3. Receivables
4. Days' sales in receivables
5. Accounts receivable turnover
6. Accounts receivable turnover in days
7. Credit sales versus cash sales
8. Inventories
9. Inventory cost

10. Days' sales in inventory
11. Merchandise inventory turnover
12. Inventory turnover in days
13. Operating cycle computed
14. Prepayments
15. Other current assets
16. Current liabilities (E15, pp. 178–206)

Current Assets Compared With Current Liabilities
Two of the most common liquidity ratios are the current ratio and the acid test or quick ratio. These both compare various liquid assets with current liabilities and provide an important picture of the balance between the left and right sides of the balance sheets. The cash ratio follows this trend, and considers only cash, cash equivalents, and marketable securities in the numerator, which is then divided by current liabilities. It is a stricter liquidity test than even the acid test ratio. The four elements in this category are:

1. Working capital
2. Current ratio
3. Acid test ratio (quick ratio)
4. Cash ratio (E15, pp. 207–213)

Other Liquidity Considerations
There are a number of other liquidity considerations that are important:

1. Sales to working capital (working capital turnover)
2. Liquidity considerations not on the face of the statements (E15, pp. 214–215)

The sales-to-working-capital ratio, which is also known as the working capital turnover, is nothing more than sales divided by working capital. There are also a number of other liquidity considerations that are not necessarily obvious from the financial statements, that indicate *increased liquidity.* A number of these include:

• Unused credit lines
• Long-term assets that might be quickly convertible to cash

- Very good long-term debt position that might allow for the issuance of more debt or stock. (E15, p. 215)

Other factors can impinge on the liquidity of a firm. Some of these include:

- Discounted notes with full recourse against the firm
- Contingent liabilities
- Bank guarantees for notes for another company (E15, p. 215)

Each of these are examples of additional potential liabilities that should be disclosed in the financial statements. Many times they are not. The possibility of such potentially undisclosed liabilities must be considered when a firm's financial statements are analyzed. This is particularly important if the firm is small and does not have audited financials.

Borrowing Capacity

One of the most important considerations next to liquidity is the ability to borrow money when needed. The long-term debt-paying ability is referred to as borrowing capacity. There are three areas to be considered. They are:

1. Income statement considerations
2. Balance sheet considerations
3. Special items needing consideration

Two issues are important when considering borrowing capacity. They are the ability to repay debt and the ability to pay interest. This ability is usually viewed as coming from one of two sources, the income statement or the balance sheet (E15, p. 242). The following sections will deal with the ability of a firm to repay long-term debt and the interest associated with it.

Income Statement Considerations When Determining Long-Term Debt-Paying Ability
Three ratios are usually considered when examining income statements for long-term debt-paying ability. They are:

1. Times interest earned
2. Fixed charge coverage
3. Variations of fixed charge coverage (E15, pp. 243–248)

All three deal with a firm's ability to generate the funds needed to cover long-term debt.

Balance Sheet Considerations When Determining Long-Term Debt-Paying Ability
Four areas should be investigated when considering balance sheet capacity for long-term debt paying ability. They are:

1. Debt ratio
2. Debt/equity
3. Debt to tangible net worth
4. Other long-term debt-paying ability ratios (E15, pp. 253–256)

The focus is on debt to total assets, debt to equity, and debt to tangible net worth. Other long-term debt-paying ratios that might be considered are the current debt/net worth ratio, the fixed assets/equity ratio, and cash flow/total debt ratio (E15, p. 256).

Special Items That Influence A Firm's Long-Term Debt-Paying Ability
There are a number of other important considerations that can influence a firm's long-term debt-paying ability. They are:

1. Long-term assets versus long-term debt
2. Long-term leasing
3. Pension plans
4. Joint ventures
5. Contingencies (E15, pp. 256–269)

These items must be seriously considered, especially in the financial statements of unaudited companies in which many of these items may not be accurately presented.

Profitability

There are four topics that should be considered under the heading of profitability. They are:

1. Various profitability measures
2. Segment reports if available
3. Gains and losses that bypass the income statement
4. Interim reports

All of these are important means of analyzing the profitability of an organization, and will be briefly addressed in the sections that follow.

Profitability Measures
There are a number of measures to gauge profitability. They include:

1. Net profit margin
2. Total asset turnover
3. Return on assets
4. DuPont return on assets
5. Operating income margin
6. Operating asset turnover
7. Return on operating assets
8. Sales to fixed assets
9. Return on investment (ROI)
10. Return on total equity
11. Return on common equity
12. Gross profit margin (E15, pp. 296–309)

These represent the standard measures that most analysts and texts usually refer to in the course of an analysis of profitability. They provide insight into the income statement. Nonrecurring items should always be eliminated from the computation of any of these ratios.

Segment Reporting
If it is available and accurate, segment reporting can be quite helpful to the analyst. In fact, any and all breakdowns of revenues, costs, or allocation of costs can be very important (E15, p. 310). However, the analyst must be wary of just how these figures were developed. If it is safe to say that all financial information is suspect, it is even more correct to be skeptical of figures and allocations included in segment reports.

Gains And Losses That Bypass The Income Statement
There are a number of items that could substantially affect income and actually might bypass the formal income statement. They include:

- Prior period adjustments
- Unrealized losses from long-term equity investments
- Foreign currency translations (E15, p. 314)

These gains and losses have the potential to be very significant. Therefore, the statement of retained earnings must be examined carefully in order to ensure that all appropriate information is included in the analysis process.

Interim Reports
Interim reports can be very helpful. If they are available, they can provide additional information. In fact, any and all information that is available should be considered in the analysis. Any inconsistencies between the various sources of information and the promulgated financial statements should be reconciled and fully investigated and understood (E15, p. 316).

Investors

There are a number of elements and ratios that are usually important to the investor. They include:

1. Leverage
2. Earnings per common share
3. Price/earnings ratio
4. Percentage of earnings retained
5. Dividend payout
6. Dividend yield
7. Book value per share
8. Stock options
9. Stock appreciation rights (E15, pp. 340–356)

These are all considered by the investor. Both the cash flow available to an investor and the potential cash flow are important. The difference is what was available versus what was actually paid out in the form of dividends.

A number of these elements are used to compare the strategy as it was implemented to the strategy that was planned. Other important considerations are various stock options outstanding or pending and other potential appreciation rights that might substantially change the position of an investor relative to other investors in that firm.

Cash Flow

Cash flow is another important consideration. In fact, it should be considered the most important area on which to focus in financial analysis. The following list presents three important cash flow ratios:

1. Cash flow/current maturities of long-term debt and current notes payable
2. Cash flow/total debt
3. Cash flow per share (E15, pp. 415–416)

The ability to generate cash is the ability to generate value. The statement of cash flows assists the investor in reconciling the differences between the other financial statements. It contains many items that do not appear anywhere else and helps to explain the cash position. These considerations are especially important when cash is tight, as in the current economy, or in start-up situations.

9.5 COMPUTERS AND THE ANALYSIS PROCESS

Much of traditional financial analysis is not only fragmented, it also does not take full advantage of the capabilities of computers in the analysis process. It has become the norm for most prospective financial statements to be prepared on a microcomputer with the use of a spreadsheet package. It is absurd not to use the original computer model for the analysis process. When reviewing prospective financial information, the analyst should use the model from which the prospective financial information was generated. (This was discussed in Chapter 2 in the section on using the process model for the analysis of prospective financial information, and it will be demonstrated in the case study that follows in Chapter 10. The use of the computer assets in integrating all of the ratios in a holistic fashion, if so desired.

9.6   INTERPRETATION

The calculations discussed earlier are the easy part of the basic analysis process. The real challenge comes with the interpretation. Such interpretation requires that:

1.   The purpose of the analysis be clearly specified,
2.   The important concepts or principles underlying the financial statements on which the ratios are based be understood, and
3.   The economics and current conditions facing the business be factored into the interpretations (E33, p. 1)

The heart of interpretation rests with an appreciation for the goals and objectives for which the analysis is being conducted. There is no one ratio or element that can be considered in isolation. Rather, it is necessary to pursue the analysis of financial information as an art form, requiring a sensitivity to the wide range of considerations that vary from company to company, and from point in time to point in time. The interrelatedness of the various data must be of paramount importance in the mind of the analyst. The ultimate validity of financial analysis is totally a function of the purpose for the analysis.

9.7   SUMMARY

This chapter introduced some of the basic concepts of financial analysis. The discussion was by no means intended to be comprehensive. Rather, it provided an overview of some of the considerations, approaches, and tools that could be employed in the analysis of prospective financial statements.

The use of the systems perspective in the analysis process as it applies to prospective financial statements will be discussed and demonstrated in Chapter 10. Chapter 2 introduced the process model for the analysis of prospective financial statements. This model integrates the materials in all of the chapters in the form of a heuristic model for the analysis process. Chapter 10 serves to illustrate this model. The systems approach can and should be used in the analysis of historical financial information.

As discussed in this chapter, there is no ideal or optimal ratio or element, nor are there any ideal or optimal benchmarks that should be used. Rather it is necessary to look at the whole context of what you hope to achieve by the analysis and to apply those tools that most appropriately serve your needs in any particular case.

A Case Study—
The Application

CHAPTER OUTLINE

- Step 3 — Discriminant (Bankruptcy) Analysis
- Step 4 — Valuation

10.5 PHASE 3— STRATEGIC (TOTAL) RESOURCES ANALYSIS

10.6 PHASE 4— SENSITIVITY ANALYSIS
- Step 1 — Qualitative Sensitivity Analysis
- Step 2 — Quantitative Sensitivity Analysis
- Step 3 — Strategic (Total) Resources Sensitivity Analysis

10.7 PHASE 5— EVALUATION AND CONCLUSIONS

10.1 INTRODUCTION

This chapter presents a case study that demonstrates the principles and procedures developed in the text.

This case study presents the actual financial projections that were used in a financing proposal for a combination flour mill and pasta plant that was to be built in western Canada with the assistance of the local, provincial, and federal governments. The projections were submitted by a consortium to these agencies. The agencies in turn submitted the financial projections to a Big 6 accounting firm, which was to conduct an examination of the statements. The discussion that follows seeks to provide guidance on how to approach the analysis component of such an engagement using the process model presented in Chapter 2. The process model is not limited in use only to AICPA-sanctioned engagements but is more general in application, and can be used by practitioners in the analysis of virtually any prospective financial statements or information.

Financial assistance from the various levels of government was predicated on two important issues: first, the vast wheat-producing capabilities of the western provinces; and second, the high level of unemployment in the region. It was felt that a locally situated plant would be able to take advantage of these conditions.

The discussion of the case study will draw together many of the points presented in the previous sections of this text, and show how they might be applied in a specific situation. It should be noted that not every single point discussed in the previous sections will be incorporated into the analysis of this case study. Rather, the analysis will emphasize the general approach that needs to be taken in applying the various techniques discussed in an actual situation.

The analysis will be conducted using documents, industry statistics, and information available as of August 1990. We will assume that this is when the analysis takes place.

10.2   THE CASE STUDY

Overview

As already discussed, the prospective financial statements in the case study were originally presented in order to secure financial assistance from the federal, provincial, and local governments in western Canada for a combination flour mill and pasta plant project. The case that we are looking at is called the Base Case. It addresses only the first phase of a potential three-phase project. The projections cover the years 1990 to 2000, and over nine full years of operations. The projections were presented to the federal government in August 1990. It is interesting to note that in fact the plan, as reflected in the projections, was technically not going to be achievable from the onset. This is because the funds could not be released in time for the start-up date, which the model set as September 1, 1990.

This is an important point. The projections were intended as a discussion document to be used in negotiations to secure financing support from the various levels of government. This is a common use of many financial projections. The particulars presented within a model often represent varying degrees of importance to the negotiators. In this case the negotiations were being carried on in the hope of obtaining subsidies from the local, provincial, and federal governments. Additionally, the consortium presenting the projections was interested in securing some participation from the local wheat producers in the form of an equity contribution. They hoped to obtain the following (in Canadian dollars): federal government loans of $9.75 million, provincial farm bonds of $6 million, and equity from the local wheat growers of $6.25 million. The federal government loan would be for 15 years at 0% interest, with repayments of the principal at $650,000 a year to be initiated after the third full year of operation. The farm bonds, to be provided by the local province, would be at 0% interest with no repayments. Basically this would be a gift of $6 million. The $6 million claim would be left on the books in case of bankruptcy at some time in the future, but effectively it was to be a 0% interest perpetual loan for as long as operations continued. The $6.25 million in equity was assumed to be contributed from local farm and wheat cooperatives interested in taking advantage of a new, readily available market for their wheat.

It is important to understand the context in which the projections were presented and in particular the specific purpose that was stipulated for its limited use. These sources of the funds would provide $22 million of the $50 million Phase I financing needed for the project. A loan structure was pursued in lieu of outright grants, although the model was designed to handle either approach. The possibility of using grants had been discussed for a period of about six months, but it was finally agreed to structure the subsidies in the form of provincial and federal loans.

There are many interesting aspects to the decision whether or not to proceed with this project. There were economic considerations (local, national, and international) that came into play. Additionally, the political implications played a prime role in the final decision. This provides a good example just how the external environment (governments) can radically affect a business venture.

Components of the Financial Model

A copy of the LOTUS 1–2–3 (V2.01) model is included with the text. The diskette included contains a file called *"Model."* The model was developed on Lotus 1–2–3 using the model format for prospective financial statements proposed in Chapter 8. A printout of the model, as submitted to the various participants for review, is included as Appendix A.

The printout included in Appendix A spans 13 pages, with about a thousand rows in the spreadsheet. Line numbers are listed along the left margin of the pages of the printout. For reference purposes, we will refer to a specific line number, and then move across horizontally on the designated line to an appropriate column. "L" will be used as the notation for a line. For example, the assumptions section starts on L4.

The LOTUS 1–2–3 model has five major sections. They are: assumptions; P&Ls (income statements); cash flows; balance sheets; and proofs. The printout contained in Appendix A shows the first four of these sections. The assumptions section runs from L4 to L793. It is ten pages long. The P&Ls run from L796 to L857, the cash flows from L857 to 921, and the balance sheets from L921 to L998.

A more detailed discussion of the particulars of the model will be pursued in the quantitative analysis section of this chapter. It is interesting to note the amount of detail presented in the model itself. The important operating statistics, investment required, and sources of financing are included on the first page of the model from L8 to L75. Various depreciation schedules and start-up costs are included along with details of the revenue (including tonnes sold, the various prices per tonne, and total revenues generated) for the years 1990 to 2000 (L97 to L252). The various costs are then detailed. The last part of the assumptions section presents loan amortization schedules for the various forms of debt.

10.3   PHASE 1—QUALITATIVE ANALYSIS

Before starting Phase 1, it is assumed that the practitioner already has a solid overview of the firm and its operations as discussed in section 10.2.

Phase 1 is concerned with an understanding of those important qualitative issues that are often overlooked by practitioners. The seven steps in Phase 1 include:

1.   Establish the general context
     - Communication issues
     - Accounting information
2.   Review the strategic plan
3.   Examine the business plan
     - Relationship to the strategic plan
     - Organization and provision for business functions
4.   Define and examine the systems and their interrelationships
5.   Determine the scope of the examination
6.   Examine the assumptions
7.   Review the preparation and presentation

Step 1—Establish the General Context

Establishing the general context focuses on providing an understanding of the basic foundation (communications) and the basic framework (accounting) for the analysis as discussed in Chapters 3 and 4.

Communication Issues
As discussed in Chapter 3, communication problems fall into a number of categories. First is the realization that the prospective financial statements themselves are a form of communication. Second is the need to accom-

modate the communication function within the systems reflected in the projections. As was already mentioned concerning the accounting systems, minimum detailed plans were developed and submitted with the projections. Additional detailed plans would be necessary if in fact there was going to be a successful implementation of the prospective financial statements as presented.

The first of the two communications issues presented is very important in that it involves the intentions of both the generators and the users of the prospective financial information. Both parties had an interest in achieving certain goals. It is apparent with this specific project that the goals of the parties involved are multifaceted. They include not only economic but also political considerations. This can present some problems, because the concerned parties might be very intent on making this project happen when in reality there might be some real question about its viability.

This often happens in business. The many savings and loan and bank failures in the United States clearly demonstrates this. Many of the business deals that we hear about on the news were bound to proceed, even before any projections or forecasts were prepared. Therefore, the practitioner might be confronted with some real ethical challenges. Whoever is employing the analyst is not necessarily going to be very pleased to hear that the deal does not make economic sense, when all the parties involved on both sides of the negotiating table are interested in making it happen. However, the analyst has a responsibility to maintain an objective, third-party stance and give a professional opinion consistent with the facts as seen, whether or not he or she is formally employed by the company presenting the projections.

In this particular case study, as we go through the various stages of the analysis process it is going to be important to be sensitive to these types of issues.

Accounting Information
The general context as it relates to accounting information is relatively straightforward. The overall presentation reflects GAAP. This is seen through an examination of the assumptions as presented in the first ten pages of the printout. The detailed schedules of depreciation show the appropriate rates for the jurisdiction. The prospective financial information reflects the accrual method of accounting as seen in the differences between cash basis and income statement amounts. The basic assumptions of GAAP as well as the basic principles, all appear to have been consistently followed.

Upon examining the conceptual framework, it appears that the objectives of financial statements, which are to assist with investment decisions, cash flow prospects, and enterprise resources, all appear to be addressed with the projections.

The qualitative characteristics of accounting numbers—in particular, reliability and relevance—need to be kept in mind throughout the whole process. Many analysis techniques focus on the reliability of information, but relevance is equally important. The primary objective of the presentation of the projections, which was to secure loan and investment funds, has already been discussed. Given this context, the generators and users of the projections have a common basis for establishing relevance. But it is possible that the analyst can be too quick to accommodate the immediate needs of both the generator and the specified users of the information.

The analyst has another responsibility, and that is to assume a global perspective, and not only to consider those elements that are most relevant to the immediate perceived needs and ends of the immediate parties involved, but also to provide an opinion about the projections taken as a whole.

The issues of reliability and relevance will continue to be an important theme throughout the rest of the analysis process.

Thus far we have discussed accounting information from the perspective of the information at hand, but the accounting systems that will accommodate the needs of the firm described in the projections are also important. What parts of the overall operational systems have been structured to address this important need within the environment? The projections were submitted with a minimum of additional information, most of which was marketing-oriented. Many details, such as descriptions of the accounting and information systems, were not addressed except for their recognition as several line items within the assumptions section of the model itself. What in fact the projections represent is the skeleton of a general plan, but additional detailed planning at all levels would be required before final implementation or start-up.

Step 2—Review the Strategic Plan

The actual combined strategic and business plan that was presented primarily focused on marketing analyses and the growth of the pasta market. It included the prospective financial statements presented in Appendix A. This is not uncommon. It is clear from the materials within the plan that the consortium presenting it was not made up of the same people who would be responsible for the day-to-day operations. Instead, the consortium members planned to hire professional managers to oversee the operations of the plant. This presented some problems, in that the analyst could not know who actually would be overseeing operations. The environmental analysis and diagnosis phase of the strategic planning process was quite adequately performed. There was a market for the product and it would continue to grow at a substantial rate. A number of deals were simultaneously being negotiated with various U.S. companies to contract for a substantial part of the output of the plant on a regular basis.

A marketing study for the project was conducted by a Big 6 accounting firm. It was used to amply support the marketing assumptions used in the strategic plan.

The strategic advantage analysis and diagnosis primarily consisted of documenting and understanding the capabilities of various specific plant configurations that were being considered. The primary decision was whether to have a plant that was dedicated entirely to winter wheat or one that might be able to process a variety of different types of wheats. The problem with using a swing configuration is that the processing yields are lower than those from a plant dedicated entirely to one type of wheat.

The other components of the strategic plan were only minimally addressed. A decision was made to pursue the packaging and selling of this specific proposal by the business consortium in order to obtain some form of public subsidy. Details of implementation, including leadership, policy, and organizational implementation, were barely covered in the plan. These decisions would be left to the discretion of the professionals who ultimately would be hired to run the plant.

Strategic choice primarily focused on the different possible technical configurations for manufacturing pasta. A number of alternative types of plants were examined. One theoretical configuration, already mentioned, consisted of a plant that was entirely dedicated to the processing of hard (winter) wheat. Another configuration was the swing plant arrangement that would allow different types of wheat to be processed. The tradeoff between the two was that the 100% winter wheat configuration plant would provide greater processing yields, whereas a swing plant would allow for alternative plant use if demand softened for pasta. Another option considered was subcontracting the milling process to other existing facilities and then using processed flour for the pasta. The problem with this alternative was that the processing costs were much more expensive than when using the other configurations. This alternative also potentially exposed the pasta plant to prices being raised and lowered by an outside company.

Step 3—Examine the Business Plan

Relationship to the Strategic Plan
The plan as developed and submitted was a combination strategic and business plan. The relationship between the business and the strategic plan primarily involved tying specific marketing targets developed in the strategic overview into the production figures presented in the projections. The specific goals articulated within the strategic plan were limited to sales targets that would allow the full utilization of the facilities proposed within the projections. Due to the simplicity of the strategic plan and because this was a start-up situation, there was a relatively high degree of consistency between the strategic plan and the detailed business plan as reflected within the projections.

The operating plans reflected appropriate costs to provide for the manufacturing and selling of the pasta, given the projected operating levels required to support the strategic plan.

Organization and Provision for Business Functions
As discussed earlier, detailed implementation was only lightly touched on in the financial model and business plan. This is an all-too-common limitation of many business plans. The market analysis provided within the strategic plan was reflected in the recognition of an appropriate level for demand, but detailed marketing and sales plans were not developed.

The operating plans basically followed the operating specifications as outlined in the technical information provided by the manufacturers of the milling and pasta equipment. A dedicated plant configuration was chosen. It was assumed that the manufacturer's statistics (L8 to L20) would be realizable and that the personnel requirements (L400 to L440) as specified in the manufacturer's materials would provide the staffing necessary to properly run the plant.

A number of other personnel were added beyond the basic manufacturing/operating requirements, including support and management personnel. These were reflected within the staffing details (L400 to L440) in the assumptions section of the projections.

The finance function was addressed by providing for the hiring of a CFO and a controller in the prospective financial statements (L543 to L576). Again this was basically limited to line items in the assumptions section of the projections. The specifics about how the function would be organized and carried out were not addressed.

A common element in all of the above provisions for the business functions is that specific personnel were not identified to fill these requirements. It was assumed that people could be hired at the salary amounts stipulated within the plan (L443 to L476 and L580 to L614) to perform these functions appropriately and that they would be able to achieve the operating results outlined within the projections.

This presents an interesting challenge for the analyst in that most business people agree that the success of any business hinges on the quality of the people involved. The plan assumed that the human resources required could be acquired for the amounts assumed in the projections. The labor market was soft at the time the projections were developed.

This assumption is a deficiency in many projections, which often discount one of the more important indicators for success, the caliber of management and staff.

Step 4—Define and Examine the Systems and Their Interrelationships

As with many other business functions, the major systems were not clearly identified or articulated within the business plan. As discussed in the previous sections, the detailed functions were addressed minimally, as were the interrelationships among the various functions.

The relationship of the firm to its external environment was pursued. The primary external environments that the firm interfaced with included the political, the national economic, the international economic, and the agricultural. The plans focused on the positioning of the pasta plant within these particular external environments and markets.

As already mentioned, the discussion of the internal operating and control systems was minimal. It was assumed that the resources provided within the business plan would be adequate to ensure the proper interfacing of all of the business functions. Another deficiency of the plans is their failure to address these important components of success. This is not uncommon. The question is always whether adequate resources have been provided in the projections to ensure the successful achievement of the goals outlined in the projections.

This deficiency demonstrates a lot about the creators of the projections. The projections were generated by a consortium looking to put together a business deal, not by the people who ultimately would have to ensure the operating success of the business on a day-to-day basis. The failure to address these important considerations within the plan clearly demonstrates this, and should be cause for some concern on the part of the analyst.

Step 5—Determine the Scope of the Examination

The procedures to determine the scope of the examination outlined in Chapter 5 require an overall knowledge of the entity's business. This was partially obtained through discussions with members of the consortium. There was no historical information for this particular firm because it was a proposed start-up. Therefore, the projections were based on the technical and industry data available.

A review of the process used in preparing the prospective financial statements showed a number of things. The statements appeared to be very adequately documented, and it seemed that most of the significant factors had been included in the assumptions. The assumptions themselves seemed to proceed logically from well-documented sources. The vast majority were third-party sources that were able to provide independent verification. A copy of the model itself was obtained and this allowed for a careful examination of the techniques that were used in the preparation of the prospective financial statements.

The parties involved in the development of the projections were very qualified and had a good degree of experience with business start-ups, financial projections, and presentations of financing proposals.

The biggest problem in limiting the scope would be with the fact that this was a start-up, with no previous history to compare to the projected results.

Step 6—Examine the Assumptions

The assumptions appeared to be relatively well documented. However, it is important not to confuse the documentation of the assumptions with the reasonableness of the assumptions. The distinction is not always self-evident. The availability of third-party support for most of the assumptions was quite helpful, but it had some important limitations. While it is possible to spread all the eight hundred odd parts that go into a motorcycle on the floor in a garage, even if all the parts work and they are all there, until they are put together they are just a jumble of parts. So too with businesses. A set of parts does not a business make. There is a danger in not using a systems approach in the analysis of assumptions. The end result may be a series of disjointed, totally appropriate parts that may never come together as a successful operating whole. The fragmented approach has been used for years in much of financial analysis, and it is one of the deficiencies that needs to be addressed in future methodologies for analysis.

The majority of the third-party support in this case was in fact from people with very solid professional standing. The assumptions and technical and engineering specifications themselves were examined in two fashions. The first was through discussions with customers who had used the configurations and systems specified in the technical information provided by the equipment suppliers. A number of users of the equipment were contacted and they were quite satisfied that the technical requirements stipulated were appropriate. The technical information from the various equipment suppliers was compared to each other and they were quite similar. This process provided additional comfort with the figures and the technical information presented in the assumptions section of the financial projections.

Step 7—Review the Preparation and Presentation

Some of the steps outlined under this topic in Chapter 5 also fit into the next section on quantitative analysis. For the sake of this discussion we will presently focus only on those elements that are usually considered qualitative in nature.

It was confirmed that the assumptions listed were in fact those assumptions that were used in driving the financial projections. This was primarily done by examining the model itself, clearly demonstrating the functional links between the assumptions and the projected figures.

The presentation used for the prospective financial statements was in conformity with guidelines presented in the *Guide for Prospective Financial Information* (F10). The projections were presented in an acceptable format. The accounting principles used were all consistent with GAAP. A full set of statements of income, cash flows, and balance sheets were presented for all the years for the projections, and the minimum presentation guidelines were met (F10, p. 36) except for a detail of significant accounting policies, which could be derived from the projections themselves.

A summary of the significant accounting policies used in the preparation of the prospective statements was not included as a separate schedule, because it was assumed that these were adequately articulated within the assumptions section of the financial projection. In general, this assumption seemed to be quite adequate except for disclosure of the fact that the inventories were stated at the lower-of-cost or market, and that inventory cost was determined by the last-in, first-out method.

10.4   PHASE 2—QUANTITATIVE ANALYSIS

Phase 2 is concerned with understanding the quantitative issues that affect the analysis. The four steps in Phase 2 include:

1.   Familiarization with and review of model
2.   Traditional financial analysis
     - Determine benchmarks and targets
     - Choose approaches and ratios
     - Conduct the analysis
3.   Discriminant (bankruptcy) analysis
4.   Valuation

Step 1—Familiarization With and Review of Model

Section 10.2, introducing the case study, presented an overview of the model. A printout of the model is included as Appendix A. The model is divided into five major sections:

1.   Assumptions
2.   Income statements
3.   Cash flows
4.   Balance sheets
5.   Proofs

Load the Lotus file (Release 2.01) entitled "Model. WK1" from the diskette included with the book. A quick review of Section 10.2 will help in understanding the format of the prospective financial statements. When the computer model (Lotus template) is loaded you can see additional computations beyond the four sections that are presented in Appendix A. A series of proofs to ensure mathematical accuracy are included just after the balance sheets. These are included to guarantee that even after the model has been set up and changes have been made it will not be possible for anyone to accidently change some of the formatting or formulas to introduce arithmetical errors. The proofs section includes obvious checks such asassets equal liabilities plus ownership equity. Additionally, all of the schedules in the various sections of the model are all footed and cross-footed—that is, totals are computed both horizontally and vertically. These amounts are then subtracted one from another. The resultant remainder should always be equal to zero. All of these "0" computations appear in columns to the right of each of the schedules. The total of all of these remainders from Row 1 through the last row of the model are then added together, and this sum should also total to zero, assuming that no errors exist in the model. This final "0" sum is also included in the proofs section of the model.

It should be noted that if loan covenants must be kept, the proofs section is the appropriate place to track them dynamically, period to period.

The first section of the model, the assumptions, starts at line L4 and extends through L793. Some elements of the assumptions have already been discussed in Section 10.2, which introduces the case study. The first part of the assumptions section focuses on important operating statistics, financial requirements, and the sources of financing (L8 to L78). The second section, starting at L97, deals with depreciation using the standard (Canadian) schedules for the various classes of equipment outlined. The soft costs and start-up costs were presented starting at L156. Revenues start at L175. It should be noted that the revenues were in Canadian dollars for each market. Revenues were detailed by tonnes sold and price per tonne, and these two amounts were then multiplied together to get the total revenue for a specific year and market.

An interesting point that should be made is the international nature of the projections. Most of the information and financial data had to be translated from various currencies and different standards for engineering information. For example, the pasta machines were to be purchased from a manufacturer in Italy, and paid for in lira. Current international exchange rates were used to translate these figures into Canadian dollars.

The same challenge existed for much of the operating information, some of which used the English, and some the metric system. For example, the operating statistics were in metric tones (tonnes), which is equal to 2204.62 lbs. Additionally, in the revenue section an inflation factor of 5% (L211) is included to reflect the anticipated increase in revenue per tonne over the course of the projections. L255 presents the accounts receivable aging schedule. These figures realistically represent expected results.

Detailed assumptions concerning costs start on L265. The ending raw material inventory was determined to be at 1/12 or 8.33% of the wheat required for production. The finished goods inventory was established at 2% of sales. Both of the inventory amounts were computed under the LIFO method. Line 284 presents the tonnes of wheat required for production, which always exceeds the tonnes of pasta produced (L280). The reason for this is the grain yields which will be found from L11 to L18. These yields reflect the production of byproducts not usable for producing pasta. Processing yields (L20) are also reflected in these figures. The yields were established using the engineering specifications provided by the manufacturer. Assuming a winter wheat (Durum) processing configuration the variable costs of a tonne of pasta manufactured start on L302. The various components of unit production costs were confirmed from engineering specifications and discussions with various utilities and suppliers.

The details for the total variable production costs begin on L333. L368 begins the presentation for the variable costs of goods sold. The difference between the two totals (L362 and L397) is the build-up or draw-down of inventories. The various schedules dealing with direct labor begin on L402. The schedule for the number of production personnel needed begins on L406, with the schedule starting on L443 identifying the individual compensation for each labor category. Notice that L446 also includes a 5% inflation increment, which is reflected in the various figures in the compensation schedule. L480 presents the schedule for total direct labor dollars. L519 details the various components of overhead.

L539 begins the sales, general and administrative salaries, and repeats the format used for the direct labor, including the number of personnel needed to staff various positions. A schedule for total sales and general and administrative (SG&A) expenses begins on L654 and includes the figures for the total SG&A labor dollars from the previous schedule (L650) as a component of this SG&A schedule on L661.

An accounts payable aging schedule is presented on L680. This schedule includes amounts for raw material inventory buildup, sales, general and administrative expenses, direct labor, overhead costs, variable production costs, and various soft and start-up costs.

The schedule of the various loans starts on L719. These figures tie into the financing schedule starting on L60. Various equity contributions are detailed on L786. L793 is the last line in the assumptions section of the projections.

The income statements start on L796, the cash flows on L857, and the balance sheets on L921.

A test of the arithmetical accuracy of the computations was made starting with the first line of the model. The initial testing was done using the computer printout (Appendix A). All the various figures tested were found to be accurate. Basic arithmetical accuracy and consistency was examined. For example, in the revenue section starting on L175, the various tonnes sold (L184) were manually multiplied by the prices per tonne sold (L208) to arrive at the total revenue figures by category (L230). Similar basic computations were repeated for all of the various schedules and sections on the printout of the prospective financial statements.

After using the printout for the initial check of arithmetical accuracy, the financial model was loaded into the computer and a detailed examination of the various formulas used within the model was undertaken. First basic clerical tests were conducted. The assumptions section was checked. All its schedules were algebraically accurate and consistent. The income statements were then examined. This was primarily done by confirming that the correct components from the assumptions section were entered into the appropriate lines of the income statements (L796).

After tracing the figures in the income statements line by line, the income statements themselves were checked for mathematical accuracy. The information from the income statements and the assumptions sections drives the schedule of cash flows. The various components of the statements of cash flows were traced back to their sources. The statements of cash flows were then checked for mathematical accuracy.

The balance sheets are driven by the previous three sections of the model: the assumptions, the income statements, and the cash flows. The components of the balance sheets and the balance sheets themselves also were checked for arithmetical accuracy.

The general logic of the model flows from top to bottom and from left to right. Although it is not technically necessary to create models this way on most spreadsheets today, it is the only sensible way to conveniently and logically organize the great volumes of data usually contained in a spreadsheet. It also makes examining the logic of the model a lot easier. With many models the flow of logic is actually chaotic. The logical flow of this model indicates a relatively sophisticated level of understanding of modeling and handling of financial information on the part of the preparer.

It should be noted that the model contains a circular reference. The reason for this was to develop a greater degree of accuracy. The credit line amounts required are ultimately a function of the total interest that has to be paid for a period. But simultaneously the total interest paid is a function of the credit line draw outstanding for the period. Making two cells mutually dependent on each other creates a circular reference. This was intentionally done in order to provide greater accuracy. Multiple iterations of the number of recalculations that the spreadsheet conducts at each recalculation were selected from the Lotus menu, thereby providing progressively more accurate "estimates" of the figures involved and limiting any error as a consequence of using this technique to under $1.

A more in-depth examination of the model was then undertaken. The details of the various components of the model were examined. The computations were then followed through for consistency with the conceptual intent of the model, as opposed to just testing for arithmetical accuracy.

The question of generalizability presents a minor problem. The model was set up, breaking costs into fixed and variable components. But not all costs vary functionally with activity levels. This is seen in the section for direct labor (L402). The number of people needed to staff the various positions is determined based on an assumed single generally appropriate level of activity, and then that number is input manually. Therefore, regardless of the level of activity within the model, these costs do not vary, but are fixed.

After checking for arithmetical and conceptual consistency and accuracy, the next step was to conduct a more detailed examination of the model itself to better understand the functional relationships among its various components. The assumptions, as outlined within the assumptions section, do drive the various financial statements. Most of the relationships among the various major elements of the model were established functionally. This means that if almost any input item was changed, the effects of that change would be automatically and accurately reflected throughout every line of the entire model, including all of the financial statements. This mathematical approach (as opposed to an arithmetical one) to modeling is important for permitting changes in input without having to rework the entire model. A model can be arithmetically accurate and yet lack the ability to mathematically respond appropriately to changes.

Overall, it appears that the model was prepared with a great degree of conceptual, mathematical, and arithmetical consistency, accuracy, and responsiveness. The flow of logic used reveals a relatively sophisticated approach to modeling and a very solid understanding of accounting principles and concepts on the part of the preparer.

The analysis process elicited a good degree of confidence in the methods used in developing the model and extrapolating, led to a similar degree of confidence with the methods used in developing the financial projections. Furthermore, it was noted that the modeling process used very detailed schedules that clearly articulated the levels of activity and costs or revenues associated with those activities on a per unit basis, as well as providing totals for each sub-category. Finally, a total cost or revenue figure for the total activity in all of the subcategories was usually presented. This micro-approach is indicative of a greater degree of attention to detail than is often used in the preparation of financial projections and in the articulation of the assumptions underlying them. It also indicates a degree of sophistication and knowledge on the part of the preparer of the projections. Often projections use very general figures. For example, cost of goods sold might be stated at 76% of sales. This approach ignores the problems encountered by using what effectively is a variable percentage to cover costs that in fact are not purely variable but include both fixed and variable components. The macro approach is acceptable for first-cut feasibility studies, but should be avoided in the development of detailed business plans. The fact that the model included this level of detail and sophistication in its development lends a greater degree of comfort with the overall model, and with the preparation of the projections generated.

Step 2—Traditional Financial Analysis

Determine Benchmarks and Targets

There is a question about whether the various benchmarks and targets that will be used should be determined before or after the appropriate ratios are chosen. In reality, these two steps are done simultaneously. If the industry or company has very peculiar characteristics that require the creation of special ratios or approaches for the analysis, then there is no question that the choice of the approaches and ratios must precede the determination of benchmarks.

It is often advisable to search available data bases—for example, *Dun & Bradstreet, Robert Morse Associates,* or *The Almanac of Business and Industrial Financial Ratios*—because the various services carry different standard industrial codes. It is also advisable to check which of the services, if any, carries the industry ratios pertinent to the particular company under examination. For example of these three services only Dun & Bradstreet carried the statistics for the Standard Industrial Code 2098, Macaroni and Spaghetti producer.

It should also be noted that in fact the facility under examination did not produce just pasta, but instead was a combination pasta plant and flour mill. The statistics for flour and other grain mill products (SIC 2041) were also found in Dun & Bradstreet. The statistics for the two SICs were relatively similar in most respects. It was decided to use the SIC 2098 figures (for macaroni and spaghetti) because they address the primary value added within the combined plant.

Additionally, it was necessary to choose a range for capitalization and discount rates. The median return on equity for SIC 2098 was 12% (E13, p. 41). The median return on equity for SIC 2041 was 9.4% (E13, p. 36).

It has been noted that the average rate of return on capital should be about 6 to 8 percent "over the return long-term government bond holders received" (A9, p. 81).

Long-term government bonds as of the date of analysis in July of 1990 (30-year Treasury bond yield) received 8.4 percent. This, when added to the 6 percent premium, yields a cost of capital of about 14.4 percent (E5, p. 177). The range for cost of capital was established at between 10 to 14 percent.

Choose Approaches and Ratios
The ratios that were chosen for analysis included:

- Current ratio
- Quick ratio
- Gross profit margin
- Net profit margin
- A/R turnover in days
- Sales to inventory
- Return on assets
- Return on common equity

These ratios, all provided in Dun & Bradstreet, give a good overview of profitability and liquidity for the financial projections. They also provide an appropriate picture of the important information needed to assess the concern in question. The ratios were computed consistent with the formats stipulated in the beginning of Dun & Bradstreet.

Conduct the Analysis
This part of the financial analysis was performed using the actual spreadsheet model, and it is included here as *Appendix B*. The traditional financial analysis appears from L1035 to L1087. The eight ratios listed above were computed for the years 1990 to 2000. Because the year 1990 was a start-up year and 1991 was assumed to include only three months of actual operations, the analysis section starting on L1063 excluded these two years. After completing the computations of the ratios for those years (L1039), an analysis of the ratios was conducted (L1063 to L1083). For each set of ratios from 1992 to 2000 the average of the ratios was computed along with the maximum and the minimum for each. Additionally the Dun & Bradstreet figures for SIC 2098 were included in the model. Fi-

nally, a variance from the average figures was computed. The minimum amounts for the years under investigation compared relatively favorably to the Dun & Bradstreet figures. Almost all of the minimum figures appeared in the year 1992, which was the first full year of operation. Focusing on the variances from average (the arithmetical setup was such that any plus figure implied a favorable variance and any negative figure implied an unfavorable variance) in rows L1063 to L1083 for the various ratios, all were found in fact to be positive except for the accounts receivable turnover. This is because the model assumed a 30-day collection period, when in fact the collection period within Dun & Bradstreet for SIC 2098 was 23 days, hence the negative variance. Even though it appears as a negative variance there is in fact a positive aspect, in that a 30-day period assumes that collections will be slower than the industry norm. This provides a worse cash flow situation in the projected financial statements than average, and thereby yields more conservative results.

On the surface, the ratios within the analysis all seemed to be relatively favorable. It should be noted that for the computation of the ratios for the years 1990 and 1991 we find a few odd results. This is because the company was not under full operation and the computation of the ratios would be expected to yield in some distortions, and thus why these two years were excluded from the average figures used in the analysis section.

Step 3—Discriminant (Bankruptcy) Analysis

The bankruptcy analysis was conducted from L1092 to L1124. The Z factor, discussed in Section 9.3—Discriminant (Bankruptcy) Analysis, was computed in two ways. The model and the projections did not reflect any dividend payouts. Therefore, the financial statements were adjusted under the first set of computations (L1103 to L1115). It was assumed that the dividend payout ratio was 80 percent (which is high for the industry). A capitalization rate of 12 percent was assumed, because the stocks were not publicly traded. This provided the means of assigning a market value, which is required in component X4 (see Chapter 9 on bankruptcy analysis). Additionally, the Z factor was computed a second time without any adjustments (L1118 to L1123). The difference between the two computations of Z factors was relatively negligible in the early years and grew in the latter years of the projections. An average Z factor was computed (L1121) for the years 1992 to 2000. This average figure was computed for the Z factor with the elements unadjusted for the hypothetical payout of dividends. A Z factor of under 2.675 usually indicates a troubled firm (see

Chapter 9). The figure that was arrived at for the average value of Z was 4.05. It should be noted that in the first two years of full operations (1992 and 1993) the Z factor was only 1.37 and 2.26, below the cutoff of 2.675. A possible reason for this was that four of the five factors used are weighted heavily toward the influence of total assets, for it is the denominator of four of the five ratios in the discriminant function. The projections under analysis were a base case scenario, assuming that only the first phase of a three-phase project (L38 to L78) would be pursued. In fact the full, three-phase project assumed $110 million of capital investment. The first phase only included $50 million (L60 to L75). Technically, only Phase I was being examined. Moreover, it was being examined as if only Phase I would ever be implemented. Some of the capital costs in the initial $50 million investment included in Phase I are actually intentionally higher than would be needed if only Phase I were going to be pursued. These extra costs allow for the easy expansion of the plant in Phases II and III. Although the actual three-phase project when completed would cost approximately $110 million, the output would be approximately three times greater than the Phase I output, or 90,000 metric tons versus 30,000 metric tons.

The bankruptcy analysis has appropriately identified some potential problems in the early years of the project. This is an important point because the operations are heavy in assets, given the relative amount of sales that are being generated. But the return on assets (L1057) was acceptable relative to other firms in the industry (L1081). Given the above explanation, this was not considered to present a major problem.

Step 4—Valuation

Two valuations were conducted (L1125–L1161). One computed the future value, the other the present value of the project. Three different figures for the cost of capital were used: 10 percent, 12 percent, and 14 percent. A separate value was computed for each rate. The range of rates was then taken and used as an indicator for both the future and the present value computations. The average future value of $211,489,819 (L1140) in the year 2000 does not seem overly impressive given the Phase I cost of $50 million, but $22 million would effectively come from subsidies. Venture capitalists would be looking for a compound return of about 45 percent to 60 percent a year (C28, p. 10), which would mean they would be expecting a minimum value of about six times their initial investment in five years and about 41 times their initial investment in ten years. The private (nonfarmer) equity contributed was $10 million. The compound return on this $10 million raised to $211 million in ten years is 36.7 percent per year, which does not reflect a return on or of the wheat growers' equity of $6.25 million. The net rate of return, when including the wheat growers' equity, would be too low for most venture capitalists. If the project were to be sold, it would probably be another consortium that was interested in these returns.

The reason potential buyers are being discussed is that the value of any business is ultimately no more than what a willing and able buyer would pay for it. This determines the real value of a business.

Looking at this from the present value perspective, (again assuming an initial investment of $10 million) the average present value is 68,472,451 (L1157). This is a $58,478,819 profit on a $10 million investment in ten years, without reflecting any amounts due to the wheat growers. These values are acceptable, assuming a substantial amount in government subsidies. Without the subsidies again there is a real question as to whether the business, in and of itself, would be profitable enough to interest most investors. But it is important to remember that this is only Phase I of what is really structured as a three-phase project.

The determining factor for the project is the interest of the various levels of government in encouraging this type of business in this region of western Canada. The business is not intended to stand as a single-phase project, but economies of scale encourage the implementation of second and third phases. The incentives provided by the government are meant to encourage this investment. Without them this project would probably not be undertaken. But the environmental situation cannot be ignored. It is an important component of these financial projections and the overall business plan. This particular environment provides a hedge against risk for any investors.

10.5   PHASE 3—STRATEGIC (TOTAL) RESOURCES ANALYSIS

As with many plans the basic strategic and business plans did not discuss or include any reference to qualitative goals or the resources required to achieve any such goals. The concept of a strategic (total) resources approach to modeling and business planning was pursued in Chapter 2. Most firms currently do not formally incorporate qualitative goals into their financial models and plans. This one is no exception.

Some of the elements that the firm perhaps should have included in its plans include: the quality of the workforce; the morale within the firm; the quality of relations with the city in which the business is to be located; the flexibility of the manufacturing process; the quality of the local environment; and, perhaps most importantly, the quality of the relations with the federal and provincial governments.

Chapter 2 outlines a process for addressing a total resource approach for planning. This methodology is valuable and in fact should be used in the business and strategic planning processes and modeling. The analysis of the above listed elements could be pursued in the fashion outlined in Chapter 2.

10.6 PHASE 4—SENSITIVITY ANALYSIS

Phase 4 is concerned with sensitivity or "what if" analysis. The three steps in phase 4 include:

1. Qualitative Sensitivity Analysis
2. Quantitative Sensitivity Analysis
3. Strategic (Total) Resources Sensitivity Analysis

Step 1—Qualitative Sensitivity Analysis

The various qualitative assumptions appeared to be relatively insensitive to change. The environmental considerations, particularly the relationship with the government and the wheat suppliers, are probably the most important; in fact, they are vital to the plan's acceptance. If these important environmental interests are not responsive to this proposal, the actual business reflected in the financial projections probably will never get off the ground.

Another important environmental consideration is grain and its availability as the raw material for the process. Part of this is dependent on climatic considerations, which are relatively difficult to project. Given the importance of this proposed business to the labor market in the region and the high profile of the government in the region's activities, it is very likely that even if there would be grain shortages at some time in the future, the government would step in to either directly or indirectly (through subsidies) ensure an adequate supply of this important resource.

The plan failed to address the detailed aspects of implementation, and this is an important deficiency. Lack of detail about specific personnel, the organization itself, and its structure and functions, is a major concern. This is especially true given the uncertainties in the external and internal environments.

Step 2—Quantitative Sensitivity Analysis

The quantitative sensitivity analysis was also conducted within the spreadsheet itself and can be found in Appendix B from L1161 to L1261. The variances from the Dun & Bradstreet median industry figures (L1063 to L1083) became an integral part of this sensitivity analysis. *The variances, if a plus, were favorable,* meaning that the performance of the company under investigation had results better than Dun & Bradstreet median statistics. If negative, they were worse than the Dun & Bradstreet median industry performance. It should be mentioned that the first part of the sensitivity analysis (L1161 to L1228) was conducted using the Data Table 1 command in Lotus. Certain inputs that were considered important to the overall performance of the firm were varied, and then the effects of these changes, first on the projected financial statements and finally on the selected ratios and other figures, were computed. Three important inputs (assumptions) were examined. They were: (1) the tonnes of pasta sold (L1164 to L1182); (2) the price that the pasta would get in the marketplace (L1185 to L1203); and (3) the cost of winter wheat, the raw material for the entire operation (L1206 to L1224). The first eight columns in each data table were variances from the Dun & Bradstreet median industry statistics. By scanning these figures and looking for the presence or absence of negative figures, the analyst can develop a good sense of the firm's projected hypothetical performance over the given range for the inputs. Additionally, the Z factor, future value, present value, and cumulative cash flow amounts were included for analysis.

For the pasta sold data table (L1166 to L1182), we examined from 30 tonnes down to 20 tonnes of pasta sold. The 30 tonne figure is an average operating figure. The maximum plant capacity is 36,000 tonnes per year.

The projections assumed that an average operating level of 30,000 tonnes would be an appropriate practical maximum operating output for the plant. The Dun & Bradstreet figures in the sensitivity analysis are all in the positive range except at the 20,000 tonne level. This ignores the accounts receivable turnover variance that was discussed earlier in this chapter which does not present any real concern. The average Z factors were all lower than would be considered acceptable at the 21,000 and 20,000 tonne levels. The present values, future values, and cash flow figures were also included. As would be expected, they all decreased with decreases in the tonnes of pasta sold. Remember that the projections contained a number of fixed costs (especially for labor) that would not reflect any changes over the tested range for tonnes sold. In fact, these fixed costs would be reduced somewhat as activity decreased, so the displayed results are conservative. The results of the computations show a favorable reaction to the changes examined in this part of the sensitivity analysis.

For the price of pasta data table (L1187 to L1203) a starting figure of $900 per tonne was used, and this was also the figure used in the model itself. The price of pasta was examined downward in decrements of $20 to $700. The $900 pasta price probably is lower than what the market would bear; therefore, the figures included were also relatively conservative. Again, as the various ratios were scanned most of them were positive. The gross profit margins went below industry norms at the $780 price per tonne for pasta (L1199). The return on assets went negative a little lower at the $720 per tonne range (L1202). The return on equity went negative in the $700 range (L1203). The accounts receivable in days are all negative, and from $740 to $700 Canadian per tonne the Z factors were below the minimum cutoff. Again the results of this sensitivity analysis, given the previous qualification on the bankruptcy analysis, were favorable.

The *cost of wheat* was examined in a third data table (L1208 to L1224). The model used a starting figure of $131.70 per tonne in 1990, which was in fact the market price less a $10 subsidy from the government. Actually an additional $10 subsidy probably was available, which would have lowered the starting price to $121.70. The cost of wheat per tonne was examined over a range of from $151.70 to $111.70 per tonne in decrements of $4.00. It is interesting to note that the price of the wheat was only slightly higher in August of 1992, a 1.2% change in two years. In July of 1990 winter wheat was selling for $3.32 (dollars US per bushel) (E5, p. 6). In August 1992 winter wheat was selling for $3.40 dollars US per bushel (E5, p. 6).

The price of wheat at $131.70 (the first figure used in the model itself) is the midpoint of the range tested in the data table (L1219). Once again the variances within the Dun & Bradstreet statistics were all positive except for the accounts receivable in days. The Z factors were all acceptable.

Another form of sensitivity analysis was conducted using the two most important assumptions within the model, which were the price of pasta and the cost of wheat. This is found from L1228 to L1261. This analysis was conducted using Lotus 1-2-3 and the Data Table 2 command. The first row and the first column in the matrix are the ranges of variation for the two inputs (assumptions). The range for the cost of wheat is found on the horizontal row (L1242) and varies from $115.70 to $151.70 per tonne. The range for varying the expected price of pasta is from $900 to $700 per tonne. This is the first column in the table.

The remaining figures in the matrix (table) are the future values for the firm, reflecting the various combinations of assumptions. Assuming the price of pasta at $900 a tonne and the cost of wheat at $131.70 per tonne, a future value of $211,489,810 is given, which is the figure arrived at in the valuation analysis section (L1140).

This table allows the analyst to scan the various results for the future values based on the variation of the two most important inputs. Under the worst-case scenario (with the price for pasta at $700 and the cost of wheat at $151.70) a future value of $66,809,799 is achieved. This should be compared with the most optimal scenario, when the price for pasta is assumed to be $900, the cost of wheat is assumed to be $115.70, and the future value of $226,114,151 is achieved. Using ranges of values for the inputs (sensitivity analysis) allows the analyst to examine a large number of possible combinations for the inputs and at the same time to see the computations for the expected future values associated with these combinations. The probability is that the price for the pasta most likely will not go much lower than about $850 and the cost of wheat will probably not go much higher than $131. This means that the worse case appears to be about $175 million for the future value, versus the $211 million figure (L1140) obtained by using the assumptions in the projections themselves as submitted for initial examination.

The projections seem to be relatively able to accept substantial variation and still yield favorable results.

It should be noted that the quantitative sensitivity analysis just conducted very graphically demonstrates the systems approach to the analysis of prospective financial information. This is especially true for the sensitivity analysis sections that used the LOTUS 1-2-3 data tables in the analysis process. No one particular element (or ratio) became the focus. Rather, the data tables themselves are arranged so that a positive figure indicates performance at better than industry norm and negatives show just the opposite. The data table effectively becomes a tapestry. The elements each individually represents a very important facet of the organization; the data table weaves them all into a systems view of the firm in which not only are all of the elements viewed together, but they are all viewed together over ranges for the inputs, effectively simulating a dynamic tapestry. These ranges span the most probable variations for the most important inputs or drivers of the proposed firm.

Step 3—Strategic (Total) Resources Sensitivity Analysis

As with the discussion in Section 10.5 above, there will be no strategic (total) resources sensitivity analysis because the consortium did not address these resources either in the prospective financial statements presented for examination or in the business plans that they prepared. The reasons for this were presented in Section 10.5 above. The aspect about the process developed in Chapter 2 for Strategic Resources Sensitivity Analysis that makes it so very valuable is that it can easily translate qualitative resources into quantifiable elements and directly use these elements in financial models. Therefore, these qualitative elements can be analyzed in exactly the same fashion as the quantitative elements discussed in the previous section, Step 2—Quantitative Sensitivity Analysis.

10.7   PHASE 5—EVALUATION AND CONCLUSIONS

When the discussion of the process for the analysis of prospective financial statements was started, the fact that the process is not one that can be reduced to a few separate disjoint rules or computations was discussed. In fact, the process requires careful consideration of all the information available, and an appreciation for both the interrelatedness among all the components in the prospective financial statements under examination and the interrelatedness among all of the procedures themselves. The analysis of prospective financial statements is more of an art than a methodology.

The evaluation of this firm's projected financial statements pointed out some important deficiencies in the projections and business plans. This was particularly true of the lack of specific provisions for the business functions and detailed plans for implementation of the proposal. As discussed earlier, this was not atypical. The plan was presented by a business consortium on a fishing expedition. In particular, they were fishing for some governmental subsidies for their project. Appreciating these limitations, the overall qualitative component of the analysis yielded a relatively favorable impression. The quantitative analysis and sensitivity analysis were also favorable. The one potential problem was posed by the bankruptcy analysis in the early years of the project, which could have presented some concern if not for the explanations previously discussed.

All the approaches taken seemed to confirm one another and taken jointly lent a good degree of comfort with the information presented.

The overall conclusions concerning the financial projections being examined, given the hypothetical assumptions articulated, were that the un-derlying assumptions provided a reasonable basis for management's pro-jections, and the projections were presented in conformity with the appropriate guidelines established by the AICPA. These are the two con-clusions permitted by the *AICPA's Guide for Prospective Financial In-formation* (F10, p. 140). The *Guide* provides an example of a complete report. If an analysis is performed on a project that is not an AICPA sanc-tioned engagement, the conclusions could vary in scope. But regardless of the type of engagement being performed, an additional conclusion remains consistently true.

> there will usually be differences between the projected and actual results, because events and circumstances frequently do not occur as expected, and those differences may be material. (F10, p. 140)

As an afterthought, it should be noted that the construction of the actual plant started in the spring of 1992, almost two years behind schedule.

CHAPTER ELEVEN

Conclusion

We have just about finished what we set out to do: to present a practitioner's guide for the analysis of prospective financial statements. This was accomplished by:

I. Setting the stage (Chapter 1):
    *   Demonstrating the need for a new model for the analysis of prospective financial statements
    *   Discussing the challenges involved in the analysis of prospective financial statements
    *   Presenting a general approach for the analysis
    *   Identifying some unique aspects of the process specifically as they apply to the practitioner
    *   Emphasizing the differences between the new approach and those presented in previous works

II. Presenting a process model for the analysis of prospective financial statements, which includes the following 5 phase approach (Chapter 2):
    *   PHASE 1 - QUALITATIVE ANALYSIS
        Step 1 - Establish the General Context
        1. Communication Issues
        2. Accounting Information
        Step 2 - Review the Strategic Plan
        Step 3 - Examine the Business Plan
        1. Its Relationship to the Strategic Plan
        2. The Organization and Provision for Business Functions

Step 4 - Define and Examine the Systems and Their Interrelationships

Step 5 - Determine the Scope of the Examination

Step 6 - Examine the Assumptions

Step 7 - Review the Preparation and Presentation

- PHASE 2 - QUANTITATIVE ANALYSIS

Step 1 - Familiarization With and Review of Model

Step 2 - Traditional Financial Analysis

1. Determine Benchmarks and Targets

2. Choose Approaches and Ratios

3. Conduct the Analysis

Step 3 - Discriminant (Bankruptcy) Analysis

Step 4 - Valuation

- PHASE 3 - STRATEGIC (TOTAL) RESOURCES ANALYSIS

- PHASE 4 - SENSITIVITY ANALYSIS

Step 1 - Qualitative Sensitivity Analysis

Step 2 - Quantitative Sensitivity Analysis

Step 3 - Strategic (Total) Resources Sensitivity Analysis

- PHASE 5 - EVALUATION AND CONCLUSIONS

III. Discussing in detail the major subsystems in the firm of particular import to the analysis process (Chapters 3–9):
- Communications (Chapter 3)
- Accounting (Chapter 4)
- Prospective Financial Statements (Chapter 5)
- Strategic Planning (Chapter 6)
- Systems (Chapter 7)
- Modeling, Forecasting and Sensitivity Analysis (Chapter 8)
- Financial Analysis (Chapter 9)

IV. Demonstrating the application of the process model through the use of a detailed case study (Chapter 10).

V. Providing a printout of a detailed 11 year set of financial projections for an actual start-up business (Appendix A).

VI. Providing a printout of the detailed quantitative analysis of the financial projections provided in Appendix A (Appendix B).

VII. Providing a computer diskette with the Lotus model containing the financial projections as presented, as well as containing the computations and formulas for the financial analysis conducted (attached in pocket provided).

VIII. Providing an exhaustive 11 topic bibliography for future reference by the reader, as well as for providing endnote references including

- Valuation (Section A)
- Marketing (Section B)
- Strategic and Business Planning (Section C)
- Computers (Section D)
- Finance (Section E)
- Accounting and AICPA Publications (Section F)
- Cost Estimating and Management Accounting (Section G)
- Systems and Operations (Section H)
- Quantitative Methods (Section I)
- Ethics and Business Responsibility (Section J)
- Communications and Logic (Section K)

The process model as presented consists of five main phases, which are each further broken down into a number of additional steps. The process described in this model is intended to help in facilitating the analysis and understanding of prospective financial statements. The model outlines the basic phases and steps in the analysis process and should assist the analyst in organizing the various topics addressed in the text in a constructive way, and in drawing reasonable and practical inferences concerning how to approach the process for the analysis of prospective financial statements.

Throughout the text I have emphasized that although there are a number of similarities between the analysis of historical financial statements and the analysis of prospective financial statements, there are many important differences as well. The most important of these differences is that the figures exactly as presented for analysis in prospective financial statements will most likely differ from the actual results achieved. This major difference creates some special needs and real challenges with the analysis of prospective financial statements. The thrust of the various chapters within this text has been to emphasize the impact that these differences have on the analysis process.

The needs and challenges that have led to the writing of this book necessitate taking a very different perspective and approach for the analysis of prospective financial statements than is used with historical financial statements. Some important aspects of this perspective and approach include integrating:

- An emphasis on what might happen
- The use of the systems paradigm throughout
- An approach using modeling, computers, and sensitivity analysis
- An emphasis on communications, qualitative issues, and assumptions
- An appreciation for art over technique
- An emphasis on risk and uncertainty
- A focus on context
- An understanding that change is the only real constant

The implications of this different perspective are far-reaching. The firm is viewed holistically as a system, rather than as a group of fragmented parts. The parts (subsystems) of the firm are seen working together as a whole, not as a series of disjoint functions. This is what we have called *The Systems View of the Firm*. The analysis process itself is viewed as a system, not a collection of disjoint procedures or methodologies. The qualitative aspects and assumptions are seen as being as important as the quantitative ones in the analysis process, if not more so.

The difference in perspective and approach facilitates focusing on the interrelatedness among all of the elements under examination, whether they are elements of the analysis process being employed or an element of the prospective financial statements being analyzed. Regardless, all of the elements are brought together, kept together, and examined in such a fashion as to determine the influence of each upon the characteristics of the whole system. We have called this the systems perspective.

This difference in perspective and approach also leads to a shifting in emphasis. Change is seen as the only constant, not the status quo. Context takes precedence over details. The whole analysis process itself is appreciated as an art form, not just a set of techniques or procedures. Qualitative issues and assumptions are emphasized over the merely quantitative—which an approach that traditional financial analysis would never consider. Communications are emphasized over mere data. Computers, modeling, and sensitivity analysis are emphasized over the use of the static presentations of data on paper. Risk and uncertainty are assumed to be focal, and therefore emphasized, while certainty is relegated only to death and taxes.

The overall emphasis is on what might happen, rather than on what someone might hope will happen. The shifts in emphasis when seen collectively lead to an entirely new way of viewing prospective financial statements, one that radically breaks with the past, and the techniques developed for merely addressing traditional historical financial statements.

Society requires stewardship over its resources from the businesses using them. Practitioners have a responsibility, a duty, to see their function as facilitating the performance of this stewardship function over society's resources. The practitioner employed in the analysis of prospective financial statements has a social as well as a professional responsibility to assist in this. Armed with the new perspective presented in this text, I hope that analysts will be better prepared to perform this function.

The text was not intended to provide all the answers to all the questions about this important topic; rather, it was intended to be a practitioner's guide to the analysis of prospective financial statements. My hope in preparing it was in some small way to help start filling the void in the professional literature on this very important topic.

Printout of Case Study Model

```
1  PASTA PLANT & FLOUR MILL COMBINED  -  TEMPLATE
2
3  ***************************************************************
4  ASSUMPTIONS                                    BASE CASE - AUG 1 UPDATE
5  ***************************************************************
6                                                   INTEREST        14.0%
7  ***************************************************************
8  OPERATING STATISTICS             *          *   RUN #  P
9                                                 ***************
10 GRAIN YIELDS            %
11
12 SEMOLINA           50.72%
13 FLOUR-PRIME        14.49%
14 MILLFEED           27.54%
15 CLEAN/FLOUR         7.25%
16
17 TOTAL             100.00%
18
19 PROCESSING YIELD   98.00%
20
21
22
23 PROPERTY PLANT & EQUIPMENT
24 ****************************
25
26 INSURANCE & PROPERTY TAX INFORMATION
27 ************************************
28
29 BUILDINGS ARE ASSUMED TO HAVE        125,000 SQFT
30
31 INSURANCE RATES
32
33 EQUIPMENT          0.33   PER $100
34 BUILDINGS          0.57   PER $100
35
36
37 BREAKDOWN OF ACQUISITIONS BY PHASE
38 **********************************
```

	PHASE I	PHASE I WITH GRANTS 0.0000%	PHASE I GRANTS	PHASE II	PHASE II WITH GRANTS 0.0000%	PHASE II GRANTS	PHASE III	PHASE III WITH GRANTS 0.0000%	PHASE III GRANTS
BUILDINGS -	7,500,000	7,500,000	0	0	0	0	0	0	0
EQUIPMENT -	200,000	200,000	0	0	0	0	0	0	0
MOBILE EQUIP -	300,000	300,000	0	0	0	0	0	0	0
PROCESS EQUIP -	42,000,000	42,000,000	0	0	0	0	0	0	0
TOTAL	50,000,000	50,000,000	0	0	0	0	0	0	0

227

		PHASE I	PHASE II	PHASE III
FINANCING				
(GOVERNMENT LOAN PERCENTAGE)		19.5000%	25.0000%	25.0000%
BANK LOANS	0	18,000,000	0	0
FEDERAL GOVERNMENT LOANS		9,750,000	0	0
FARM BONDS		6,000,000		
EQUITY	0	16,250,000	0	0
TOTAL LT FINANCING		50,000,000	0	0

DEPRECIATION

	1990	1991	1992	1993	1994	1995	1996	1997	1998	1999	2000
BUILDINGS - CLASS 3 5.00%											
NBV - BEGINNING OF YEAR	0	0	7,437,500	7,065,625	6,712,344	6,376,727	6,057,890	5,754,996	5,467,246	5,193,884	4,934,189
ADDITIONS	0	7,500,000	0	0	0	0	0	0	0	0	0
GRANTS	0	0	0	0	0	0	0	0	0	0	0
DEPRECIATION	0	62,500	371,875	353,281	335,617	318,836	302,895	287,750	273,362	259,694	246,709
NBV - END OF YEAR	0	7,437,500	7,065,625	6,712,344	6,376,727	6,057,890	5,754,996	5,467,246	5,193,884	4,934,189	4,687,480
EQUIPMENT - CLASS 8 20.00%											
NBV - BEGINNING OF YEAR	0	0	193,333	154,667	123,733	98,987	79,189	63,351	50,681	40,545	32,436
ADDITIONS	0	200,000	0	0	0	0	0	0	0	0	0
GRANTS	0	0	0	0	0	0	0	0	0	0	0
DEPRECIATION	0	6,667	38,667	30,933	24,747	19,797	15,838	12,670	10,136	8,109	6,487
NBV - END OF YEAR	0	193,333	154,667	123,733	98,987	79,189	63,351	50,681	40,545	32,436	25,949
MOBILE EQ - CLASS 10 30.00%											
NBV - BEGINNING OF YEAR	0	0	285,000	199,500	139,650	97,755	68,429	47,900	33,530	23,471	16,430
ADDITIONS	0	300,000	0	0	0	0	0	0	0	0	0
GRANTS	0	0	0	0	0	0	0	0	0	0	0
DEPRECIATION	0	15,000	85,500	59,850	41,895	29,327	20,529	14,370	10,059	7,041	4,929
NBV - END OF YEAR	0	285,000	199,500	139,650	97,755	68,429	47,900	33,530	23,471	16,430	11,501
PROCESS EQ- CLASS 29 25.00%											
NBV - BEGINNING OF YEAR	0	0	40,250,000	30,187,500	22,640,625	16,980,469	12,735,352	9,551,514	7,163,635	5,372,726	4,029,545
ADDITIONS	0	42,000,000	0	0	0	0	0	0	0	0	0
GRANTS	0	1,750,000	10,062,500	7,546,875	5,660,156	4,245,117	3,183,838	2,387,878	1,790,909	1,343,182	1,007,386
DEPRECIATION	0	40,250,000	30,187,500	22,640,625	16,980,469	12,735,352	9,551,514	7,163,635	5,372,726	4,029,545	3,022,159
NBV - END OF YEAR											
TOTAL ADDITIONS	0	50,000,000	0	0	0	0	0	0	0	0	0
TOTAL PP&E GRANTS	0	0	0	0	0	0	0	0	0	0	0
TOTAL DEPRECIATION	0	1,834,167	10,558,542	7,990,940	6,062,415	4,613,077	3,523,099	2,702,668	2,084,466	1,618,026	1,265,512
TOTAL NBV - END OF YEAR	0	48,165,833	37,607,292	29,616,352	23,553,937	18,940,860	15,417,761	12,715,092	10,630,626	9,012,600	7,747,088

SOFT COSTS & START UP

	1990	1991	1992	1993	1994	1995	1996	1997	1998	1999	2000
SOFT COST & START UP EXPENSES	750,000	1,850,000	0	0	0	0	0	0	0	0	0
TOTAL SOFTCOST PROV GRANTS	0	50,000	0	0	0	0	0	0	0	0	0
TOTAL SOFTCOST FED GRANTS	250,000	0	0	0	0	0	0	0	0	0	0

REVENUES

	1990	1991	1992	1993	1994	1995	1996	1997	1998	1999	2000
TONS (M) OF PASTA SOLD	0	5,000	30,000	30,000	30,000	30,000	30,000	30,000	30,000	30,000	30,000

TONS (M) SOLD (detailed)

	1990	1991	1992	1993	1994	1995	1996	1997	1998	1999	2000
PASTA - DOMESTIC	0	350	2,100	2,100	2,100	2,100	2,100	2,100	2,100	2,100	2,100
PASTA - US	0	1,500	9,000	9,000	9,000	9,000	9,000	9,000	9,000	9,000	9,000
PASTA - PACIFIC RIM	0	1,250	7,500	7,500	7,500	7,500	7,500	7,500	7,500	7,500	7,500
PASTA - SOUTH AMERICA	0	900	5,400	5,400	5,400	5,400	5,400	5,400	5,400	5,400	5,400
PASTA - THIRD WORLD	0	400	2,400	2,400	2,400	2,400	2,400	2,400	2,400	2,400	2,400
PASTA - EEC & N AFRICA	0	600	3,600	3,600	3,600	3,600	3,600	3,600	3,600	3,600	3,600
BY-PRODUCT MILLFEED	0	2,111	12,667	12,667	12,667	12,667	12,667	12,667	12,667	12,667	12,667
BY-PRODUCT CLEAR/FLOUR	0	556	3,333	3,333	3,333	3,333	3,333	3,333	3,333	3,333	3,333
TOTAL	0	7,667	46,000	46,000	46,000	46,000	46,000	46,000	46,000	46,000	46,000

PRICE PER TON (M) SOLD

INFLATION 5.0%	1990	1991	1992	1993	1994	1995	1996	1997	1998	1999	2000
PASTA - DOMESTIC	900	945	992	1,042	1,094	1,149	1,206	1,266	1,330	1,396	1,466
PASTA - US	900	945	992	1,042	1,094	1,149	1,206	1,266	1,330	1,396	1,466
PASTA - PACIFIC RIM	900	945	992	1,042	1,094	1,149	1,206	1,266	1,330	1,396	1,466
PASTA - SOUTH AMERICA	900	945	992	1,042	1,094	1,149	1,206	1,266	1,330	1,396	1,466
PASTA - THIRD WORLD	900	945	992	1,042	1,094	1,149	1,206	1,266	1,330	1,396	1,466
PASTA - EEC & N AFRICA	900	945	992	1,042	1,094	1,149	1,206	1,266	1,330	1,396	1,466
BY-PRODUCT MILLFEED	100	105	110	116	122	128	134	141	148	155	163
BY-PRODUCT CLEAR/FLOUR	800	840	882	926	972	1,021	1,072	1,126	1,182	1,241	1,303

TOTAL REVENUE

	1990	1991	1992	1993	1994	1995	1996	1997	1998	1999	2000
PASTA - DOMESTIC	0	330,750	2,083,725	2,187,911	2,297,307	2,412,172	2,532,781	2,659,420	2,792,391	2,932,010	3,078,611
PASTA - US	0	1,417,500	8,930,250	9,376,763	9,845,601	10,337,881	10,854,775	11,397,513	11,967,389	12,565,759	13,194,046
PASTA - PACIFIC RIM	0	1,181,250	7,441,875	7,813,969	8,204,667	8,614,901	9,045,646	9,497,928	9,972,824	10,471,465	10,995,039
PASTA - SOUTH AMERICA	0	850,500	5,358,150	5,626,058	5,907,360	6,202,728	6,512,865	6,838,508	7,180,433	7,539,455	7,916,428
PASTA - THIRD WORLD	0	378,000	2,381,400	2,500,470	2,625,494	2,756,768	2,894,607	3,039,337	3,191,304	3,350,869	3,518,412
PASTA - EEC & N AFRICA	0	567,000	3,572,100	3,750,705	3,938,240	4,135,152	4,341,910	4,559,005	4,786,956	5,026,303	5,277,619
BY-PRODUCT MILLFEED	0	221,667	1,396,500	1,466,325	1,539,641	1,616,623	1,697,454	1,782,327	1,871,444	1,965,016	2,063,267
BY-PRODUCT CLEAR/FLOUR	0	466,667	2,940,000	3,087,000	3,241,350	3,403,418	3,573,588	3,752,268	3,939,881	4,136,875	4,343,719
TOTAL	0	5,413,333	34,104,000	35,809,200	37,599,660	39,479,643	41,453,625	43,526,306	45,702,622	47,987,753	50,387,140

ACCOUNTS RECEIVABLE AGING

% RECEIVED IN:

YEAR 1	YEAR 2	NEVER	TOTAL
92%	8%	0%	100%

COSTS

RAW MAT & WIP INVENTORY (DURUM COMPONENT ONLY)

8.33% OF PRODUCTION

	1990	1991	1992	1993	1994	1995	1996	1997	1998	1999	2000
$ RM & WIP INV BUILD UP	0	91,955	480,870	-9,939	0	0	0	0	0	0	0

FINISHED GOODS INVENTORY

2.00% OF SALES

	1990	1991	1992	1993	1994	1995	1996	1997	1998	1999	2000
TONS (M) OF PASTA PRODUCED	0	5,100	30,500	30,000	30,000	30,000	30,000	30,000	30,000	30,000	30,000

TONS (M) OF DURUM REQUIRED FOR PROD

	1990	1991	1992	1993	1994	1995	1996	1997	1998	1999	2000
DURUM	0	7,980	47,721	46,939	46,939	46,939	46,939	46,939	46,939	46,939	46,939
TOTAL	0	7,980	47,721	46,939	46,939	46,939	46,939	46,939	46,939	46,939	46,939

VARIABLE COST PER TON (M) OF PASTA PRODUCED (EXCEPT DURUM WHICH IS PER TON OF INPUT REQUIRED)

INFLATION 5.0%

	1990	1991	1992	1993	1994	1995	1996	1997	1998	1999	2000
DURUM	131.70	138.29	145.20	152.46	160.08	168.09	176.49	185.32	194.58	204.31	214.53
	0.00	0.00	0.00	0.00	0.00	0.00	0.00	0.00	0.00	0.00	0.00
NATURAL GAS	3.74	3.92	4.12	4.33	4.54	4.77	5.01	5.26	5.52	5.80	6.09
ELECTRICITY	12.41	13.03	13.68	14.37	15.08	15.84	16.63	17.46	18.34	19.25	20.21
WATER & SEWER	0.09	0.09	0.10	0.10	0.11	0.11	0.12	0.12	0.13	0.13	0.14
CHEMICALS	1.45	1.52	1.60	1.68	1.76	1.85	1.94	2.04	2.14	2.25	2.36
PACKAGING	95.00	99.75	104.74	109.97	115.47	121.25	127.31	133.67	140.36	147.38	154.74
TRANSPORTATION	100.00	105.00	110.25	115.76	121.55	127.63	134.01	140.71	147.75	155.13	162.89
MAINTENANCE	10.31	10.83	11.37	11.94	12.53	13.16	13.82	14.51	15.23	15.99	16.79
	0.00	0.00	0.00	0.00	0.00	0.00	0.00	0.00	0.00	0.00	0.00
	0.00	0.00	0.00	0.00	0.00	0.00	0.00	0.00	0.00	0.00	0.00

TOTAL VARIABLE PRODUCTION COST

	1990	1991	1992	1993	1994	1995	1996	1997	1998	1999	2000
DURUM	0	1,103,458	6,929,066	7,156,249	7,514,061	7,889,764	8,284,252	8,698,465	9,133,388	9,590,058	10,069,561
	0	0	0	0	0	0	0	0	0	0	0
	0	0	0	0	0	0	0	0	0	0	0
NATURAL GAS	0	20,008	125,639	129,759	136,247	143,059	150,212	157,723	165,609	173,889	182,584
ELECTRICITY	0	66,456	417,302	430,984	452,533	475,160	498,918	523,863	550,057	577,559	606,437
WATER & SEWER	0	463	2,905	3,001	3,151	3,308	3,474	3,647	3,830	4,021	4,222
CHEMICALS	0	7,765	48,758	50,357	52,875	55,518	58,294	61,209	64,269	67,483	70,857
PACKAGING	0	508,725	3,194,494	3,299,231	3,464,193	3,637,402	3,819,273	4,010,236	4,210,748	4,421,285	4,642,350
TRANSPORTATION	0	535,500	3,362,625	3,472,875	3,646,519	3,828,845	4,020,287	4,221,301	4,432,366	4,653,985	4,886,684
MAINTENANCE	0	55,210	346,687	358,053	375,956	394,754	414,492	435,216	456,977	479,826	503,817
	0	0	0	0	0	0	0	0	0	0	0
	0	0	0	0	0	0	0	0	0	0	0
TOTAL	0	2,297,584	14,427,476	14,900,508	15,645,534	16,427,810	17,249,201	18,111,661	19,017,244	19,968,106	20,966,511

	1990	1991	1992	1993	1994	1995	1996	1997	1998	1999	2000
DURUM	0	1,081,821	6,815,475	7,156,249	7,514,061	7,889,764	8,284,252	8,698,465	9,133,388	9,590,058	10,069,561
	0	0	0	0	0	0	0	0	0	0	0
NATURAL GAS	0	19,616	123,580	129,759	136,247	143,059	150,212	157,723	165,609	173,889	182,584
ELECTRICITY	0	65,153	410,461	430,984	452,533	475,160	498,918	523,863	550,057	577,559	606,437
WATER & SEWER	0	454	2,858	3,001	3,151	3,308	3,474	3,647	3,830	4,021	4,222
CHEMICALS	0	7,613	47,959	50,357	52,875	55,518	58,294	61,209	64,269	67,483	70,857
PACKAGING	0	498,750	3,142,125	3,299,231	3,464,193	3,637,402	3,819,273	4,010,236	4,210,748	4,421,285	4,642,350
TRANSPORTATION	0	525,000	3,307,500	3,472,875	3,646,519	3,828,845	4,020,287	4,221,301	4,432,366	4,653,985	4,886,684
MAINTENANCE	0	54,128	341,003	358,053	375,956	394,754	414,492	435,216	456,977	479,826	503,817
	0	0	0	0	0	0	0	0	0	0	0
TOTAL	0	2,252,533	14,190,960	14,900,508	15,645,534	16,427,810	17,249,201	18,111,661	19,017,244	19,968,106	20,966,511

DIRECT LABOR

STAFFING

	1990	1991	1992	1993	1994	1995	1996	1997	1998	1999	2000
EXEC VP OPERATIONS	0	0.5	1	1	1	1	1	1	1	1	1
SUPER - PASTA	0	0.5	1	1	1	1	1	1	1	1	1
SUPER - MILL	0	0.5	1	1	1	1	1	1	1	1	1
SHIFT FOREMEN	0	0.5	3	3	3	3	3	3	3	3	3
FOOD TECH / QC	0	0.5	1	1	1	1	1	1	1	1	1
SUPPORT STAFF	0	3	3	3	3	3	3	3	3	3	3
PASTA - SKILLED	0	2	9	9	9	9	9	9	9	9	9
PASTA - UNSKILLED	0	4	19	19	19	19	19	19	19	19	19
MILL - SKILLED	0	1	6	6	6	6	6	6	6	6	6
MILL - UNSKILLED	0	1	5	5	5	5	5	5	5	5	5
MAINTENANCE	0	0.5	1	1	1	1	1	1	1	1	1
TOTAL	0	14	50	50	50	50	50	50	50	50	50

DIRECT LABOR ANNUAL COMPENSATION

INFLATION 5.0%

	1990	1991	1992	1993	1994	1995	1996	1997	1998	1999	2000
EXEC VP OPERATIONS	80,000	84,000	88,200	92,610	97,241	102,103	107,208	112,568	118,196	124,106	130,312
SUPER - PASTA	35,000	36,750	38,588	40,517	42,543	44,670	46,903	49,249	51,711	54,296	57,011
SUPER - MILL	35,000	36,750	38,588	40,517	42,543	44,670	46,903	49,249	51,711	54,296	57,011
SHIFT FOREMEN	27,000	28,350	29,768	31,256	32,819	34,460	36,183	37,992	39,891	41,886	43,980
FOOD TECH / QC	40,000	42,000	44,100	46,305	48,620	51,051	53,604	56,284	59,098	62,053	65,156
SUPPORT STAFF	14,000	14,700	15,435	16,207	17,017	17,868	18,761	19,699	20,684	21,719	22,805
	0	0	0	0	0	0	0	0	0	0	0
PASTA - SKILLED	27,600	28,980	30,429	31,950	33,548	35,225	36,987	38,836	40,778	42,817	44,957
PASTA - UNSKILLED	15,600	16,380	17,199	18,059	18,962	19,910	20,905	21,951	23,048	24,201	25,411
	0	0	0	0	0	0	0	0	0	0	0
MILL - SKILLED	27,600	28,980	30,429	31,950	33,548	35,225	36,987	38,836	40,778	42,817	44,957
MILL - UNSKILLED	15,600	16,380	17,199	18,059	18,962	19,910	20,905	21,951	23,048	24,201	25,411
	0	0	0	0	0	0	0	0	0	0	0
MAINTENANCE	30,000	31,500	33,075	34,729	36,465	38,288	40,203	42,213	44,324	46,540	48,867

TOTAL DIRECT LABOR DOLLARS

	1990	1991	1992	1993	1994	1995	1996	1997	1998	1999	2000
EXEC VP OPERATIONS	0	42,000	88,200	92,610	97,241	102,103	107,208	112,568	118,196	124,106	130,312
SUPER - PASTA	0	18,375	38,588	40,517	42,543	44,670	46,903	49,249	51,711	54,296	57,011
SUPER - MILL	0	18,375	38,588	40,517	42,543	44,670	46,903	49,249	51,711	54,296	57,011
SHIFT FOREMEN	0	14,175	89,303	93,768	98,456	103,379	108,548	113,975	119,674	125,658	131,940
FOOD TECH / QC	0	21,000	44,100	46,305	48,620	51,051	53,604	56,284	59,098	62,053	65,156
SUPPORT STAFF	0	44,100	46,305	48,620	51,051	53,604	56,284	59,098	62,053	65,156	68,414
	0	0	0	0	0	0	0	0	0	0	0
PASTA - SKILLED	0	57,960	273,861	287,554	301,932	317,028	332,880	349,524	367,000	385,350	404,617
PASTA - UNSKILLED	0	65,520	326,781	343,120	360,276	378,290	397,204	417,065	437,918	459,814	482,804
	0	0	0	0	0	0	0	0	0	0	0
MILL - SKILLED	0	28,980	182,574	191,703	201,288	211,352	221,920	233,016	244,667	256,900	269,745
MILL - UNSKILLED	0	16,380	85,995	90,295	94,809	99,550	104,527	109,754	115,242	121,004	127,054
	0	0	0	0	0	0	0	0	0	0	0
MAINTENANCE	0	15,750	33,075	34,729	36,465	38,288	40,203	42,213	44,324	46,540	48,867

OVERHEAD

	Param	1990	1991	1992	1993	1994	1995	1996	1997	1998	1999	2000
521 INFLATION	5.00%											
523 MISC		0	0	0	0	0	0	0	0	0	0	0
527 SALARIES	1.00	0	0	0	0	0	0	0	0	0	0	0
528 TAXES		0	21,875	137,813	144,703	151,938	159,535	167,512	175,888	184,682	193,916	203,612
529 EQPT RENTAL	15.00%	0	0	0	0	0	0	0	0	0	0	0
530 INSURANCE		0	31,679	199,580	209,559	220,037	231,039	242,591	254,720	267,456	280,829	294,871
531 BENEFITS		0	51,392	187,105	196,461	206,284	216,598	227,428	238,799	250,739	263,276	276,440
532 TRAINING		0	2,500	15,750	16,538	17,364	18,233	19,144	20,101	21,107	22,162	23,270
534 TOTAL		0	107,447	540,248	567,260	595,623	625,404	656,675	689,508	723,984	760,183	798,192

SG&A SALARIES

SG&A STAFFING

	1990	1991	1992	1993	1994	1995	1996	1997	1998	1999	2000
547 BOARD OF DIRECTORS	0	0.0	10	10	10	10	10	10	10	10	10
549 PRESIDENT & CEO	0	1.0	1.0	1.0	1.0	1.0	1.0	1.0	1.0	1.0	1.0
551 CFO	0	0.5	1.0	1.0	1.0	1.0	1.0	1.0	1.0	1.0	1.0
553 VP DISTRIBUTION	0	0.5	1.0	1.0	1.0	1.0	1.0	1.0	1.0	1.0	1.0
555 PROJECT MANAGER	0	1.0	1.0	1.0	1.0	1.0	1.0	1.0	1.0	1.0	1.0
558	0		0	0	0	0	0	0	0	0	0
560 CONTROLLER	0	0.5	1.0	1.0	1.0	1.0	1.0	1.0	1.0	1.0	1.0
562 SALES MANAGER	0	0.5	1.0	1.0	1.0	1.0	1.0	1.0	1.0	1.0	1.0
564 DP MANAGER	0	0.5	1.0	1.0	1.0	1.0	1.0	1.0	1.0	1.0	1.0
566 HUMAN RESOURCES MGR	0	0.5	1.0	1.0	1.0	1.0	1.0	1.0	1.0	1.0	1.0
568 GRAIN PURCHASING AGENT	0	0.4	1.0	1.0	1.0	1.0	1.0	1.0	1.0	1.0	1.0
570 A/R CLERK	0	0.4	1.0	1.0	1.0	1.0	1.0	1.0	1.0	1.0	1.0
572 A/P CLERK	0	0.4	1.0	1.0	1.0	1.0	1.0	1.0	1.0	1.0	1.0
574 SUPPORT STAFF	0	3.0	3.0	3.0	3.0	3.0	3.0	3.0	3.0	3.0	3.0
576 TOTAL	0	9	24	24	24	24	24	24	24	24	24

SG&A SALARIES

INFLATION 5.0%

	1990	1991	1992	1993	1994	1995	1996	1997	1998	1999	2000
BOARD OF DIRECTORS	10,000	10,500	11,025	11,576	12,155	12,763	13,401	14,071	14,775	15,513	16,289
PRESIDENT & CEO	150,000	157,500	165,375	173,644	182,326	191,442	201,014	211,065	221,618	232,699	244,334
CFO	50,000	52,500	55,125	57,881	60,775	63,814	67,005	70,355	73,873	77,566	81,445
VP DISTRIBUTION	50,000	52,500	55,125	57,881	60,775	63,814	67,005	70,355	73,873	77,566	81,445
PROJECT MANAGER	60,000	63,000	66,150	69,458	72,930	76,577	80,406	84,426	88,647	93,080	97,734
	0	0	0	0	0	0	0	0	0	0	0
CONTROLLER	35,000	36,750	38,588	40,517	42,543	44,670	46,903	49,249	51,711	54,296	57,011
SALES MANAGER	60,000	63,000	66,150	69,458	72,930	76,577	80,406	84,426	88,647	93,080	97,734
DP MANAGER	30,000	31,500	33,075	34,729	36,465	38,288	40,203	42,213	44,324	46,540	48,867
HUMAN RESOURCES MGR	35,000	36,750	38,588	40,517	42,543	44,670	46,903	49,249	51,711	54,296	57,011
GRAIN PURCHASING AGENT	35,000	36,750	38,588	40,517	42,543	44,670	46,903	49,249	51,711	54,296	57,011
A/R CLERK	29,000	30,450	31,973	33,571	35,250	37,012	38,863	40,806	42,846	44,989	47,238
A/P CLERK	20,000	21,000	22,050	23,153	24,310	25,526	26,802	28,142	29,549	31,027	32,578
SUPPORT STAFF	14,000	14,700	15,435	16,207	17,017	17,868	18,761	19,699	20,684	21,719	22,805

TOTAL SG&A LABOR DOLLARS

	1990	1991	1992	1993	1994	1995	1996	1997	1998	1999	2000
BOARD OF DIRECTORS	0	0	110,250	115,763	121,551	127,628	134,010	140,710	147,746	155,133	162,889
PRESIDENT & CEO	0	157,500	165,375	173,644	182,326	191,442	201,014	211,065	221,618	232,699	244,334
CFO	0	26,250	55,125	57,881	60,775	63,814	67,005	70,355	73,873	77,566	81,445
VP DISTRIBUTION	0	26,250	55,125	57,881	60,775	63,814	67,005	70,355	73,873	77,566	81,445
PROJECT MANAGER	0	63,000	66,150	69,458	72,930	76,577	80,406	84,426	88,647	93,080	97,734
	0	0	0	0	0	0	0	0	0	0	0
CONTROLLER	0	18,375	38,588	40,517	42,543	44,670	46,903	49,249	51,711	54,296	57,011
SALES MANAGER	0	31,500	66,150	69,458	72,930	76,577	80,406	84,426	88,647	93,080	97,734
DP MANAGER	0	15,750	33,075	34,729	36,465	38,288	40,203	42,213	44,324	46,540	48,867
HUMAN RESOURCES MGR	0	18,375	38,588	40,517	42,543	44,670	46,903	49,249	51,711	54,296	57,011
GRAIN PURCHASING AGENT	0	18,375	38,588	40,517	42,543	44,670	46,903	49,249	51,711	54,296	57,011
A/R CLERK	0	12,180	31,973	33,571	35,250	37,012	38,863	40,806	42,846	44,989	47,238
A/P CLERK	0	8,400	22,050	23,153	24,310	25,526	26,802	28,142	29,549	31,027	32,578
SUPPORT STAFF	0	44,100	46,305	48,620	51,051	53,604	56,284	59,098	62,053	65,156	68,414
TOTAL	0										

SALES, GENERAL & ADMIN

	INFLATION	1990	1991	1992	1993	1994	1995	1996	1997	1998	1999	2000
	5.00%											
EXPENSES:												
TELEPHONE		0	6,111	38,500	40,425	42,446	44,569	46,797	49,137	51,594	54,173	56,882
SALARIES		0	440,055	767,340	805,707	845,992	888,292	932,707	979,342	1,028,309	1,079,724	1,133,711
BENEFITS	15.0%	0	66,008	115,101	120,856	126,899	133,244	139,906	146,901	154,246	161,959	170,057
ADVERTISING		0	41,667	262,500	275,625	289,406	303,877	319,070	335,024	351,775	369,364	387,832
MKT DEV		0	13,889	87,500	91,875	96,469	101,292	106,357	111,675	117,258	123,121	129,277
LEG/ACCOUNT.	0.6%	0	2,778	17,500	18,375	19,294	20,258	21,271	22,335	23,452	24,624	25,855
TRAVEL	0.0%	0	32,480	204,624	214,855	225,598	236,878	248,722	261,158	274,216	287,927	302,323
INSURANCE	0.0%	0	0	0	0	0	0	0	0	0	0	0
POST & SUP		0	1,389	8,750	9,188	9,647	10,129	10,636	11,167	11,726	12,312	12,928
RES & DEV		0	556	3,500	3,675	3,859	4,052	4,254	4,467	4,690	4,925	5,171
CONSULTING		0	150,000	50,000	52,500	55,125	57,881	60,775	63,814	67,005	70,355	73,873
COMMISSIONS	5.0%	0	270,667	1,705,200	1,790,460	1,879,983	1,973,982	2,072,681	2,176,315	2,285,131	2,399,388	2,519,357
TOTAL		0	1,025,599	3,260,515	3,423,541	3,594,718	3,774,454	3,963,176	4,161,335	4,369,402	4,587,872	4,817,266

ACCOUNTS PAYABLE AGING (RAW MAT INV BUILDUP, SGA, DIRECT LABOR, OVERHEAD, VAR PROD COSTS, & SOFT COSTS & START UP)

% PAID IN:

	YEAR 1	YEAR 2	NEVER	TOTAL
	92%	8%	0%	100%

PRODUCTION COSTS - ADD'S

	1990	1991	1992	1993	1994	1995	1996	1997	1998	1999	2000
RAW MATERIAL BUILD-UP	0	91,955	480,870	-9,939	0	0	0	0	0	0	0
VARIABLE CGS	0	2,297,584	14,427,476	14,900,508	15,645,534	16,427,810	17,249,201	18,111,661	19,017,244	19,968,106	20,966,511
DIRECT LABOR	0	342,615	1,247,369	1,309,737	1,375,224	1,443,985	1,516,184	1,591,993	1,671,593	1,755,173	1,842,931
OVERHEAD	0	107,447	540,248	567,260	595,623	625,404	656,675	689,508	723,984	760,183	798,192
DEPRECIATION	0	1,834,167	10,558,542	7,990,940	6,062,415	4,613,077	3,523,099	2,702,668	2,084,466	1,618,026	1,265,512
TOTAL PRODUCTION COSTS	0	4,673,767	27,254,504	24,758,506	23,678,796	23,110,277	22,945,158	23,095,831	23,497,287	24,101,488	24,873,147

TOTAL COST OF GOODS SOLD

	1990	1991	1992	1993	1994	1995	1996	1997	1998	1999	2000
VARIABLE CGS	0	2,252,533	14,190,960	14,900,508	15,645,534	16,427,810	17,249,201	18,111,661	19,017,244	19,968,106	20,966,511
DIRECT LABOR	0	342,615	1,247,369	1,309,737	1,375,224	1,443,985	1,516,184	1,591,993	1,671,593	1,755,173	1,842,931
OVERHEAD	0	107,447	540,248	567,260	595,623	625,404	656,675	689,508	723,984	760,183	798,192
DEPRECIATION	0	1,834,167	10,558,542	7,990,940	6,062,415	4,613,077	3,523,099	2,702,668	2,084,466	1,618,026	1,265,512
TOTAL CGS	0	4,536,762	26,537,118	24,768,445	23,678,796	23,110,277	22,945,158	23,095,831	23,497,287	24,101,488	24,873,147

LOANS
====

PHASE I BANK LOAN — PRIN 18,000,000 · YEARS 10 · RATE 14.00% · PAYMTS 3,450,844

	2000	1999	1998	1997	1996	1995	1994	1993	1992	1991	1990
BEG BAL	5,682,368	8,011,589	10,054,766	11,847,026	13,419,184	14,798,270	16,007,994	17,069,156	18,000,000	18,000,000	0
INTEREST	795,532	1,121,623	1,407,667	1,658,584	1,878,686	2,071,758	2,241,119	2,389,682	2,520,000	1,260,000	0
PRINCIPAL	2,655,312	2,329,221	2,043,177	1,792,260	1,572,158	1,379,086	1,209,725	1,061,162	930,844	0	0
END BAL	3,027,056	5,682,368	8,011,589	10,054,766	11,847,026	13,419,184	14,798,270	16,007,994	17,069,156	18,000,000	0

PHASE II BANK LOAN — PRIN 0 · YEARS 10 · RATE 14.00% · PAYMTS 0

	2000	1999	1998	1997	1996	1995	1994	1993	1992	1991	1990
BEG BAL	0	0	0	0	0	0	0	0	0	0	0
INTEREST	0	0	0	0	0	0	0	0	0	0	0
PRINCIPAL	0	0	0	0	0	0	0	0	0	0	0
END BAL	0	0	0	0	0	0	0	0	0	0	0

PHASE III BANK LOAN — PRIN 0 · YEARS 10 · RATE 14.00% · PAYMTS 0

	2000	1999	1998	1997	1996	1995	1994	1993	1992	1991	1990
BEG BAL	0	0	0	0	0	0	0	0	0	0	0
INTEREST	0	0	0	0	0	0	0	0	0	0	0
PRINCIPAL	0	0	0	0	0	0	0	0	0	0	0
END BAL	0	0	0	0	0	0	0	0	0	0	0

PHASE I GOVERNMENT LOAN — PRIN 9,750,000 · YEARS 15 · RATE 0.00% · PAYMTS 650,000

	2000	1999	1998	1997	1996	1995	1994	1993	1992	1991	1990
BEG BAL	5,850,000	6,500,000	7,150,000	7,800,000	8,450,000	9,100,000	9,750,000	9,750,000	9,750,000	9,750,000	0
INTEREST	0	0	0	0	0	0	0	0	0	0	0
PRINCIPAL	650,000	650,000	650,000	650,000	650,000	650,000	650,000	0	0	0	0
END BAL	5,200,000	5,850,000	6,500,000	7,150,000	7,800,000	8,450,000	9,100,000	9,750,000	9,750,000	9,750,000	0

PHASE I FARM BONDS — PRIN 6,000,000 · YEARS N/A · RATE 0.00% · PAYMTS N/A

	2000	1999	1998	1997	1996	1995	1994	1993	1992	1991	1990
BEG BAL	6,000,000	6,000,000	6,000,000	6,000,000	6,000,000	6,000,000	6,000,000	6,000,000	6,000,000	6,000,000	0
INTEREST	0	0	0	0	0	0	0	0	0	0	0
PRINCIPAL	0	0	0	0	0	0	0	0	0	0	0
END BAL	6,000,000	6,000,000	6,000,000	6,000,000	6,000,000	6,000,000	6,000,000	6,000,000	6,000,000	6,000,000	0

PHASE III GOVERNMENT LOAN — PRIN 0 · YEARS 15 · RATE 0.00% · PAYMTS 0

	2000	1999	1998	1997	1996	1995	1994	1993	1992	1991	1990
BEG BAL	0	0	0	0	0	0	0	0	0	0	0
INTEREST	0	0	0	0	0	0	0	0	0	0	0
PRINCIPAL	0	0	0	0	0	0	0	0	0	0	0
END BAL	0	0	0	0	0	0	0	0	0	0	0

CREDIT LINE — ANN RATE 14.00%

	2000	1999	1998	1997	1996	1995	1994	1993	1992	1991	1990
BALANCE	0	0	0	0	0	0	0	0	149,914	2,141,624	0
INTEREST ***	0	0	0	0	0	0	0	0	0	149,914	0

LOANS SUMMARY:

	2000	1999	1998	1997	1996	1995	1994	1993	1992	1991	1990
TOTAL INTEREST	795,532	1,121,623	1,407,667	1,658,584	1,878,686	2,071,758	2,241,119	2,389,682	2,669,914	1,409,914	0
TOTAL PRIN ADD (W/O CL)	0	0	0	0	0	0	0	0	0	33,750,000	0
TOTAL PRIN REPAY	3,305,312	2,979,221	2,693,177	2,442,260	2,222,158	2,029,086	1,859,725	1,061,162	930,844	0	0
ENDING BALANCE (W/O C/L)	14,227,056	17,532,368	20,511,589	23,204,766	25,647,026	27,869,184	29,898,270	31,757,994	32,819,156	33,750,000	0

EQUITY ADDITIONS (REDUCTIONS)

	2000	1999	1998	1997	1996	1995	1994	1993	1992	1991	1990
COMMON	0	0	0	0	0	0	0	0	0	15,750,000	500,000
PREFERRED	0	0	0	0	0	0	0	0	0	0	0

BASE CASE - AUG 1 UPDATE
INTEREST 14.0%
RUN # P

P&L

	1990	1991	1992	1993	1994	1995	1996	1997	1998	1999	2000
REVENUES	0	5,413,333	34,104,000	35,809,200	37,599,660	39,479,643	41,453,625	43,526,306	45,702,622	47,987,753	50,387,140
COST OF SALES											
VARIABLE CGS	0	2,252,533	14,190,960	14,900,508	15,645,534	16,427,810	17,249,201	18,111,661	19,017,244	19,968,106	20,966,511
DIRECT LABOR	0	342,615	1,247,369	1,309,737	1,375,224	1,443,985	1,516,184	1,591,993	1,671,593	1,755,173	1,842,931
OVERHEAD	0	107,447	540,248	567,260	595,623	625,404	656,675	689,508	723,984	760,183	798,192
DEPRECIATION		1,834,167	10,558,542	7,990,940	6,062,415	4,613,077	3,523,099	2,702,668	2,084,466	1,618,026	1,265,512
TOTAL CGS	0	4,536,762	26,537,118	24,768,445	23,678,796	23,110,277	22,945,158	23,095,831	23,497,287	24,101,488	24,873,147
GROSS PROFIT	0	876,572	7,566,882	11,040,755	13,920,864	16,369,366	18,508,467	20,430,475	22,205,335	23,886,265	25,513,994
INTEREST	0	1,409,914	2,669,914	2,389,682	2,241,119	2,071,758	1,878,686	1,658,584	1,407,667	1,121,623	795,532
S G & A	0	1,025,599	3,260,515	3,423,541	3,594,718	3,774,454	3,963,176	4,161,335	4,369,402	4,587,872	4,817,266
SOFT COST & START UP EXPENSES	750,000	1,850,000	0	0	0	0	0	0	0	0	0
INCOME (LOSS) FROM OPERATIONS	-750,000	-3,408,941	1,636,453	5,227,532	8,085,027	10,523,155	12,666,605	14,610,557	16,428,266	18,176,770	19,901,197
OTHER INCOME (EXPENSE)											
SOFT COST GRANTS	250,000	50,000	0	0	0	0	0	0	0	0	0
INCOME BEFORE PROV FOR TAXES	-500,000	-3,358,941	1,636,453	5,227,532	8,085,027	10,523,155	12,666,605	14,610,557	16,428,266	18,176,770	19,901,197
PROVISION FOR TAXES * 40.00%	0	0	0	1,202,018	3,234,011	4,209,262	5,066,642	5,844,223	6,571,306	7,270,708	7,960,479
NET INCOME (LOSS)	-500,000	-3,358,941	1,636,453	4,025,515	4,851,016	6,313,893	7,599,963	8,766,334	9,856,959	10,906,062	11,940,718
CUM NET INCOME (LOSS)	-500,000	-3,858,941	-2,222,488	1,803,027	6,654,043	12,967,936	20,567,899	29,334,233	39,191,192	50,097,254	62,037,972

CASH FLOW

BASE CASE - AUG 1 UPDATE

RUN #   P

INTEREST   14.0%

	1990	1991	1992	1993	1994	1995	1996	1997	1998	1999	2000
CASH, beginning balance	0	62,500	5,000	7,206,026	18,048,710	27,038,211	35,867,809	44,697,013	53,648,470	62,817,670	72,279,536
RECEIPTS:											
ON ACCOUNTS RECEIVABLE	0	4,962,222	31,713,111	35,667,100	37,450,455	39,322,978	41,289,127	43,353,583	45,521,262	47,797,325	50,187,191
GRANTS	250,000	50,000	0	0	0	0	0	0	0	0	0
ADDITIONS TO LOANS	0	33,750,000	0	0	0	0	0	0	0	0	0
ADDITIONS TO EQUITY	500,000	15,750,000	0	0	0	0	0	0	0	0	0
TOTAL RECEIPTS	750,000	54,512,222	31,713,111	35,667,100	37,450,455	39,322,978	41,289,127	43,353,583	45,521,262	47,797,325	50,187,191
TOTAL CASH AVAILABLE	750,000	54,574,722	31,718,111	42,873,126	55,499,165	66,361,189	77,156,936	88,050,596	99,169,732	110,614,995	122,466,727
DISBURSEMENTS:											
A/P	687,500	5,301,433	18,769,704	20,171,554	21,126,099	22,183,274	23,292,437	24,457,059	25,679,912	26,963,908	28,312,103
PP&E	0	50,000,000	0	0	0	0	0	0	0	0	0
TAXES	0	0	0	1,202,018	3,234,011	4,209,262	5,066,642	5,844,223	6,571,306	7,270,708	7,960,479
PRINCIPAL REPAID	0	0	930,844	1,061,162	1,859,725	2,029,086	2,222,158	2,442,260	2,693,177	2,979,221	3,305,312
INTEREST	0	1,409,914	2,669,914	2,389,682	2,241,119	2,071,758	1,878,686	1,658,584	1,407,667	1,121,623	795,532
TOTAL DISBURSEMENTS	687,500	56,711,346	22,370,461	24,824,416	28,460,954	30,493,379	32,459,923	34,402,126	36,352,062	38,335,460	40,373,426
INCREASE (DECREASE) IN CASH	62,500	-2,199,124	9,342,650	10,842,684	8,989,501	8,829,598	8,829,204	8,951,457	9,169,200	9,461,865	9,813,766
END CASH BAL (PRE C/L)	62,500	-2,136,624	9,347,650	18,048,710	27,038,211	35,867,809	44,697,013	53,648,470	62,817,670	72,279,536	82,093,301
CREDIT LINE DRAW (REPAY)	0	2,141,624	-2,141,624	0	0	0	0	0	0	0	0
CASH, end of period (W C/L)	62,500	5,000	7,206,026	18,048,710	27,038,211	35,867,809	44,697,013	53,648,470	62,817,670	72,279,536	82,093,301
CUM CASH FLOW (W/O C/L)	62,500	-2,136,624	7,206,026	18,048,710	27,038,211	35,867,809	44,697,013	53,648,470	62,817,670	72,279,536	82,093,301

RUN #   P   INTEREST   14.0%

	DEC 89	1990	1991	1992	1993	1994	1995	1996	1997	1998	1999	2000
ASSETS												
CASH	0	62,500	5,000	7,206,026	18,048,710	27,038,211	35,867,809	44,697,013	53,648,470	62,817,670	72,279,536	82,093,301
ACC/REC	0	0	451,111	2,842,000	2,984,100	3,133,305	3,289,970	3,454,469	3,627,192	3,808,552	3,998,979	4,198,928
RAW MAT INV	0	0	91,955	572,824	562,885	562,885	562,885	562,885	562,885	562,885	562,885	562,885
FG INV	0	0	45,051	281,567	281,567	281,567	281,567	281,567	281,567	281,567	281,567	281,567
PREPAIDS	0	0	0	0	0	0	0	0	0	0	0	0
TOT CURRENT ASSETS	0	62,500	593,117	10,902,417	21,877,261	31,015,968	40,002,231	48,995,934	58,120,114	67,470,674	77,122,967	87,136,682
PP&E	0	0	48,165,833	37,607,292	29,616,352	23,553,937	18,940,860	15,417,761	12,715,092	10,630,626	9,012,600	7,747,088
TOTAL ASSETS	0	62,500	48,758,950	48,509,708	51,493,613	54,569,905	58,943,091	64,413,694	70,835,207	78,101,300	86,135,567	94,883,770
LIABILITIES & STOCKHOLDERS' EQUITY												
ACCTS PAYABLE	0	62,500	476,267	1,663,040	1,682,592	1,767,592	1,855,971	1,948,770	2,046,208	2,148,519	2,255,944	2,368,742
CREDIT LINE	0	0	2,141,624	0	0	0	0	0	0	0	0	0
TOT CUR LIAB (EXCL LT LOANS)	0	62,500	2,617,891	1,663,040	1,682,592	1,767,592	1,855,971	1,948,770	2,046,208	2,148,519	2,255,944	2,368,742
LT DEBT	0	0	33,750,000	32,819,156	31,757,994	29,898,270	27,869,184	25,647,026	23,204,766	20,511,589	17,532,368	14,227,056
TOTAL LIABILITIES	0	62,500	36,367,891	34,482,196	33,440,587	31,665,861	29,725,155	27,595,796	25,250,974	22,660,108	19,788,313	16,595,798
STOCKHLDS' EQUITY												
CONTRIBUTED	0	500,000	16,250,000	16,250,000	16,250,000	16,250,000	16,250,000	16,250,000	16,250,000	16,250,000	16,250,000	16,250,000
RET EARNINGS	0	-500,000	-3,858,941	-2,222,488	1,803,027	6,654,043	12,967,936	20,567,899	29,334,233	39,191,192	50,097,254	62,037,972
TOTAL STOCKHLDS' EQ	0	0	12,391,059	14,027,512	18,053,027	22,904,043	29,217,936	36,817,899	45,584,233	55,441,192	66,347,254	78,287,972
TOT LIA & STHLD EQ	0	62,500	48,758,950	48,509,708	51,493,613	54,569,905	58,943,091	64,413,694	70,835,207	78,101,300	86,135,567	94,883,770

Printout of Case Study Quantitative Analysis

```
FINANCIAL ANALYSIS - TRADITIONAL                                    BASE CASE - AUG 1 UPDATE
```

COMPUTATION OF RATIOS

	1990	1991	1992	1993	1994	1995	1996	1997	1998	1999	2000
CURRENT RATIO	1.00	0.17	4.00	6.18	8.17	9.81	11.16	12.26	13.16	13.87	15.36
QUICK RATIO	1.00	0.13	3.69	5.94	7.95	9.60	10.97	12.09	12.99	13.72	15.21
GROSS PROFIT MARGIN	#DIV/0!	16.19%	22.19%	30.83%	37.02%	41.46%	44.65%	46.94%	48.59%	49.78%	50.64%
NET PROFIT MARGIN	#DIV/0!	-62.05%	4.80%	11.24%	12.90%	15.99%	18.33%	20.14%	21.57%	22.73%	23.70%
A/R TURNOVER IN DAYS	#DIV/0!	15	18	30	30	30	30	30	30	30	30
SALES TO INVENTORY	#DIV/0!	79	69	42	45	47	49	52	54	57	60
RETURN ON ASSETS	-1600.00%	-13.76%	3.36%	8.05%	9.15%	11.12%	12.32%	12.96%	13.24%	13.28%	13.19%
RETURN ON COMMON EQUITY	#DIV/0!	-54.22%	12.39%	25.10%	23.69%	24.23%	23.02%	21.28%	19.51%	17.91%	16.51%

ANALYSIS OF RATIOS

	AVERAGE (EXCL '90 & '91)	MAXIMUM (EXCL '90 & '91)	MINIMUM (EXCL '90 & '91)	DUNN & BRADSTREET (SIC 2098 - MAC & SPAG)	VARIANCE (FROM AVERAGE)
CURRENT RATIO	10.44	15.36	4.00	2.10	8.34
QUICK RATIO	10.24	15.21	3.69	1.50	8.74
GROSS PROFIT MARGIN	41.34%	50.64%	22.19%	33.30%	8.04%
NET PROFIT MARGIN	16.82%	23.70%	4.80%	2.60%	14.22%
A/R TURNOVER IN DAYS	28.35	29.69	17.62	23.00	-5.35
SALES TO INVENTORY (TIMES)	52.61	68.80	42.16	30.90	21.71
RETURN ON ASSETS	10.74%	13.28%	3.36%	6.50%	4.24%
RETURN ON COMMON EQUITY	20.40%	25.10%	12.39%	12.00%	8.40%

```
*************************************************************
FINANCIAL ANALYSIS - BANKRUPTCY ANALYSIS & VALUATION          BASE CASE - AUG 1 UPDATE
*************************************************************
```

BANKRUPTCY ANALYSIS

		1990	1991	1992	1993	1994	1995	1996	1997	1998	1999	2000
CAP RATE	12.00%											
DIV PAY RATIO	80.00%											
$X1 =$		0.00%	-6.06%	14.55%	29.40%	40.75%	49.39%	55.86%	60.58%	63.91%	66.08%	68.17%
$X2 =$		-800.00%	-7.91%	-7.48%	-5.81%	-3.80%	-1.09%	2.29%	6.28%	10.88%	16.13%	22.10%
$X3 =$		-800.00%	-4.00%	9.12%	16.22%	22.37%	27.69%	32.41%	36.74%	40.85%	44.91%	49.08%
$X4 =$		-6666.67%	-76.97%	39.55%	100.32%	127.66%	177.01%	229.50%	289.31%	362.49%	459.28%	599.59%
$X5 =$		0.00	0.11	0.72	0.76	0.81	0.87	0.92	0.98	1.05	1.12	1.19
Z FACTOR (ADJ FOR DIV PAY)		-77.60	-0.67	1.33	2.17	2.75	3.42	4.07	4.75	5.49	6.37	7.54
Z FACTOR (UNADJUSTED)		-77.60	-0.67	1.37	2.26	2.85	3.48	4.04	4.59	5.17	5.86	6.79
Z FACTOR - AVE ('92 TO '00) (UNADJUSTED)		4.05										

VALUATION ANALYSIS

FUTURE VALUE

RATE	TOTAL FUTURE VALUE ($ CAN)	1990	1991	1992	1993	1994	1995	1996	1997	1998	1999	2000
10.00%	200,724,167	162,109	-5,185,420	20,026,799	21,129,324	15,925,450	14,220,157	12,926,837	11,914,390	11,094,732	10,408,052	88,101,738
12.00%	211,171,946	194,116	-6,098,344	23,132,057	23,969,720	17,743,681	15,560,769	13,892,923	12,576,153	11,501,844	10,597,289	88,101,738
14.00%	222,573,343	231,701	-7,151,439	26,650,716	27,131,310	19,731,709	17,000,638	14,912,173	13,261,978	11,916,292	10,786,527	88,101,738
AVERAGE	211,489,819											

PRESENT VALUE

RATE	TOTAL PRESENT VALUE	1990	1991	1992	1993	1994	1995	1996	1997	1998	1999	2000
10.00%	77,387,856	62,500	-1,999,204	7,721,198	8,146,269	6,139,950	5,482,486	4,983,855	4,593,513	4,277,499	4,012,755	33,967,034
12.00%	67,991,715	62,500	-1,963,504	7,447,903	7,717,608	5,712,991	5,010,151	4,473,149	4,049,185	3,703,286	3,412,044	28,366,402
14.00%	60,037,781	62,500	-1,929,056	7,188,866	7,318,503	5,322,506	4,585,817	4,022,466	3,577,336	3,214,346	2,909,599	23,764,898
AVERAGE	68,472,451											

FINANCIAL ANALYSIS - SENSITIVITY ANALYSIS

BASE CASE - AUG 1 UPDATE

//————————VARIANCES FROM D & B MEDIAN INDUSTRY STATS————————//

30000

PASTA SOLD (TONNES)	CURRENT RATIO	QUICK RATIO	GROSS PROF MARGIN	NET PROF MARGIN	A/R TURNS DAYS	SALES TO INV	RETURN ON ASSETS	RETURN ON EQUITY	Z FACTOR	FUTURE VALUE	PRESENT VALUE	CUM CASH FLOW
30,000	8.34	8.74	8.04%	14.22%	-5.35	21.71	4.24%	8.40%	4.05	211,489,819	68,472,451	82,093,301
29,000	7.99	8.40	7.46%	13.72%	-5.35	21.71	3.89%	7.91%	3.91	201,121,216	65,114,910	78,160,402
28,000	7.64	8.04	6.83%	13.18%	-5.35	21.71	3.52%	7.38%	3.76	190,752,612	61,757,369	74,227,502
27,000	7.26	7.67	6.15%	12.59%	-5.35	21.71	3.14%	6.82%	3.62	180,286,975	58,369,229	70,294,603
26,000	6.87	7.28	5.42%	11.96%	-5.35	21.71	2.74%	6.21%	3.46	169,789,691	54,971,111	66,361,703
25,000	6.47	6.89	4.63%	11.27%	-5.35	21.71	2.32%	5.56%	3.31	159,292,406	51,572,992	62,428,803
24,000	6.04	6.47	3.78%	10.52%	-5.35	21.71	1.89%	4.85%	3.14	148,717,423	48,150,321	58,495,904
23,000	5.59	6.02	2.86%	9.70%	-5.35	21.71	1.44%	4.09%	2.97	138,048,948	44,698,107	54,563,004
22,000	5.13	5.56	1.85%	8.81%	-5.35	21.71	0.96%	3.25%	2.79	127,380,473	41,245,894	50,630,104
21,000	4.62	5.06	0.74%	7.80%	-5.35	21.71	0.47%	2.35%	2.60	116,511,110	37,730,067	46,697,205
20,000	4.10	4.54	-0.48%	6.70%	-5.35	21.71	-0.05%	1.34%	2.40	105,637,257	34,212,822	42,764,305

900

//————————VARIANCES FROM D & B MEDIAN INDUSTRY STATS————————//

PASTA PRICE ($ CAN / TONNE)	CURRENT RATIO	QUICK RATIO	GROSS PROF MARGIN	NET PROF MARGIN	A/R TURNS DAYS	SALES TO INV	RETURN ON ASSETS	RETURN ON EQUITY	Z FACTOR	FUTURE VALUE	PRESENT VALUE	CUM CASH FLOW
900	8.34	8.74	8.04%	14.22%	-5.35	21.71	4.24%	8.40%	4.05	211,489,819	68,472,451	82,093,301
880	7.82	8.22	6.75%	13.35%	-5.35	20.58	3.82%	7.83%	3.89	199,417,974	64,563,671	77,513,127
860	7.30	7.69	5.40%	12.45%	-5.35	19.44	3.38%	7.21%	3.73	187,337,438	60,652,151	72,932,952
840	6.75	7.15	3.99%	11.49%	-5.35	18.31	2.93%	6.54%	3.56	175,116,743	56,696,434	68,352,777
820	6.21	6.61	2.51%	10.48%	-5.35	17.17	2.44%	5.81%	3.39	162,896,048	52,740,717	63,772,602
800	5.66	6.06	0.96%	9.43%	-5.35	16.04	1.94%	5.01%	3.22	150,814,450	48,772,197	59,192,427
780	5.08	5.48	-0.67%	8.31%	-5.35	14.91	1.41%	4.14%	3.03	138,214,837	44,753,927	54,612,252
760	4.51	4.91	-2.38%	7.13%	-5.35	13.77	0.85%	3.18%	2.84	125,782,382	40,730,860	50,032,077
740	3.90	4.30	-4.18%	5.87%	-5.35	12.64	0.27%	2.11%	2.64	113,126,189	36,537,373	45,451,902
720	3.27	3.67	-6.07%	4.54%	-5.35	11.50	-0.35%	0.90%	2.42	100,378,133	32,514,736	40,871,727
700	2.61	3.01	-8.07%	3.10%	-5.35	10.37	-0.98%	-0.45%	2.19	87,304,582	28,288,244	36,254,298

131.7

//————————VARIANCES FROM D & B MEDIAN INDUSTRY STATS————————//

COST OF WHEAT ($ CAN / TONNE)	CURRENT RATIO	QUICK RATIO	GROSS PROF MARGIN	NET PROF MARGIN	A/R TURNS DAYS	SALES TO INV	RETURN ON ASSETS	RETURN ON EQUITY	Z FACTOR	FUTURE VALUE	PRESENT VALUE	CUM CASH FLOW
151.70	7.35	7.73	5.01%	12.41%	-5.35	15.84	3.59%	7.53%	3.82	193,209,403	62,554,357	75,153,618
147.70	7.54	7.93	5.62%	12.78%	-5.35	16.91	3.73%	7.71%	3.87	196,865,485	63,737,975	76,541,555
143.70	7.74	8.13	6.22%	13.14%	-5.35	18.02	3.86%	7.89%	3.91	200,521,568	64,921,594	77,929,491
139.70	7.94	8.33	6.83%	13.50%	-5.35	19.19	3.99%	8.07%	3.96	204,177,652	66,105,213	79,317,428
135.70	8.14	8.53	7.44%	13.86%	-5.35	20.42	4.12%	8.24%	4.00	207,833,735	67,288,832	80,705,365
131.70	8.34	8.74	8.04%	14.22%	-5.35	21.71	4.24%	8.40%	4.05	211,489,818	68,472,451	82,093,301
127.70	8.54	8.95	8.65%	14.58%	-5.35	23.06	4.37%	8.57%	4.09	215,145,902	69,656,069	83,481,238
123.70	8.75	9.16	9.26%	14.95%	-5.35	24.49	4.49%	8.73%	4.14	218,801,988	70,839,688	84,869,175
119.70	8.96	9.37	9.86%	15.31%	-5.35	26.00	4.61%	8.88%	4.18	222,458,069	72,023,307	86,257,111
115.70	9.17	9.58	10.47%	15.67%	-5.35	27.59	4.73%	9.04%	4.23	226,114,152	73,206,926	87,645,048
111.70	9.38	9.80	11.08%	16.03%	-5.35	29.27	4.85%	9.19%	4.27	229,770,236	74,390,545	89,032,985

FINANCIAL ANALYSIS - SENSITIVITY ANALYSIS - CONTINUED   BASE CASE - AUG 1 UPDATE

WHEAT 131.7
PASTA 900

FUTURE VALUE

COST OF WHEAT ($ / TONNE)

($ CAN / TONNE)

211,489,819

	116	120	124	128	132	136	140	144	148	152
P R I C E 900	226,114,151	222,458,061	218,801,977	215,145,894	211,489,810	207,833,727	204,177,644	200,521,560	196,865,477	193,209,393
880	214,042,308	210,386,225	206,730,141	203,074,058	199,417,974	195,761,891	192,105,807	188,449,724	184,755,985	181,055,448
860	201,970,463	198,314,379	194,658,296	191,002,212	187,337,438	183,636,901	179,936,364	176,235,827	172,535,290	168,834,753
840	189,898,617	186,218,354	182,517,817	178,817,280	175,116,743	171,416,206	167,715,669	164,015,132	160,314,595	156,614,057
820	177,698,196	173,997,659	170,297,122	166,596,585	162,896,048	159,195,510	155,494,973	151,774,585	148,014,938	144,255,291
F 800	165,477,501	161,776,963	158,076,426	154,375,889	150,634,837	146,875,191	143,115,544	139,355,898	135,596,251	131,836,604
O R 780	153,254,737	149,495,090	145,735,444	141,975,797	138,216,150	134,456,857	130,696,857	126,937,211	123,116,414	119,285,873
760	140,836,050	137,076,403	133,316,757	129,557,110	125,782,382	121,951,842	118,191,301	114,290,761	110,460,220	106,629,679
P A 740	128,417,363	124,617,810	120,787,270	116,956,729	113,126,189	109,295,648	105,465,107	101,570,822	97,660,068	93,703,253
S T A 720	115,792,157	111,961,617	108,131,076	104,288,886	100,378,133	96,467,379	92,503,900	88,503,936	84,468,143	80,378,503
700	103,096,197	99,185,443	95,274,690	91,304,546	87,304,582	83,237,955	79,148,315	75,058,674	70,969,033	66,809,799

Bibliography

BIBLIOGRAPHY OUTLINE

A   Valuation
B   Marketing
C   Strategic and Business Planning
D   Computers
E   Finance
F   Accounting and AICPA Publications
G   Cost Estimating and Management Accounting
H   Systems and Operations
I   Quantitative Methods
J   Ethics and Business Responsibility
K   Communications and Logic

A. *VALUATION*

1. American Institute of Certified Public Accountants [AICPA]. *Valuation of Businesses and Professional Practices with Revenues under $20 Million.* New York: The American Institute of Certified Public Accountants, Inc., 1986.
2. American Institute of Certified Public Accountants [AICPA]. *Valuation of a Closely Held Business.* New York: AICPA Inc., 1987.
3. Bishop, John A., and Idelle A. Howitt. *Federal Tax Valuation Digest.* 1988/1989 Cumulative Edition. Boston, MA: Warren, Gorham & Lamont, 1988.
4. Blum, Robert R., C.P.A. *Business Valuation.* Milwaukee, WI: Aardvark/McGraw-Hill, 1984.

5. Coxe, Weld. *Managing Architectural And Engineering Practice.* New York: John Wiley & Sons. 1980 (Chapter 10).

6. Desmond, Glenn M. *How To Value Professional Practices.* Los Angeles: Valuation Press, 1980.

7. Desmond, Glenn M., and Richard E. Kelly. *Business Valuation Handbook.* Los Angeles: Valuation Press, 1989.

8. Desmond, Glenn M., and John Marcello. *Handbook Of Small Business Valuation Formulas.* Los Angeles: Valuation Press, 1988.

9. Fishman, Jay E., and Roger J. Grabowski. *Closely Held Corporations: Valuation.* Okemos, MO: Steven C. Dilley's Federal Tax Workshops, Inc., 1986.

10. Goldberg, Barth H. *Valuation of Divorce Assets.* New York: West, 1987.

11. Horn, Thomas. *Business Valuation Manual.* Lancaster, PA: Charter Oak Press, 1987.

12. Internal Revenues Service. *IRS Valuation Guide for Income, Estate and Gift Taxes.* Chicago: Commerce Clearing House, 1987.

13. Kinnard, William N. Jr. *Income Property Valuation.* Lexington MA: D.C. Heath, 1971.

14. Krahmer, Johannes R., Esq. Valuation of Shares of Closely Held Corporations. Wilmington, DE: Tax Management Inc., 1985.

15. Miles, Raymond C. *Basic Business Appraisal.* New York: John Wiley & Sons, 1984.

16. Miles, Raymond C. *How To Price A Business.* Englewood Cliffs, NJ: Institute for Business Planning, Prentice Hall, 1982.

17. Stegall, Donald P., D.B.A., Lawrence L. Steinmetz, Ph.D., and John B. Kline, J.D. *Managing the Small Business.* Homewood IL: Richard D. Irwin, 1976.

18. Thornton, Roy C. "A Practical Guide to Valuation," *The Practical Accountant.* Boston, MA: Warren, Gorham & Lamont, 9 November, 1984, pp. 55–66.

19. Zipp, Alan S., CPA. *Handbook of Tax and Financial Planning for Divorce and Separation.* Englewood Cliffs, NJ: Prentice-Hall, 1984.

B. MARKETING

1. Caples, John. *Tested Advertising Methods,* Fourth Edition. Englewood Cliffs, NJ: Prentice-Hall, 1974.

2. Hartly, Robert F. *Marketing Fundamentals for Responsive Management.* New York: Dun-Donnelley, 1976.

3. Heidingsfield, Myron S., and A. B. Blankenship. *Marketing.* New York: Barnes and Noble Books, 1974.

4. Hopkins, Thomas. *How to Master the Art of Selling,* Second Edition. NY: Warner Books, 1982.

5. Lemmon, Wayne A. *Market Analysis Workbook*. New York: AMACOM, 1980.

6. Lewis, Herschell Gordon. *How to Make Your Advertising Twice as Effective at Half The Cost*. Englewood Cliffs, NJ: Prentice-Hall, 1986.

7. Little, John D.C., and Michael N. Cassettari. *Decision Support Systems for Marketing Managers*. New York: Management Decision Systems, Inc., 1984.

8. McCarthy, Jerome E. *Basic Marketing*, Fourth Edition. Homewood IL: Richard D. Irwin, 1971.

9. McNair, Malcom P., and Harry L. Hanson. *Readings In Marketing*. New York: McGraw-Hill, 1949.

10. Urban, Glen L., and John R. Hauser. *Design and Marketing of New Products*. Englewood Cliffs, NJ: Prentice-Hall, 1980.

C. *STRATEGIC AND BUSINESS PLANNING*

1. Bangs, David H., Jr., and William R. Osgood. *Business Planning Guide*. Portsmouth, NH: Upstart Publishing Company, 1978.

2. Beischel, Mark E., CMA, and K. Richard Smith, CMA. "Linking the Shop Floor to the Top Floor," *Management Accounting*. Montvale, NJ: Institute of Management Accountants, October, 1991, pp. 25–29.

3. Bennett, Robert E., and James A. Hendricks. "Justifying the Acquisition of Automated Equipment," *Management Accounting*. Montvale, NJ: National Association of Accountants, July, 1987, pp. 39–46.

4. Boardroom. *Shrewd Business*. New York: Boardroom Reports, 1981.

5. Bromwich, Michael, and Al Bhimani. "Strategic Investment Appraisal," *Management Accounting*. Montvale, NJ: National Association of Accountants, March, 1991, pp. 45–48.

6. Cunningham, Barton J. "Approaches to the Evaluation of Organizational Effectiveness," *Academy of Management Review*. Victoria, British Columbia, Canada: University of Victoria, School of Public Administration, July 1977, pp. 463–473.

7. Doyle, A. Conan. *Casebook of Sherlock Holmes*. Santa Rosa, CA: Classic Press Inc., 1968.

8. Ellsworth, Richard R. "Capital Markets and Competitive Decline," *Harvard Business Review*. Boston: Graduate School of Business Administration, Harvard University. September–October 1985, pp. 171–183.

9. Ellsworth, Richard R. "Financial Policies as if Corporate Strategy Mattered." Boston: Harvard University. Unpublished working paper.

10. Fox, Phillip J., and Joseph R. Mancuso. *402 Things You Must Know Before Starting a New Business*. Englewood Cliffs, NJ: Prentice-Hall, 1980.

11. Fraser, William M. "To Buy or Not to Buy?" *Management Accounting.* Montvale, NJ: National Association of Accountants, December 1989, pp. 34–37.

12. Glueck, William F. *Business Policy and Strategic Management.* New York: McGraw-Hill, 1980.

13. Haller, Terry. *Secrets of the Master Business Strategists.* Englewood Cliffs, NJ: Prentice Hall, 1983.

14. Hammermesh, Richard, G. "A Note on Implementing Strategy," Boston: Harvard Business School, 1982. Working paper.

15. Hammermesh, Richard, G. "Administrative Issues Posed by Contemporary Approaches to Strategic Planning: The Case of the Dexter Corporation," Boston: Harvard Business School. Working paper.

16. Hammermesh, Richard, G., M.J. Anderson, Jr., and J.E. Harris. "Strategies for Low Market Share Businesses," *Harvard Business Review.* Boston: May–June, 1978.

17. Hammermesh, Richard, and Roderick E. White. "Managing Organizational Context—A Key to Business Unit Profitability," Boston: Harvard Business School. Working paper.

18. Hanan, Mark. *Growth Partnering.* New York: American Management Association, 1986.

19. Heghitt, C. F. *Your Own Business.* Washington: U.S. Government Printing Office, 1950.

20. Hendricks, James A., Robert C. Bastian, and Thomas L. Sexton. "Bundle Monitoring of Strategic Projects," *Management Accounting.* Montvale, NJ: Institute of Management Accountants, February, 1992, pp. 31–35.

21. Hudson, William J. *Business Without Economists.* New York: AMACOM, 1987.

22. Inc. Magazine. *Small Business Success.* Boston: Inc. Publishing Company, 1987.

23. Koehler, Robert W. "Triple-Threat Strategy," *Management Accounting.* Montvale, NJ: Institute of Management Accountants, October 1991, pp. 30–34.

24. Lindhe, Richard. *Forecasting and the Information Process.* Unpublished paper.

25. Mancuso, Joseph R. *Check List For Starting a Successful Business.* Worcester, MA: Center For Entrepreneurial Management, 1979.

26. Mancuso, Joseph R. *How to Prepare and Present a Business Plan.* Englewood Cliffs, NJ: Prentice Hall, 1983.

27. Mancuso, Joseph R. *How to Start, Finance, and Manage Your Own Small Business.* Englewood Cliffs, NJ: Prentice Hall, 1984.

28. Mancuso, Joseph R. *How to Write a Winning Business Plan.* Englewood Cliffs, NJ: Prentice Hall, 1985.

29. Mintzberg, Henry, and James Brian Quinn. *The Strategy Process,* Second Edition. Englewood Cliffs, NJ: Prentice-Hall, 1991.

30. Parisi, Anthony J. (special edition editor). "The Quality Imperative," *Business Week: Special Issue 1991.* New York: McGraw-Hill, October 25, 1991.

31. Randolph, Robert M. *Planagment—Moving Concept into Reality.* Austin, TX: Learning Concepts, 1975.

32. Skinner, Wickham. "Manufacturing—The Missing Link in Corporate Strategy," *Harvard Business Review.* Boston: Graduate School of Business Administration, Harvard University, May-June 1969, pp. 136–145.

33. Test, Darrell L., John D. Hawley, and Michael F. Cotright. "Determining Strategic Value," *Management Accounting.* Montvale, NJ: National Association of Accountants, June 1987, pp. 39–42.

34. The Company Company. *Planning the Business Venture.* Alpine, UT: The Company Co., 1989.

35. Toffler, Alvin. *Future Shock.* New York: Random House, 1970.

36. Vandermerwe, Sandra, and Michael Oliff. "Corporate Challenges for an Age of Reconsumption," *Business Edge.* Seattle, WA: American Passage Media Corporation, May, 1992, pp. 23–28.

37. Welsh, John A., and Jerry F. White. *The Entrepreneur's Master Planning Guide.* Englewood Cliffs, NY: Prentice-Hall, 1983.

38. White, Richard M. *The Entrepreneur's Manual.* Radnor, PA: Chilton Book Company, 1977.

39. White, Roderick E., and Richard G. Hammermesh. "Toward a Model of Business Unit Performance: An Integrative Approach," (reprinted from the *Academy of Management Review,* Vol 6, No. 2, April 1981.) Boston, MA: Harvard Business School.

40. Wolfensberger, Beth. "Entrepreneur," *New England Business.* Boston, MA: April, 1991, pp. 29–31.

41. Wright, Bruce J. *Total Financial Planning.* New York: American Management Association, 1983.

D. COMPUTERS

1. Bonelli, Robert Allen. *Increasing Profitability With Minicomputers.* New York: Petrocelli Books, 1981.

2. Bradley, James. *File and Data Base Techniques.* New York: Holt, Rinehart, and Winston, 1982.

3. Date, C.J. *Database.* Reading, MA: Addison-Wesley Company, 1983.

4. Kenney, Donald P. *Personal Computers in Business.* New York: AMACOM, 1985.

5. Price Waterhouse. *Managing Microcomputers.* New York: Price Water-house, 1984.

6. Sambridge, Edward R. *Purchasing Computers: A Practical Guide for Buyers of Computers and Computing Equipment.* New York: AMACOM, 1979.

7. Simpson, Alan. *Data File Programing on Your IBM PC.* Berkeley, CA: Sybex, 1984.

8. Texas Instruments Learning Center. *Calculator Decision-Making Sourcebook,* Second Edition. Texas: Texas Instruments, 1981.

E. *FINANCE*

1. Baker, John C., and Deane W. Malott. *Introduction to Corporate Finance.* New York: McGraw-Hill, 1936.

2. Blecke, Curtis J., and Daniel L. Gotthilf. *Financial Analysis for Decision Making, Second Edition.* Englewood Cliffs, NJ: Prentice-Hall, 1980.

3. Brandt, Louis K. *Business Finance.* Englewood Cliffs, NJ: Prentice-Hall, 1965.

4. Bridwell, Rodger W. *High-Tech Investing.* New York: Truman Talley Books, 1983.

5. "Business Week Index," *Business Week,* July 16, 1990, p6.

6. "Business Week Index," *Business Week,* August 17, 1992, p6.

7. Casey, Douglas. *Strategic Investing.* New York: Simon and Schuster, 1982.

8. Cole, Robert H., Ph.D. *Consumer and Commercial Credit Management.* Homewood, IL: Irwin, 1988.

9. Compton, Eric N. *Principles of Banking,* Third Edition. Washington: American Bankers Association, 1986.

10. Copeland, Thomas E., and J. Fred Weston. *Financial Theory and Corporate Policy.* Reading, MA: Addison-Wesley Publishing Company, 1979.

11. Davis, Carlisle R., and Edward F. Gee. *Analyzing Financial Statements.* New York: American Institute of Banking, 1965.

12. Dooner, William, and William Proctor. *How to Go From Rags to Riches in Real Estate.* New York: William Morrow and Company, 1982.

13. Dun & Bradstreet. *Industry Norms and Key Business Ratios.* NY: Dunn & Bradstreet Information Services. 1989–1990.

14. Foster, George. *Financial Statement Analysis.* Englewood Cliffs, NY: Prentice-Hall, 1978.

15. Gibson, Charles H. *Financial Statement Analysis,* Fourth Edition. Boston: PWS-KENT Publishing Company, 1989.

16. Gould, Dr. Bruce G. *How to Make Money in Commodities.* Seattle, WA: Bruce Gould Publications, 1982.

17. Graham, Benjamin, and David L. Dodd. *Security Analysis.* New York: McGraw-Hill, 1940.

18. Grant, Eugene L. *Principals of Engineering Economy*. New York: The Ronald Press Company, 1950.

19. Hawken, Paul. *The Next Economy*. New York: Holt, Rinehart and Winston, 1983.

20. Helfert, Erich A. *Techniques of Financial Analysis*. Homewood, IL: Richard D Irwin, Inc., 1977.

21. Hennessy, John H. Jr. *Handbook of Long-Term Financing*. Englewood Cliffs, NJ: Prentice-Hall, 1986.

22. Kirshman, John Emmett, Ph.D. *Principals of Investment*. New York: McGraw-Hill, 1933.

23. Mark M. *ESOPs in the 1980's*. New York: American Management Association, 1985.

24. Maness, Terry S., and James W. Henderson. *Financial Analysis and Forecasting*. Englewood Cliffs, NJ: Prentice Hall, 1991.

25. Moskowitz, Louis A. *Modern Factoring and Commercial Finance*. New York: Thomas Y. Crowell, 1977.

26. Mullins, David W. Jr. "Does the Capital Asset Pricing Model Work?" *Harvard Business Review*, January–February 1982, pp. 103–113.

27. Naisbitt, John, and Patricia Aburdene. *Re-inventing the Corporation*. New York: Warner Books, 1985.

28. Neun, Stephen P., and Rexford E. Santerre. *Corporate Control and Performance in the 1930's*. Eastern Economic Association, Conference in Pittsburg Pennsylvania, William Penn Hotel, March 1991.

29. Predicasts. *Predicast Forecasts*. Cleveland, OH: August 6, 1991.

30. Sinai, Allen. *Financial and Real Business Cycles*. Boston: The Boston Company Economic Advisors, March 16, 1991.

31. Smith, Adam. *The Money Game*. New York: Random House, 1968.

32. Solomon, Ezra, and John J. Pringle. *An Introduction to Financial Management*. California: Goodyear Publishing Company, 1977.

33. Stickney, Clyde P. *Financial Statement Analysis—A Strategic Perspective*. San Diego, CA: Harcourt Brace Jovanovich, 1990.

34. The Halcyon Group. *Profiting from Financial Statements—A Business Analysis System*. Charleston, SC: 1989.

35. Toney, Albert, and Thomas Tilling. *High-Tech: How to Find and Profit From Today's New Super Stocks*. New York: Simon and Schuster, 1983.

36. Viscione, Jerry A., and George A. Aragon. *Cases in Financial Management*. Boston: Houghton Mifflin, 1980.

37. Warfield, Gerald. *How to Read and Understand the Financial News*. New York: Harper & Row, 1986.

38. Warren, Gorham & Lamont, Inc. *Seven Sources of New Income and Savings for Corporations and Individuals*. Boston: Warren, Gorham & Lamont, 1981.

39.   Waterman, Merwin H. *Essays on Business Finance.* Michigan: Mastero Press, 1953.
40.   Weston, J. Fred, and Eugene F. Brigham. *Essentials of Managerial Finance,* Fourth Edition. Chicago, IL: Dryden, 1977.
41.   Weston, J. Fred, and Eugene F. Brigham. *Essentials of Managerial Finance,* Sixth Edition. Chicago: Dryden, 1982.
42.   Zweig, Martin E., Ph.D. *The ABC's of Market Forecasting.* New York: Dow Jones & Company, 1980.

F.   *ACCOUNTING AND AICPA PUBLICATIONS*

1.   Accounting Principles Board. *Statement #1,* "Fundamentals of Financial Accounting," April 13, 1962.
2.   Accounting Principles Board. *Statement #4,* "Basic Concepts and Principles Underlying Financial Statements of Business Enterprises," October, 1970.
3.   Ameiss, Albert P., and Nicholas A. Kargas. *Accountant's Desk Handbook.* Englewood Cliffs, NJ: Prentice-Hall, 1981.
4.   American Institute of Certified Public Accountants [AICPA]. *AICPA Professional Standards, Accounting,* Volumes 1–3. New York: AICPA, 1981.
5.   AICPA. *Assisting Clients in Determining Pricing For Manufactured Products.* New York: AICPA, 1985.
6.   AICPA. *Assisting Small Business Clients in Obtaining Funds.* New York: AICPA, 1982.
7.   AICPA. *Codification of Statements on Auditing Standards—Numbers 1–33.* New York: AICPA, 1981.
8.   AICPA. *Comparing Attest and Management Advisory Services,* "A Guide for the Practitioner." New York: AICPA, 1988.
9.   AICPA. *Developing an MAS Engagement Control Program.* New York: AICPA, 1984.
10. AICPA. *Guide for Prospective Financial Information.* New York: AICPA, 1993.
11. AICPA. *Guide for Prospective Financial Statements.* New York: AICPA, 1986.
12. AICPA. *Guide for Review of a Financial Forecast.* New York: AICPA, 1980.
13. AICPA. *Operational Audit Engagements.* New York: AICPA, 1982.
14. AICPA. *Proposed Audit and Accounting Guide Exposure—Audits of Credit Unions.* Washington, DC: AICPA, Federal Government Division, March 20, 1992. Exposure draft.
15. AICPA. *Proposed Statement on Responsibilities in Personal Financial Planning Practice—Basic PFP Engagement Functions and Responsibilities.* New York: AICPA, March 31, 1992. Exposure draft.

16.   AICPA. *Proposed Statement on Standards for Accounting and Review Services—Omnibus Statement on Standards for Accounting and Review Services—1992*. New York: AICPA, March 18, 1992. Exposure draft.

17.   AICPA. *Proposed Statement on Standards for Attestation Engagements—Reporting on an Entity's Internal Control Structure Over Financial Reporting*. New York: AICPA, April 20, 1992. Exposure draft.

18.   AICPA. *Statement on Auditing Standards #52*. "Omnibus Statement on Auditing Standards—1987." New York: AICPA 1985.

19.   AICPA. "Statement on Auditing Standards No. 69," *Journal of Accountancy*. New York: AICPA, March 1992, pp. 108–111.

20.   AICPA. *Statement on Auditing Standards #69*, "The Meaning of Present Fairly in Conformity with Generally Accepted Accounting Principles in the Independent Auditor's Report." New York: AICPA, 1992.

21.   AICPA. *Statement on Quality Control Standards, Statement #1*, "System of Quality Control for A CPA Firm" New York: AICPA, 1979.

22.   AICPA. *Statements on Standards for Accountants' Services on Prospective Financial Information*, "Financial Forecasts and Projections." New York: AICPA, 1985.

23.   AICPA. *Statement on Standards for Attestation Engagements*, "Attest Services Related to MAS Engagements." New York: AICPA, 1987.

24.   AICPA. *Statement on Standards for Attestation Engagements*, "Attestation Standards." New York: AICPA, 1986.

25.   AICPA. *Statement on Standards for Attestation Engagements*, "Reporting on Pro Forma Financial Information." New York: AICPA, 1988.

26.   AICPA. *Statement of Standards for Management Advisory Services, Statement #1*, "Definitions and Standards for MAS Practice." New York: AICPA, 1981.

27.   AICPA. *Statement of Standards for Management Advisory Services, Statement #2*, "MAS Engagements." New York: AICPA, 1982.

28.   AICPA. *Statement of Standards for Management Advisory Services, Statement #3*, "MAS Consultations." New York: AICPA, 1982.

29.   Ball, Ray, and Philip Brown. "An Empirical Evaluation of Accounting Income Numbers," *Journal of Accounting Research*, Vol. 6, No. 2, Autumn 1968, pp. 159–177.

30.   Beams, Floyd A., Ph.D. *Advanced Accounting*, Second Edition. Englewood Cliffs, NJ: Prentice-Hall, 1982.

31.   Beaver, William H., Roger Clarke, and William F. Wright. "The Association Between Unsystematic Security Returns and the Magnitude of Earnings Forecast Errors," *Journal of Accounting Research*, Vol. 17, No. 2, Autumn 1979, pp. 316–340.

32.   Burton, John C., and Robert J. Sack. "Standard Setting Process in Trouble (Again)," *Accounting Horizons*, Vol. 4, No. 4. Sarasota, Florida: American Accounting Association, December 1990, pp. 117–120.

33. Burton, John C., and Robert J. Sack. "Time for Some Lateral Thinking," *Accounting Horizons,* Vol. 5, No. 2. Sarasota, Florida: American Accounting Association, June, 1991, pp. 118–122.

34. Cameron, Alex, and Gordon Chapman. "Providing Forecasts and Projections: A Guide to the Complex New Rules," *The Practical Accountant.* Boston: Warren, Gorham & Lamont, August, 1987, pp. 94–107.

35. Davidson, Sidney, and Roman L. Weil. *Handbook of Modern Accounting.* New York: McGraw-Hill, 1977.

36. Edwards, James Don, Ph.D., C.P.A., John R. Johnson, and Roger A. Roemmich, Ph.D. *Intermediate Accounting.* Texas: Business Publications, Inc., 1981.

37. Elliot, Robert K., and Peter D. Jacobson. "U.S. Accounting: A National Emergency," *Journal of Accountancy.* New York: AICPA, November, 1991, pp. 54–58.

38. Feltman, Gerald A. *Studies in Accounting Research #5,* "Information Evaluation." Sarasota, FL: American Accounting Association, 1972.

39. Financial Accounting Standards Board. *Accounting Standards, Original Pronouncements July 1973–June 1, 1988.* Stamford, CT: FASB, 1988.

40. Financial Accounting Standards Board. *Exposure Draft: Financial Accounting Series—New Basis Accounting.* Financial Accounting Foundation, Norwalk, CT: December 18, 1991.

41. Financial Accounting Standards Board. *Exposure Draft: Financial Accounting Series—Recognition and Measurement of Financial Instruments.* Financial Accounting Foundation, Norwalk, CT: November 18, 1991.

42. Financial Accounting Standards Board, *Statement of Financial Accounting Concepts #1,* "Objectives of Financial Reporting by Business Enterprises." Stamford, CT: Financial Accounting Foundation, November, 1978.

43. Financial Accounting Standards Board, *Statement of Financial Accounting Concepts #2,* "Qualitative Characteristics of Accounting Information." Stamford, CT: Financial Accounting Foundation, May, 1980.

44. Financial Accounting Standards Board, *Statement of Financial Accounting Concepts #3,* "Elements of Financial Statements of Business Enterprises." Stamford, CT: Financial Accounting Foundation, December, 1980.

45. Financial Accounting Standards Board, *Statement of Financial Accounting Concepts #4,* "Objectives of Financial Reporting by Non-Business Organizations." Stamford, CT: Financial Accounting Foundation, December, 1980.

46. Financial Accounting Standards Board, *Statement of Financial Accounting Concepts #5,* "Recognition and Measurement in Financial Statements of Business Enterprises." Stamford, CT: Financial Accounting Foundation, December, 1984.

47. Financial Accounting Standards Board, *Statement of Financial Accounting Concepts #6,* "Elements of Financial Statements (A replacement of FASB concepts statement #3- incorporating an amendment of FASB concept state-

ment #2)." Stamford, CT: Financial Accounting Foundation, December, 1985.

48. Financial Accounting Standards Board. "Statement of Financial Accounting Standards No. 107—Disclosures About Fair Value of Financial Instruments," *Journal of Accountancy*. New York: AICPA, May 1992, pp. 139–167.

49. Gentry, James A. Jr., Ph.D., and Glenn L. Johnson, Ph.D. *Finney and Miller's Principles of Accounting*, Sixth Edition. Englewood Cliffs, NJ: Prentice-Hall, 1971.

50. Harsha, Phillip, and Peacock, Eileen. "Auditing Accounting Estimates," *Management Accounting*. New Jersey: National Association of Accountants, September, 1989, pp. 31–33.

51. Hill, Henry P. "Rational Expectations and Accounting Principles," *Journal of Accounting, Auditing & Finance*, Vol. 5, No. 2. Boston: Warren, Gorham & Lamont, 1982, pp. 99–109.

52. Holder, William W., and Kimberly Ham Eudy. "A Framework for Building an Accounting Constitution," *Journal of Accounting, Auditing & Finance*, Vol. 5, No. 2. Boston: Warren, Gorham & Lamont, 1982, pp. 110–125.

53. Kieso, Donald E., and Jerry J. Weygandt. *Intermediate Accounting*, Third Edition. New York: John Wiley and Sons, 1980.

54. Lindhe, Richard. "Accounting for the Systems." Unpublished article.

55. Lindhe, Richard. "Mathematics as the Language of Accounting." Unpublished article.

56. Lindhe, Richard. "Mathematics, The Science of Relationships, and Accounting." Unpublished article.

57. Meigs, Walter B., A.N. Mosich, and Charles E. Johnson. *Intermediate Accounting*, Fourth Edition. New York: McGraw-Hill, 1978.

58. Murphy, Maureen M. *FIRREA: The Financial Institutions Reform, Recovery, and Enforcement Act of 1989: A Summary*. Washington, DC: The Library of Congress, August 28, 1989.

59. Okopny, Robert D., and Jerry R. Strawser. "A Management Guide to Prospective Financial Statements," *Corporate Accounting*, Vol. 6, No. 2., Spring 1988, pp. 52–57.

60. Pate, Gwen Richardson, and Keith G. Stanga. "Applications in Accounting," *Journal of Accountancy*. New York: AICPA, August 1989, pp. 28–31.

61. Sheppard, Howard R. *Litigation Services Resource Directory*. New York: John Wiley & Sons, 1991.

62. "The Thrift Bailout," *The American Banker*. Washington, DC: Library of Congress, August 10, 1989, pp. 1–5.

63. Wyatt, Arthur R. "Accounting Standards Setting at a Crossroads," *Accounting Horizons*, Vol. 5, No. 3. Sarasota, Florida: American Accounting Association, September 1991, pp. 110–114.

G. COST ESTIMATING AND MANAGEMENT ACCOUNTING

1. Anderson, Anker V., Ph.D. *Graphing Financial Information.* New York: National Association of Accountants, 1983.
2. Anthony, Robert N., and James S. Reece. *Management Accounting, Text and Cases.* Homewood, IL: Richard D. Irwin, 1975.
3. Backer, Morton, and Martin L. Gosman. *Financial Reporting and Business Liquidity.* Montvale, NJ: National Association of Accountants, 1978.
4. Caplan, Edwin H., and Stephan Landekich. *Human Resource Accounting: Past, Present and Future.* New York: National Association of Accountants, 1974.
5. Cooper, Robin, and Robert S. Kaplan. *The Design of Cost Management Systems.* Englewood Cliffs, NJ: Prentice-Hall, 1991.
6. Dearden, John. *Management Accounting—Text and Cases.* Englewood Cliffs, NJ: Prentice-Hall, 1988.
7. Demski, Joel S. *Information Analysis.* Reading, MA: Addison-Wesley, 1972.
8. Department of Defense. *ASPM, Armed Services Pricing Manual, Vol. 1.* Chicago, IL: Commerce Clearing House, 1986.
9. Department of Defense. *ASPM, Armed Services Pricing Manual, Vol. 2.* Chicago, IL: Commerce Clearing House, 1987.
10. Department of Defense. *ASPM No. 1, Armed Services Procurement Regulation Manual for Contract Pricing.* Chicago, IL: Commerce Clearing House, 1975.
11. Dickenson, Daniel. *It's Their Business, Too—A Manager's Guide to Employee Awareness.* New York: American Management Association, 1985.
12. Dudick, Thomas S. *Cost Accounting Desk Reference Book.* New York: Van Nostrand Reinhold, 1986.
13. Dudick, Thomas S. *Dudick on Manufacturing Cost Controls.* Englewood Cliffs, NJ: Prentice-Hall, 1985.
14. Dunn & Bradstreet. *How to Control Accounts Receivable for Greater Profits.* New York: Dunn & Bradstreet. Pamphlet.
15. Ferrara, William L. "More Questions Than Answers—The New Cost/Management Accounting," *Management Accounting.* Montvale, NJ: National Association of Accountants, October 1990, pp. 48–52.
16. Fitz-Enz, Jac. "White-Collar Effectiveness—Part 2: The Organization Side," *Management Review.* New York: American Management Association Membership Publications, June 1986, pp. 52–56.
17. Fremgen, James M., and Shu S. Liao. *The Allocation of Corporate Indirect Costs.* Montvale, NJ: National Association of Accountants, 1981.
18. Gambino, Anthony J., and Morris Gartenberg. *Industrial R & D Management.* New York: National Association of Accountants, 1979.
19. Garrison, Ray H., D.B.A., CPA. *Managerial Accounting.* Dallas, TX: Business Publications, 1979.

20. Gordon, Lawrence A., Danny Miller, and Henry Mintzberg. *Normative Models in Managerial Decision-Making.* New York: National Association of Accountants, 1975.

21. Gordon, Myron J., and Gordon Shillinglaw. *Accounting: A Management Approach,* Third Edition. Homewood, IL: Richard D. Irwin, 1964.

22. Heckert, J. Brooks. *The Analysis and Control of Distribution Costs.* New York: The Ronald Press, 1940.

23. Horngren, Charles T., Ph.D., CPA. *Cost Accounting, A Managerial Emphasis,* Fifth Edition. Englewood Cliffs, NJ: Prentice-Hall, 1980.

24. Horngren, Charles T., Ph.D., CPA. *Introduction to Management Accounting,* Fourth Edition. Englewood Cliffs, NJ: Prentice-Hall, 1978.

25. Horngren, Charles T., Ph.D., CPA. *Introduction to Management Accounting,* Fifth Edition. Englewood Cliffs, NJ: Prentice-Hall, 1981.

26. Kaplan, Robert S., and Anthony A. Atkinson. *Advanced Management Accounting,* Second Edition. Englewood Cliffs, NJ: Prentice-Hall, 1989.

27. Keegan, Daniel P., G. Eiler, and Charles R. Jones. "Are Your Performance Measures Obsolete?" *Management Accounting.* Montvale, NJ: National Association of Accountants, June 1989, pp. 45–50.

28. Matz, Adolph, Ph.D., and Milton F. Usry. *Cost Accounting, Planning and Control.* Cincinnati, OH: South-Western Publishing, 1980.

29. Mendlowitz, Edward, CPA. *24 Common Financial Problems . . . And How to Solve Them.* Boca Raton: Newsletter Management Corporation, 1982.

30. Merchant, Kenneth A. *Control in Organizations: A Literature Review.* Boston: Harvard Business School, 1983. Cambridge, MA: MIT Press, 1980. Working paper.

31. Merchant, Kenneth A. *The Control Function of Management.* Cambridge, MA: Sloan Management Review Association, 1982.

32. Merchant, Kenneth A., and William J. Bruns, Jr. *Measure Better, Manage Better—A Cure for Management Myopia.* Boston, MA: Harvard Business School, July, 1983. Working paper.

33. National Association of Accountants. *Financial Analysis to Guide Capital Expenditure Decisions.* New York: National Association of Accountants, 1967.

34. National Association of Accountants. *Managing the Cash Flow.* New York: National Association of Accountants, 1974.

35. National Association of Accountants. *Return on Capital as a Guide to Managerial Decisions.* New York: National Association of Accountants, 1959.

36. National Association of Accountants. *Techniques in Inventory Management.* New York: National Association of Accountants, 1964.

37. National Association of Accountants. *The Pricing Decision.* New York: National Association of Accountants, 1981.

38. National Association of Accountants. *Use of Graphs in Internal Reporting.* New York: National Association of Accountants, 1961.

39.	Sherwood, J. F., CPA, and Franklin T. Chace, CPA. *Principles of Cost Accounting,* Second Edition. Cincinnati, OH: South-Western, 1949.
40.	Simmons, John D. *Long-Range Profit Planning: Research Report 42.* New York: National Association of Accountants, 1973.
41.	Symonds, Curtis W. *Pricing for Profit.* New York: AMACOM, 1982.
42.	Willson, James D., CPA. *Budgeting.* New York: AICPA, 1983.
43.	Wilson, Gerald E. "Theory Z: Implications for Management Accountants," *Management Accounting.* Montvale, NJ: National Association of Accountants, November 1983, pp. 58–62.

## H.	SYSTEMS AND OPERATIONS

1.	Abdel-Hamid, Tarek K., and Stuart E. Madnick. *The Dynamics of Software Project Scheduling: A System Dynamics Perspective.* Cambridge, MA: Center for Information Systems Research, Sloan School of Management, 1982.
2.	Alloway, Robert M., and Jerome T. Nolte. *Planning Skill Development for Systems Analysts.* Cambridge, MA: Center for Information Systems Research, Sloan School of Management, 1979.
3.	Beckett, John A. *Management Dynamics—The New Synthesis* New York: McGraw-Hill, 1971.
4.	Bellman, Richard, and Robert Kalaba. *Dynamic Programming and Modern Control Theory.* New York: Academic Press, 1965.
5.	Boguslaw, Robert. *The New Utopians.* Englewood Cliffs, NJ: Prentice-Hall, 1965.
6.	Bradshaw-Camball, Patricia, and Victor V. Murray. "Illusions and Other Games: A Trifocal View of Organizational Politics," *Organization Science,* Vol. 2, No. 4, Institute of Management Sciences, November 1991, pp. 379–396.
7.	Bullen, Christine V., and John F. Rockart. *A Primer on Critical Success Factors.* Cambridge, MA: Center for Information Systems Research, Sloan School of Management, 1981.
8.	Carroll, Phill Jr., M.E. *Timestudy for Cost Control.* New York: McGraw-Hill, 1948.
9.	Coyle, R.G. *Management System Dynamics.* New York: John Wiley & Sons, 1977.
10.	De Long, David W., and John F. Rockart. *A Survey of Current Trends in the Use of Executive Support Systems.* Cambridge, MA: Center for Information Systems Research, Sloan School of Management, 1984.
11.	DeMasi, Ronald J. *An Introduction to Business Systems Analysis.* Reading, MA: Addison-Wesley, 1969.
12.	Fitzgerald, Jerry, and Andra Fitzgerald. *Fundamentals of Systems Analysis,* Third Edition. New York: John Wiley & Sons, 1987.

13. Forrester, Jay W. *Collected Papers of Jay W. Forrester.* Cambridge, MA: Wright-Allen Press, 1975.
14. Gharajedaghi, Jamshid. *Toward a Systems Theory of Organization.* Seaside, CA: Intersystems Publications, 1985.
15. Grindley, Kit. *Systematics—A New Approach to Systems Analysis.* New York: PBI Books, 1975.
16. Howard, Ronald A. *Dynamic Probabilistic Systems, Volume I: Markov Models.* New York: John Wiley & Sons, 1971.
17. Howard, Ronald A. *Dynamic Probabilistic Systems, Volume II: Semimarkov and Decision Processes.* New York: John Wiley & Sons, 1971.
18. Jarett, Irwin M. *Computer Graphics and Reporting Financial Data.* New York: John Wiley & Sons, 1983.
19. Keen, Peter G. W. *Decision Support Systems and Managerial Productivity Analysis.* Cambridge, MA: Center for Information Systems Research, Sloan School of Management, 1980.
20. Levinson, Eliot. *The Implementation of Executive Support Systems.* Cambridge, MA: Center for Information Systems Research, Sloan School of Management, 1984.
21. Lindhe, Richard, and Steven D. Grossman. *Accounting Information Systems.* Houston, TX: Dame Publications, 1980.
22. Lowry, Stewart M., Harold B. Maynard, and G.F. Stegemerten. *Time and Motion Study,* Third Edition. New York: McGraw-Hill, 1940.
23. Lyneis, James E. *Corporate Planning and Policy Design.* Cambridge, MA: MIT Press, 1980.
24. Marshall, Paul W., William J. Abernathy, Jeffrey G. Miller, Richard P. Rosenbloom, and D. Darly Wycoff. *Operations Management.* Homewood, IL: Richard D. Irwin, 1975.
25. Maynard, H.B. *Industrial Engineering Handbook,* Third Edition. New York: McGraw-Hill, 1971.
26. McDowall, Robert L. *The Impact of Business Systems Technologies on the Financial Function.* Montvale, NJ: National Association of Accountants, 1988.
27. Mitchell, William N. *Organization and Management of Production.* New York: McGraw-Hill, 1939.
28. Monks, Joseph G. *Operations Management, Theory and Problems.* New York: McGraw-Hill, 1977.
29. Moore, Franklin G., Ph.D. *Manufacturing Management,* Third Edition. Homewood, IL: Richard D. Irwin, 1961.
30. Morgan, Gareth. *Images of Organization.* Beverly Hills, CA: Sage Publications, 1986.
31. Muther, Richard. *Production-Line Technique.* New York: McGraw-Hill, 1944.
32. Naylor, Thomas H. *Corporate Planning Models.* Reading, MA: Addison-Wesley, 1979.

33. Optner, Stanford L. *Systems Analysis.* Englewood Cliffs, NJ: Prentice-Hall, 1960.

34. Orlicky, Joseph. *Material Requirements Planning.* New York: McGraw-Hill, 1975.

35. Padulo, Louis, and Michael A. Arbib. *System Theory—A Unified State–Space Approach to Continuous and Discrete Systems.* Philadelphia: W.B. Saunders, 1974.

36. Ramlow, Donald E., and Eugene H. Wall. *Production Planning and Control.* Englewood Cliffs, NJ: Prentice-Hall, 1967.

37. Randers, Jorgen. *Elements of the System Dynamics Method.* Cambridge, MA: MIT Press, 1980.

38. Richardson, George P., and Alexander L. Pugh III. *Introduction to System Dynamics Modeling With DYNAMO.* Cambridge, MA: MIT Press, 1981.

39. Schwarzenbach, J., and K.F. Gill. *System Modelling and Control.* New York: John Wiley & Sons, 1978.

40. Shubik, Martin. "On Concepts of Efficiency," *Policy Sciences.* Scotland: Elsevier Scientific Publishing Company, 1978, pp. 121–126.

41. Shumard, F.W. *A Primer of Time Study.* New York: McGraw-Hill, 1940.

42. Stamps, Jeffrey S. *Holonomy: A Human Systems Theory.* Seaside, CA: Intersystems Publications, 1980.

43. Sylvester, L. Arthur. *Advanced Time-Motion Study.* New York: Funk & Wagnalls, 1950.

44. Randolph, Robert M. *Planagement—Moving Concept Into Reality.* Austin, TX: Learning Concepts, 1979.

45. Rockart, John F. *A New Approach to Defining the Chief Executive's Information Needs,* Revised Edition. Cambridge, MA: Center for Information Systems Research, Sloan School of Management, 1978.

46. Tyran, Michael R. *Computerized Accounting Methods and Controls,* Second Edition. Englewood Cliffs, NJ: Prentice-Hall, 1978.

47. Vichas, Robert P. *Handbook of Annotated Financial Forms.* Englewood Cliffs, NJ: Prentice-Hall, 1981.

48. Vollmann, Thomas E., William L. Berry, and D. Clay Whybark. *Manufacturing Planning and Control Systems.* Homewood, IL: Dow Jones–Irwin, 1984.

49. Wallace, Thomas F. *MRP II: Making it Happen.* Brattleboro, VT: Oliver Wright Limited Publications, 1985.

50. Wright, Oliver W. *Manufacturing Resource Planning: MRP II,* Revised Edition. New York: Van Nostrand Reinhold, 1984.

51. Wright, Oliver W. *The Executive's Guide to Successful MRP II.* Englewood Cliffs, NJ: Prentice-Hall, 1986.

I. QUANTITATIVE METHODS

1. Anderson, Dick, and Douglas Ford Cobb. *1–2–3: Tips, Tricks, and Traps.* Indianapolis, IN: Que Corporation, 1984.
2. Armstrong, J. Scott. *Long-Range Forecasting.* New York: John Wiley & Sons, 1978.
3. Buckley, John W., Marlene H. Buckley, and Hung-Fu Chiang. *Research Methodology & Business Decisions.* Montvale, NJ: National Association of Accountants, 1976.
4. Chernoff, Herman, and Lincoln E. Moses. *Elementary Decision Theory.* New York: John Wiley & Sons, 1959.
5. Cobb, Douglas Ford, and Leith Anderson. *1–2–3 for Business.* Indianapolis, IN: Que Corporation, 1984.
6. Cosenza, Robert M., and Daune Davis. *Business Research for Decision Making.* Boston, MA: PWS-Kent Publishing Company, 1988.
7. Cross, K. Patricia, and Thomas A. Angelo. *Classroom Assessment Techniques,* Second Edition. Ann Arbor, MI: University of Michigan, 1988.
8. Emory, C. William. *Business Research Methods,* Third Edition. Homewood, IL: Irwin, 1985.
9. Esterby-Smith, Mark, Richard Thorpe, and Andy Lowe. *Management Research—An Introduction.* London: Sage Publications, 1991.
10. Hayen, Roger L., and Richard M. Peters. "Spreadsheet Integrity," *Management Accounting.* Montvale, NJ: National Association of Accountants, April 1989, pp. 30–33.
11. Palisade Corporation. *@ Risk Version 1.55.* Reading, MA: Addison-Wesley Publishing Company, 1991.
12. Parsons, James A., Ph.D. *Practical Mathematical and Statistical Techniques for Production Managers.* Englewood Cliffs, NJ: Prentice-Hall, 1973.
13. Piattelli-Palmarini, Massimo. "Probability—Neither Rational nor Capricious," *Bostonia.* March–April 1991, pp. 28–35.
14. Riaffa, Howard. *Decision Analysis.* Reading, MA: Addison-Wesley, 1968.
15. Riaffa, Howard, and Rich Schaifer. *Applied Statistical Decision Theory.* Boston: Harvard University Graduate School of Business Administration, Division of Research, 1961.
16. Russo, Joe. *Sensitivity Analysis—An Introduction for Managers—Working Papers No. 96.* New York: Pace University, Nov. 1990.
17. Smith, Bernard T. *Focus Forecasting: Computer Techniques for Inventory Control.* Essex Junction, VT: Oliver Wight Publications, 1984.
18. Starfield, Anthony M., Karl A. Smith, and Andrew L. Bleloch. *How to Model It: Problem Solving for the Computer Age.* New York: McGraw-Hill, 1990.
19. Sullivan, William G., and W. Wayne Claycombe. *Fundamentals of Forecasting.* Reston, VA: Reston Publishing Company, 1977.

20. Watson, Hugh J., M.B.A., D.B.A. *Computer Simulation in Business.* New York: John Wiley & Sons, 1981.
21. Zikmund, William G. *Business Research Methods,* Second Edition. Chicago, IL: Dryden Press, 1988.

J. *ETHICS AND BUSINESS RESPONSIBILITY*

1. Axelson, John. *Counseling and Development in a Multicultural Society.* Monterrey, CA: Brooks/Cole, 1987.
2. Callahan, Joan C. *Ethical Issues in Professional Life.* New York: Oxford University Press, 1988.
3. Cross, Patricia K., and Thomas A. Angelo. *Classroom Assessment Techniques.* Ann Arbor, MI: The University of Michigan, 1988.
4. De George, Richard T., and Joseph A. Pichler. *Ethics, Free Enterprise, and Public Policy: Original Essays on Moral Issues in Business.* New York: Oxford University Press, 1978.
5. Dewey, Robert E., Francis W. Gramlich, and Donald Loftsgordon. *Problems of Ethics.* New York: Macmillan, 1965.
6. Epstein, Marc J., Eric G. Flamholtz, and John J. McDonough. *Corporate Social Performance: The Measurement of Product and Service Contributions.* New York: National Association of Accountants, 1977.
7. Ermann, David M., Mary B. Williams, and Claudio Gutierrez. *Computers, Ethics, & Society.* New York: Oxford University Press, 1990.
8. Farmer, Richard N., and W. Dickerson Hogue. *Corporate Social Responsibility.* Chicago: Science Research Associates, 1973.
9. Girvetz, Harry K. *Contemporary Moral Issues.* Belmont, CA: Wadsworth Publishing Company, 1963.
10. Hoffman, W. Michael, and Jenifer Mills Moore. *Business Ethics,* Second Edition. New York: McGraw-Hill, 1990.
11. Kant, Immanuel. *First Introduction to the Critique of Judgement.* Indianapolis, IN: Bobs-Merrill, 1965.
12. Kant, Immanuel. *Fundamental Principles of the Metaphysic of Morals.* Indianapolis, IN: Bobbs-Merrill, 1949.
13. Nikolai, Loren A., John D. Bazley, and R. Lee Brummet. *The Measurement of Corporate Environment Activity.* New York: National Association of Accountants, 1976.
14. Quine, W.V., and J.S. Ullian. *The Web of Belief,* Second Edition. New York: Random House, 1978.
15. Raymond, Diane. *Business Ethics: Readings and Cases in Corporate Morality,* Second Edition. New York: McGraw-Hill, 1990.
16. Richardson, John E. *Business Ethics 91/92.* Guilford, CT: The Dushkin Publishing Group, 1991.

17. Schaefer, Francis. *How Then Should We Live?* Old Tappan, NJ: Fleming H. Revell Company, 1976.
18. Walton, Clarence C. *Corporate Encounters—Ethics, Law & the Business Environment.* Fort Worth, TX: Dryden Press, 1992.

K. COMMUNICATIONS AND LOGIC

1. Berger, Arthur Asa. *Media USA,* Second Edition. New York: Longman, 1991.
2. Cherry, Colin. *On Human Communication,* Second Edition. Cambridge, MA: The M.I.T. Press, 1966.
3. Copi, Irving, and Carl Cohen. *Introduction to Logic.* New York: Macmillan, 1990.
4. Crandal, Robert H. "Information Economics and Its Implications for the Further Development of Accounting Theory," *The Accounting Review,* XLIV, July 1969, pp. 457–46.6
5. DeFleur, Melvin L., and Everette E. Dennis. *Understanding Mass Communication,* Fourth Edition. Boston: Houghton Mifflin, 1991.
6. Demski, Joel S., Ph.D., and Gerald A. Feltham, Ph.D. *Cost Determination.* Ames, IA: The Iowa State University Press, 1976.
7. Fogelin, Robert J. *Understanding Argument.* New York: Harcourt Brace Jovanovich, 1978.
8. Forester, Tom. *The Information Technology Revolution.* Cambridge, MA: MIT Press, 1985.
9. George, Frank. *Machine Takeover.* New York: Pergamon Press, 1977.
10. Goldberg, Louis. *An Inquiry Into The Nature of Accounting.* Menasha, WI: American Accounting Association, 1965.
11. Hilton, Ronald W. "The Determinants of Cost Information Value: An Illustrative Analysis," *Journal of Accounting Research,* Vol. #2, Autumn 1979, pp. 411–435.
12. Lament, Thomas B., and Robert Ehrsam. "The Human Element," *Management Accounting.* Montvale, NJ: National Association of Accountants, July 1987, pp. 32–38.
13. Laver, Murray. *Computers and Social Change.* London: Cambridge University Press, 1980.
14. Lee, Lucy C., and Norton M. Bedford. "An Information Theory Analysis of the Accounting Process," *The Accounting Review,* XLIV April 1969, pp. 256–276.
15. Lucas, Henry C. Jr. *Computer Based Information Systems in Organizations.* Chicago: Science Research Associates, 1973.
16. Magee, Robert P. "Equilibria in Budget Participation," *Journal of Accounting Research,* Vol. 18, No 2, Autumn 1980, pp. 551–573.

17. Nora, Simon, and Alain Minc. *The Computerization of Society.* Cambridge, MA: The MIT Press, 1980.

18. Otto, Herbert R. "Applying A Symbolic Logic: Two Aspects," *Philosophic Research and Analysis,* Vol. VIII, No. 5, Late Fall 1980, pp. 7–12.

19. Otto, Herbert R. "Bringing Logic Down to Earth," *Philosophic Research and Analysis,* Vol. VII, No. 4, Early Fall 1978, pp. 2–4.

20. Otto, Herbert R. "Meaning Making: Some Functional Aspects," (included as a major paper in the following book)

21. Otto, Herbert R. *The Linguistic Basis of Logic Translation.* Washington, D.C.: University Press of America, 1978.

22. Otto, Herbert R., and J.A. Tuedio. *Perspectives on Mind.* Dordrect, Holland: D. Reidel Publishing Company, 1988.

23. Roszak, Theodore. *The Cult of Information.* New York: Pantheon Books, 1986.

24. Shannon, Claude, E., and Warren Weaver. *The Mathematical Theory of Communication.* Urbana, IL: University of Illinois Press, 1949.

25. Shannon, Claude E., and Warren Weaver. *The Mathematical Theory of Communications.* Urbana, IL: University of Illinois Press, 1964.

26. Simons, Geoff. *Eco-Computer—The Impact of Global Intelligence.* New York: John Wiley & Sons, 1987.

27. Singh, Jagjit. *Great Ideas in Information Theory, Language and Cybernetics.* New York: Dover Publications, 1966.

28. Sundem, Gary L. "A Game Theory Model of the Information Evaluator and the Decision Maker," *Journal of Accounting Research,* Vol. 17, No. 1, Spring 1979, pp. 243–261.

29. Whetmore, Edward Jay. *MEDIAMERICA,* Updated Third Edition. Belmont, CA: Wadsworth, 1987.

30. Williams, Frederick. *The New Communications,* Second Edition. Belmont, CA: Wadsworth, 1989.

Index

Disk Content

The enclosed diskette contains a Lotus 1-2-3 file of the case study model discussed in Chapter 10 and printed in Appendix A and B. This file, **MODEL.WK1**, is formatted in Lotus 1-2-3 version 2.01.

Computer Requirements

To read the file, you will need an IBM PC or compatible computer with DOS version 4.1 or later, a 3.5″ floppy drive, and Lotus 1-2-3 version 2.01 or later. If you have a different spreadsheet software, consult your user manual for information on using Lotus files in your package. Most popular spreadsheet programs, including Microsoft Excel and Borland/Novell Quattro Pro, are capable of reading files formatted for Lotus. Using the index in your software manual, refer to the section on "Converting Lotus Files" or "Loading Files from Other Programs."

Copying the Disk

We suggest that you copy the file to your hard drive and work from the copy on your hard drive.

DOS:
1. Insert the diskette into Drive A.
2. At the prompt **A:\>**, type **copy *.* c:** (or replace **c:** with another desired destination drive).

WINDOWS:
1. Insert the diskette into Drive A.
2. From your Windows Program Manager, open the File Manager icon.
3. Click on the **a:** drive icon on the menu bar.
4. Click on the filename **MODEL.WK1**.
5. Pull down the File Menu and choose Copy.
6. In the pop-up menu **To:** field type **c:** (or another desired destination drive). Click on OK.

User Assistance and Information

John Wiley and Sons, Inc., is pleased to answer questions regarding installation of the diskette. If you have any problems please call our technical support number at (212) 850-6194, weekdays between 9 A.M. and 4 P.M. Eastern Standard Time.

To place additional orders or to request general information about orders or other Wiley products, please call Wiley customer service at (800) 879-4539.